WELLNESS ISSUES FOR
HIGHER EDUCATION

Wellness Issues for Higher Education is an essential resource that addresses a range of student wellness issues confronting professionals in college and university settings. Organized around five dimensions of wellness—emotional, social, intellectual, physical, and spiritual—this book comprehensively covers key topics that contribute to students' success in college. Each topical chapter includes proactive wellness advice and is designed to prepare the reader to better understand the facts, and strategies appropriate for addressing the issues.

Each chapter features:

- Background information, theory, and research
- Historical and emerging issues
- Common questions, controversies, challenging situations, and misconceptions
- Practical applications for the campus

This practical guide prepares practitioners to understand and deal with the wellness and health promotion issues contributing to their students' overall success and well-being. Armed with this valuable resource, higher education and student affairs professionals can work to improve academic performance, retention, satisfaction, and quality of life. This thorough resource will guide those working at any level in residence life, student activities, orientation, health education, student leadership, advising, instruction, and other areas of student development.

David S. Anderson is Professor of Education and Human Development and Director of the Center for the Advancement of Public Health at George Mason University.

Wellness Issues for Higher Education

A Guide for Student Affairs and Higher Education Professionals

Edited by David S. Anderson

Routledge
Taylor & Francis Group

NEW YORK AND LONDON

First published 2016
by Routledge
711 Third Avenue, New York, NY 10017

and by Routledge
2 Park Square, Milton Park, Abingdon, Oxon, OX14 4RN

Routledge is an imprint of the Taylor & Francis Group, an informa business

© 2016 Taylor & Francis

The right of David S. Anderson to be identified as the author of the editorial
material, and of the authors for their individual chapters, has been asserted
in accordance with sections 77 and 78 of the Copyright, Designs and Patents
Act 1988.

Library of Congress Cataloging-in-Publication Data
A catalog record has been requested for this book

ISBN: 978-1-138-02096-2 (hbk)
ISBN: 978-1-138-02097-9 (pbk)
ISBN: 978-1-315-77812-9 (ebk)

Typeset in Minion
by Apex CoVantage, LLC

Contents

Preface

When I set out to prepare this resource, my aim was to maximize the opportunities for success encountered by students at colleges and universities nationwide. This learning focuses on the traditional classroom learning, the structured and semi-structured out-of-classroom experiences, and self-directed opportunities faced by students. My experience as a student affairs administrator and faculty member at several institutions of higher education demonstrated to me that many students miss out on the opportunities made available for them. While I know that a lot of the responsibility lies with the students themselves, much of the responsibility rests with the professionals on the campus who genuinely want students to succeed, to flourish, to excel, and to take full advantage of the college experience.

My emphasis with this book is proactive. I seek to prepare, and perhaps inspire, more systematically, the professionals working with college students as these student affairs practitioners, faculty members, and other professionals deal with the students on a range of issues. Many times, these issues are outside the normal and expected purview of the professional: an academic advisor who senses a student's mental anguish over a changed relationship, a residence hall staff member who observes a student's prioritization of game-playing on a smartphone, a coach who notices several students' diminished grades, a faculty member who hears about the regular abuse of drugs or alcohol, or a chief student affairs officer who observes staff indifference to incessant student complaints about the campus climate. How can campus professionals best serve their students and their institutions, while maintaining their personal and professional commitment through their work, their service, their research, and their professional development? Campus professionals are increasingly placed in challenging positions, whether through the changing nature of the student body, consistently diminished resources, modified priorities, and varied and competing mandates. What would benefit them to continue to serve multiple needs with varying priorities, and to continue to believe that they, in fact, are making a difference in the lives of students?

This book is designed for professionals serving colleges and universities, regardless of the nature or size of the institution, regardless of the professional position, and regardless of the level of experience. The chapters compiled here are designed to provide substantive, current, and insightful knowledge helpful to professionals as they strive to help students succeed in college. Whether incorporated in a graduate preparation program in higher education or student development, utilized as part of staff training activities, referred to on an as-needed basis, provided to new staff and faculty, or serving to anchor discussions and training seminars, this resource can be used to enhance the lives of students.

Overview of This Resource

Wellness Issues for Higher Education is designed to accomplish several things for each of 12 wellness issues:

- Provide current research, including correct misperceptions, identify controversies, and suggest future directions in the field of study.
- Make suggestions appropriate for implementation by a variety of campus professionals in a range of campus settings.
- Offer issues and questions for consideration on campus.
- Identify resources for further information and study.

With each of the topics, an obvious challenge is one of knowledge. Each field of study has extensive research, and many have volumes and volumes prepared about the topic area. Further, many controversies and differences of opinion exist, and new knowledge continues to emerge. Within this context, how can a professional staff member or faculty member be expected to be fully knowledgeable on a topic, or more accurately, a variety of topics? The answer is that she or he is not expected to be fully knowledgeable on all topics; however, since this vast network of professionals has the primary contact with students on campus, and since specialists on numerous topical areas are available on or near campus, some basic knowledge is viewed as essential. This book is designed to provide the requisite overview of the necessary content for the identified topic areas.

Similarly, while many suggestions and issues are raised by the chapters' authors, this book is not designed to suggest that "one size fits all." Rather, the chapter authors are, intentionally, offering their best wisdom and insights. They are often quite provocative with their suggestions, seeking to facilitate progress with regard to their specific topic areas.

The design of the book is around 12 distinct wellness topics. Indeed, dozens of wellness topics could have been included. These 12 were selected based on two overarching criteria: representation of the wellness schema, and significant affiliation with students' success in college. For the first, numerous schema or classifications exist regarding wellness: the five dimensions of wellness, the six aspects of wellness, the seven components of wellness; this volume identifies five main wellness areas within which the 12 topics are aligned. The issue of student success served as the second organizing principle, as most institutions seek to retain students who enroll; retention is a topic priority. Thus, while tobacco use and body image are significant health issues among college students, they were not identified as among the top ones that might affect a student's success. Issues surrounding study skills, stress, mental health, alcohol, and technology are among those identified for the focused attention in this volume. The 12 topical areas selected are important in the lives of students, and often contribute to students' nonsuccess or withdrawal from college. The premise is that if these issues were better addressed and/or were less of a problem among students, improvement would be found in academic performance, retention, satisfaction, and quality of life.

What's special about this book? First, it focuses on praxis, the intersection between theory and practice. For this book, the theory is represented by current knowledge. Second, it addresses an audience from various professional roles; these are not just student affairs, not just residence hall professionals, and not just those in an instructional position. Third, this book is written for professionals with various levels of experience, including the very seasoned, senior professional, the middle career person, and the graduate student who is preparing to embark on his or her career. Fourth, many of the chapters have specific questions or queries that can serve as the basis of discussion or further exploration. Some have checklists, some have case studies, some incorporate specific examples for use on campus, and some include testimonials. Finally, this book can provide a new foundation for academic preparation programs, primarily in higher education and student affairs, whether as the foundation for a specific course on wellness issues or through being woven into existing courses.

The Book's Audiences and Context

As documented in the introduction, only 1 of 180 masters-level preparation programs in higher education nationwide has a required course on wellness issues. That raises questions about where the emerging professionals (and soon-to-be midcourse professionals) are obtaining their preparation on these issues. Are they gaining appropriate knowledge and skills on these key wellness issues in other coursework, seminars, or discussions? Are their skills enhanced through professional development sessions? Does this occur with in-service training, or is it accomplished through self-learning or personal experience? An opportunity exists for reexamining the professional preparation programs for these graduate students, as well as to review current in-service and professional development opportunities for other student affairs professionals.

Beyond the student affairs profession, where much of the responsibility for addressing these issues often tends to fall, the question is raised about what preparation is available for other professionals on campus, who may not be formally or informally part of the student affairs staff. What expectations are made, and what preparation is available, for faculty? How about other professional staff members?

The intent of this book is to be proactive, and to prepare more broadly and completely those professionals who serve in various roles and capacities on our campuses. It is this wide number of individuals who serve, in essence, on the front lines with students. This book is designed to serve as a practical resource for those working in residence life, student activities, orientation, health education, student leadership, advising, and other areas of student development; it is designed to aid and guide those in various other roles on campus, such as with athletics teams, instructional faculty, and research faculty. This book is not designed at all to diminish the important role played by specialists: the counselors who address mild and more serious mental health concerns; the health professionals who diagnose and treat physical symptoms; the nutritional specialists and athletic trainers who provide specialized services; the career counselor who links individual attributes, job markets and potentials, and skills preparation; the faculty member and academic advisor who help students better understand content and prepare for examinations. Each of these individuals, and countless more, has significant and vital roles to play in the growth and development of students. However, many of these specialists are typically not on the "front lines" with the general student body; they are consumed with their focused professional responsibilities.

With this resource, all professionals working with college students have the opportunity to be exposed to and better prepared to address these various wellness issues. They can identify earlier, and refer, students to the appropriate professionals who can best address the specific needs and issues. These numerous professionals, better prepared on the range of wellness issues, can redirect, advise, and assist students. The intent, then, is for the wide range of professionals on campus—student affairs, faculty, or other staff—to be better equipped from both a proactive and reactive perspective. The proactive efforts are wellness-based, seeking to promote healthier, safer, and more productive campus environments. From this proactive approach, these professionals can help shape the campus environment to promote healthy decision-making by students, and to acquaint students with and nurture students to access the range of services and stimuli that help them, the students, to maximize their own potential. From a reactive point of view, these professionals can better and earlier identify problems or issues faced by students, and refer them to appropriate specialists as needed. Reactive approaches incorporate earlier intervention, so that appropriate campus specialists can be engaged as needed, and at the earliest possible time (e.g., the counseling center staff will get engaged with a student on mental health concerns earlier than otherwise would be achieved, because the student affairs professional would be better prepared to identify and refer at the earlier time). A potential and likely consequence of each of these thrusts is that more students will be seeking services of specialists so that minor issues and problems do not then escalate into larger ones. Further, a likely consequence is that larger, problematic, and potentially dire situations will be minimized and, ideally, averted.

For each topic area, authors provide a better understanding for student affairs professionals in a variety of roles and settings, so they are better prepared to address the issue from both proactive perspectives and reactive approaches. Currently, without basic content knowledge, many wellness issues and opportunities go unaddressed and can ultimately contribute to students' lack of satisfaction, poor academic performance, attrition, substance abuse, or other problematic behavior.

The Book's Contents

The organization of this book is around five dimensions of wellness: emotional, social, intellectual, physical, and spiritual. Within these dimensions, 12 key topics are identified, with a range from one to four topics. These topics can also be viewed as those most central for students' success in college; that is, healthy decisions in the topical area can contribute to students' success, and unwise or inappropriate decisions in a topical area can result in harmful or negative consequences for the student. While numerous other wellness topics do exist, these 12 are chosen because of their strong relationship to students' success or nonsuccess in college. The aim of this book is to better prepare professional staff members to understand and deal with these issues, thus contributing to students' overall success and well-being.

There is undoubtedly overlap among the identified topics. While each topic will be developed and presented as a distinct wellness issue, obvious linkages among them exist (e.g., students drink alcohol or use illicit drugs to deal with stress, alcohol abuse affects sexual decision-making, prescription drug abuse links to study skills as well as sleep, and technology involvement can affect relationship health as well as study skills).

The introduction grounds the need for increased and focused attention to wellness issues within the context of the mission and role of institutions of higher education. The growing numbers of college students, an overview of wellness, and current ways in which wellness is addressed with professional preparation activities are highlighted. Most important, the opportunity that exists for campuses and their personnel to make a difference in the lives of students, and ultimately our culture, is emphasized.

Emotional Wellness is the initial section of this book. The section starts with a chapter on *stress management*, where the authors examine stressors within the lives of different types of students: millennials, nontraditional, international, veterans, and those in recovery. Using several examples, the authors highlight ways of developing appropriate outcomes and methods to assess stress on campus. The chapter on *mental health*, a critical area of increasing importance, emphasizes some of the current issues among students; critical to this discussion is an examination of, and call to action for, the important role of colleges and universities. Collaboration toward building a caring community and a resiliency framework is a major point of this author. *Technology* is the third area within this section; while this could be included within the *Social Wellness* section as well, the author highlights current young adult usage patterns and shows research on linkages with mental health, interpersonal communication, cyberbullying, and other issues.

The second section emphasizes four topics associated with social wellness. Its first chapter, *Relationship Health*, offers current research as well as recommendations on self and self-identity, families, friends and peers, significant others, and faculty and staff. The author also provides some insights about the Internet and technology as they affect relationship health. The next chapter, *Sexual Decision-Making*, addresses topics from sexual orientation and gender identity to contraception and safer sex strategies, social norms, and sexual health educators. Numerous campus applications, with appropriate scenarios, provide a rich foundation for discussion and further examination. The chapter on *alcohol abuse* reviews current patterns of college student alcohol use, and highlights several common myths surrounding alcohol use. The authors address peer approaches, screening, outreach, and suggestions for changing the campus culture. Complementing this chapter is one on *prescription and illicit drug abuse*, which addresses student drug use and areas of concern, constructs for understanding how drugs affect the body, drug classifications, and an overview of substance abuse disorder, treatment, and recovery issues. Focused attention is provided on marijuana, heroin, and prescription drugs as "study aids."

The third section, *Intellectual Wellness*, includes a chapter on *study and writing skills*. The author emphasizes the importance of a well-prepared workforce, and how quality academic activity can prepare students with career readiness. Healthy strategies for traditional and nontraditional students are highlighted, with habits designed to better prepare a student to be successful. The role of technology, time management, research, and writing skills is highlighted.

Physical wellness is the construct for the fourth wellness dimension. The author of the *Sleep* chapter highlights the role of sleep in quality of life, and the need to promote healthy living and learning environments. With tips and case studies, the author provides recommendations for faculty, administrators, staff members, students, and family members. The chapter on *nutrition* addresses numerous myths associated with nutrition, providing an overview of food, nutrition, and sustenance. Strategies for higher education professionals as well as individual students are highlighted in this provocative chapter. In much the same vein, the authors of the *Exercise* chapter examine fitness trends and emphasize ways cardiovascular exercise, strength training, stretching and flexibility, and hydration and nutrition can be incorporated in healthy and appropriate ways. They also address weight control and motivation for maximum results.

Spiritual Wellness is the last section of the book, with a single chapter on *spirituality*. In this chapter, the author emphasizes the ways in which discussions about spirituality, while often uncomfortable for professionals, are an important part of students' lives. She provides an understanding of spirituality, and posits how much spirituality and wellness are actually partners. With the use of case studies, she also makes recommendations for the campus as well as for professionals themselves.

Summing Up

While this book does not encompass all wellness issues, it does provide attention to a dozen key topics important to the lives of students. Grounded in the context of student success and retention, these 12 wellness topics are offered with current research, noted controversies, and specific and global action steps for campuses to consider.

Each of the authors responded well to a tall order: summarize the current science, and discuss ways in which campus professionals, from all walks of life on campus, can incorporate this in the individual as well as campus-wide perspective. Plus, they were advised, it is important to do this in a relatively short space of a single chapter. Indeed, entire books and book series have been written on these topics; some of these are identified in the references at the end of each chapter. In addition, resources for students, faculty, staff, and administrators are shared in the online resources. These resources are available for download at: www.routledge. com/books/details/9781138020979/.

The reader is encouraged to examine these topics, and identify ways in which they can be best addressed with his or her own life, and on the campus. Further professional development and discovery are anticipated.

Will this make a difference? Time will tell. It's the opportunity we have with ourselves and with our students, for a healthier tomorrow. I think our opportunity, indeed our challenge, is best summed up by the campus motto inscribed at the entrance of Radford University's Hurlburt Student Center: "Investing in Lifetimes."

1

Introduction

A Mandate for Higher Education

DAVID S. ANDERSON

Overview

College students' health and wellness are, to a large extent, vital for the overall success of students while enrolled as a student. Called "survival skills," "approaches to enhance college success," or simply "wellness strategies," positive results with these issues can make a difference with students' growth and goal attainment in various areas, from intellectual success to emotional balance, from life health skills of exercise, nutrition, and sleep to study skills and stress management approaches.

Further, students' success with wellness affects the achievement of their college's mission. Institutions of higher education have the growth and development of students as a central part of their missions, regardless of institutional size, religious affiliation, private or public status, urban or rural setting, or years of existence. Typical mission statements articulate the development of sound minds, critical thinking, strong values, career-oriented skills, a worldview, cultural appreciation, and skills, all designed to last a lifetime. Thus, students' skills surrounding wellness issues and topics are beneficial to both the individual students as well as to the institution itself.

Attention to the lives of students outside the academic classroom has long been rooted within the academy in the United States. The traditional role of the faculty serving all aspects of students' lives, to the highly fully developed profession of student affairs found throughout higher education institutions, has been a continuous evolution over decades and even centuries.

> American higher education as we know it today represents the end product of a long period of interaction between the Western European university heritage and the native American physical and social environment. From this process of transplantation and continuous adaptation have emerged those aspects of academic culture which we have come to recognize as "characteristically American."
>
> (Brubacher & Rudy, 1968, p. 390)

The evolution of supportive services, meaningful activities, prepared professionals, and healthy engagement of students in their institutions of higher learning will undoubtedly continue. This evolution is not necessarily one of increased activities and services (although that may be part of a redesigned future), particularly during years of financial constraints and a reexamination of services; the evolution anticipated, and needed, is based on a careful assessment of the nature and scope of interaction between the students and the institution where they are enrolled. Drawing upon the mission statements found at our colleges and universities, it is appropriate and timely to assess ways in which students can be supported, and encouraged, to maximize the opportunities they have for education and growth. The evolution, then, is one of determining how best to achieve these needs, and how best to facilitate students' actualization of their own potential.

The opportunities and responsibilities of institutions of higher education were highlighted well by Sanford (1962) over a half-century ago: "If our culture and our society are to be changed at all by the deliberate application of intelligence and foresight, no agency has a better chance of initiating change than our institutions of higher learning" (p. 19).

College Students

According to the National Center for Education Statistics (NCES), over 21 million individuals are enrolled in degree-granting institutions in the United States. This is a significant increase over the nearly 16 million enrolled in 2001, which was up 11% over 1991. During the 2001–2011 decade, full-time students increased 38%, and the number of part-time students rose 23%. During this same time period, the percentage of traditional-age college students (18 to 24 years old) enrolled in college reached a level of 41% from a level of 36% in 2001. For students over age 25, enrollment rose by 41 over the 2001–2011 decade. The NCES estimates, for the decade 2011–2021, an enrollment rise of 13% for students under age 25, and 14% for those age 25 and above.

The "traditional" college student arrives on campus having recently graduated from high school. This young person is eager to participate in the academic, social, cultural, recreational, and personal life opportunities and challenges that abound on the college campus. Many college students live on a residential campus, having experiences in the residence halls and much that a life on campus offers. Many other students are commuters, sometimes traveling to campus solely for classes, and often becoming involved with campus life at varying levels. Many college students work, sometimes remaining as full-time students, and other times managing college studies as a supplement to their full-time employment. Some students transfer from one school to another, sometimes enrolling in a community college for the first year or two before relocating to a four-year institution. Still others are what is referred to as "nontraditional," including those who have provided service to the nation and arrive at, or return to, college as a veteran; some students work after high school, and/or were not prepared to attend or desirous of attending college, and then arrive on campus at an older age.

Regardless of the background of the student, and whether the individual is a first-generation college student or comes from a family where enrollment in college has been a way of life for many generations, students have health and wellness needs. The issues associated with student success or nonsuccess in college abound;

these include, but are not limited to, handling the newfound stress, developing appropriate ways to study and write, gaining new understanding about such common topics as sleep or nutrition, and learning about alcohol or drugs in ways not previously heard. Ultimately, the aim is to succeed in college, and to make the investment of time, money, and effort worthwhile.

While the aims of academic, social, cultural, and personal growth abound for students, various factors can get in the way. For students who seek academic success or progress in various other areas of their lives, any of a range of concerns can block the attainment of these goals. While some of these can be anticipated, others are totally unexpected.

- Consider study skills: Could a student do better on exams or with written assignments if greater time was taken or academic preparation was more appropriate? Absolutely.
- Consider a student whose participation with an athletic team or student organization is important to his or her self-esteem, and believes that drugs or alcohol are necessary to succeed; is this an appropriate or helpful strategy? Definitely not.
- Could students be provided with skills and attitudes that aid them in these and similar situations, on campus and throughout life? Definitely.
- Alternatively, the unexpected loss of funding for college, whether through personal employment or parents' or others' financial assistance being dropped, is a challenge for which few are prepared.
- Similarly, stressors abound with changes in assignments, new grading criteria, departure of friends and trusted mentors, health issues, and even fluctuations in the weather.

Each of these issues, anticipated and unanticipated, affects the lives of our students, the culture of our campuses, and the lives of professionals. College professionals, whether student affairs, faculty, staff, or other individuals, are well served to be as acquainted as possible with the issues facing students, and identifying ways of minimizing the impact of these on the lives of students. This doesn't mean making things easier or negating many aspects of the "real world"; it means that it is appropriate, and, in fact, the obligation of college professionals, to connect students with the resources and services that do exist, and to facilitate their engagement with these resources. This doesn't translate to a guarantee that everything will go well, and that the student will demonstrate exemplary work and skills in all aspects of life in college; what it does do is connect students with resources, and further reminds them of the importance of self-responsibility for maximizing their own success.

What Is Wellness?

Before turning to specific needs surrounding wellness, it is helpful to provide a brief overview of wellness. Wellness is a concept that goes by varying definitions. Some view wellness as the state of not having disease or not being ill; that is, if someone is not sick then they must be well. Others view wellness as a measure of reducing the incidence of negative behaviors or attitudes, such as stress, low self-esteem, lack of exercise, poor nutrition, drug abuse, or sleep disorders.

A starting point is with the World Health Organization, which nearly 70 years ago articulated, "Health is a state of complete positive physical, mental and social well-being and not merely the absence of disease or infirmity" (Preamble to the Constitution of the World Health Organization, 1946). Further, its Universal Declaration of Human Rights (1948) states the following:

- All human beings are born free and equal in dignity and rights. They are endowed with reason and conscience and should act towards one another in a spirit of brotherhood. (Article 1)
- Everyone has the right to a standard of living adequate for the health and well-being of himself and of his family, including food, clothing, housing and medical care and necessary social services, and the right to security in the event of unemployment, sickness, disability, widowhood, old age or other lack of livelihood in circumstances beyond his control. (Article 25 [1])
- Everyone has the right to rest and leisure, including reasonable limitation of working hours and periodic holidays with pay. (Article 24 [1])
- Everyone has the right freely to participate in the cultural life of the community, to enjoy the arts and to share in scientific advancement and its benefits. (Article 27 [1])

All of these elements are important parts of wellness.

Over three decades ago, health was reconceptualized as being not the absence of disease but rather overall fitness that applies to the body, mind, and spirit. This quality health concept was named "wellness" and emphasized healthy living. Powers and Dodd (2003, p. 8) define wellness as "a state of healthy living" and emphasize that it is "achieved by the practice of a healthy lifestyle, which includes regular physical activity, proper nutrition, eliminating unhealthy behaviors, and maintaining good emotional and spiritual health."

The focus with wellness is on optimum health and well-being, and includes multiple dimensions. *Emotional wellness* addresses feelings and ways of problems and situations that occur throughout one's daily life. *Intellectual wellness* emphasizes cognitive abilities, problem-solving, adaptability, creativity, and critical thinking. *Occupational wellness* blends one's professional productivity and skills with making a living and contributing to society as a whole. *Social wellness* includes communications and relationship skills. *Spiritual wellness* links one's personal needs to the larger societal and world context.

A more forward-looking view is espoused by Seligman (2008, p. 3), with an emphasis on positive health that combines "excellent status on excellent biological, subjective and functional measures." In essence, wellness is about being positive and proactive. Wellness is preventive. Wellness is optimistic. Wellness is never-ending. Wellness is a journey. While wellness doesn't have a defined "endpoint" (e.g., a person is never completely "there"), a state of wellness is one of relative balance and productivity in a person's life. It's about actualized potential, knowing that one can always get better and be better throughout the range of aspects of life.

The former director of the Centers for Disease Control and Prevention from 1977 to 1983, William Foege, MD, summed up prevention well decades ago. He said, "The rationale for prevention is clearly the improvement of life quality; nonetheless, when prevention programs can be shown not only to improve life quality but also to reduce health-care expenditures and provide savings in other ways, a decision by budget makers to avoid adequate funding of such programs is already a decision to increase expenditures for that condition and simultaneously to increase human suffering. It is a decision to tolerate fraud, waste and abuse."

Student Issues With Wellness

Just as a range of knowledge, skills, and attitudes can be helpful for students to achieve their goals and dreams, a range of issues can also get in the way of their success. A helpful starting point is to understand the nature and scope of some of the issues facing students today. Undoubtedly, numerous other issues are not currently assessed or identified, thus providing a tremendous research opportunity.

One of the primary sources of information and data about college students' health and wellness is the American College Health Association's (ACHA) National College Health Assessment (NCHA). Conducted since 2000, the data provides a rich compilation of students' issues surrounding health (ACHA, 2014). Noteworthy, as a starting point, is that over one-half (58.6%) of students described their health as very good or excellent, and over 9 in 10 students (91.2%) described it as good, very good, or excellent.

Students were asked about the extent to which various factors affected their academic performance, all within the last year. For 2014, top among that listing were stress (30.8%), anxiety (21.8%), sleep difficulties (21.0%), cold/flu, sore throat (15.1%), work (13.8%), depression (13.5%), Internet use/computer games (11.6%), concern for a troubled friend or family member (10.9%), and participation in extracurricular activities (10.5%). While some may not have been identified as particularly high (e.g., relationship difficulties were 9.5%, alcohol use was 4.1%, and finances were 6.2%), these issues may actually be having greater impact, yet not be acknowledged by students through this self-report survey process.

Among the students citing alcohol use, over one in five (22%) reported consuming seven or more drinks at a time, with the average number of drinks being 4.82 per person. Nearly one in seven (14.0%) students reported using one or more prescription drugs not prescribed for them during the last year, with 8.3% reporting the use of stimulants, 6.2% using pain killers, and 3.6% using sedatives. This is consistent with other data, from the Monitoring the Future Study, which documents that, on a monthly basis, 63.1% of full-time college students drink alcohol, 14.0% use tobacco, and 20.6% use marijuana; further, 35.2% of students consumed five or more drinks at least once in the past two weeks (Johnston, O'Malley, Bachman, & Schulenberg, 2012).

From an overall contextual perspective, students reported feeling, in the last two weeks, overwhelmed by all they had to do (51.4%), feeling exhausted, and

not from physical activity (50.1%), feeling very sad (24.7%), feeling very lonely (24.1%), feeling overwhelming anxiety (22.1%), and feeling things were hopeless (16.6%). Reflecting on the past year, six in seven students (86.4%) reported feeling overwhelmed, and four in five (82.1%) felt exhausted. One in six students (17.3%) reported having received a verbal threat over the past year, with 1 in 11 (9.1%) citing an emotionally abusive intimate relationship. Beyond this, nearly one-half (49.1%) of students reported 3 or more of 12 issues being traumatic or very difficult to handle during the past year. These issues included academics (with 47.4% citing this one alone), finances (33.2%), intimate relationships (30.7%), family problems (27.6%), and sleep difficulties (27.1%). Noteworthy is that less than one in four (24.9%) cited none of these issues. Translating that slightly, three in four students reported having some issue, over the past year, that was traumatic or very difficult to handle.

Similar results surrounding wellness issues are found with the well-regarded research done by the Higher Education Research Institute (HERI) at UCLA, founded by Alexander Astin. HERI's studies provide insights regarding freshmen as well as seniors enrolled at colleges and universities nationwide. Among freshmen, one-third (33.1%) reported being overwhelmed by all they had to do, 8.9% felt depressed, at a level of "frequently" during the past year; further 45.1% reported falling asleep in class, "frequently" or "occasionally" during the past year (Eagan, Lozano, Hurtado, & Case, 2013). Approximately two-thirds of respondents, however, cited as "a major strength" or "somewhat strong" their critical thinking skills (63.7%) and problem-solving skills (69.7%); interpersonal skills were rated at these levels by 50.4% of respondents, and ability to manage time effectively by 52.9% (Eagan et al., 2013).

HERI's (2014) study of college seniors provides further insights. "Whether through formal mentorship programs, classroom interactions, or informal encounters, faculty and staff play an important role in students' academic, social, and personal growth. Among graduating seniors, 40.6% responded that faculty frequently provided them with emotional support and encouragement. Additionally, 45.5% of students "strongly agree[d]" that at least one faculty member took an interest in their development, while 83.2% of students "agree[d]" or "strongly agree[d]" that faculty showed concern about their progress" (p. 2). It reports that the majority of respondents felt overwhelmed by all they had to do during their senior year (96% of women and 87.2% of men); among women, 46.1% cited that this happened frequently, and 26.8% of men reported this.

The concern, cited by this HERI report, is that college students' emotional health and well-being have changed, with fall 2010 having the lowest self-ratings of emotional health since 1985. "There is a growing demand for campus support services and resources that provide important forms of emotional health and personal counseling for students throughout their college years" (HERI, 2014, p. 4).

Students' wellness considerations are not limited to emotional health, stress, and their coping mechanisms with the use of substances. Attention to basics of a more physiological nature is also noted with the ACHA survey. Nutritional standards of three or more servings of fruits and vegetables per day were met by one in three students (36.7%), and one-half (50.4%) met the recommendation for moderate-intensity and/or vigorous-intensity exercise.

These data document that wellness issues are very much a part of students' lives and often hamper students' basic success or survival. Further, they can easily thwart the achievement of students' goals and dreams. This can be coupled with an anticipatory and forward-looking approach, that identifies the skills needed for this twenty-first century. These skills include, among others, critical thinking, ethical leadership, interpersonal relationships, innovation, balance, and engineered planning. Different skills are needed for various different careers today, and emerging skills—some the same and some as yet unidentified—will be needed for the world of the next decade and beyond.

The Collegiate Response to Wellness Issues

To have students expressing concerns about being overwhelmed, or citing ways in which various issues have affected their academic performance, provides impetus for leaders at our institutions of higher education to examine the ways in which colleges currently best address students' needs regarding these various wellness issues. Further self-reflection can identify ways of improving necessary resources.

Most campuses have services that help students with the various physical and mental health issues. The campus-based counseling and psychological services offices, or counseling centers, are a tremendous resource available for students who address their mental health issues. Based on the nature of the situation, some campuses will address these issues with personnel on campus, and some campuses will refer to outside resources as needed. For health issues and needs, a campus health center is typically the location where these medical and health needs are addressed. Similarly, career planning needs are addressed by career planning services, and recreational and exercise needs are addressed by facilities and resources that accommodate these needs. Substance use prevention services are, increasingly, handled with the designation of a campus coordinator, with over 90% of four-year campuses now having such an individual, a significant increase from 14% in 1979 and 74% in 1994 (Anderson & Gadaleto, 2012). Many of these offices, whether counseling, health services, career planning, wellness prevention, recreation, food services, campus activities, or others, will offer proactive approaches to help students to identify and refer themselves and others when in need.

A key question, however, revolves around the proactive nature of the campus services and resources overall. For example, a counseling or mental health service will see students by appointment, and on an as needed basis. Similarly, health clinics see students who access their services. It is actually other personnel on campus, such as the faculty, student affairs staff, advisors, and others (e.g., coaches and trainers for student-athletes, and residence hall directors and resident advisors for residential students), who see students on a more regular basis, often day-to-day. These individuals are likely the ones who see students at their best as well as at their lowest or more challenging points. The focus, then, is one of enhancing the preparedness of these individuals for promoting healthy wellness choices by students, as well as identifying areas of concern and making referrals as appropriate.

Professional Preparation for Wellness

While many campuses have a range of programs, services, and resources regarding these and other wellness issues, students' needs typically exceed the professional staff members' preparation. Consensus exists among student affairs administrators that the problems facing students for each of a dozen wellness issues are greater than the professional preparation among staff members. Anderson and Kretovics (2013) examined 13 wellness areas, and found that, with one exception (disability awareness), student affairs professionals surveyed believed the needs experienced by students exceeded their own preparedness. Further, this same study examined masters-level professional preparation programs in higher education and student affairs; among these 180 programs only 1 has a required course on wellness issues (Anderson & Kretovics, 2013). This is not to suggest that student affairs practitioners are ill-prepared; what it does show is that student affairs professionals believe their students' needs exceed their own preparation. It also shows that professional preparation programs, at the masters level, do not currently systematically address wellness issues. What remains unknown is where student affairs professionals get the preparation and training that they do have; also unknown is the level of knowledge, skill, awareness, and overall preparation among faculty with the range of issues associated with students' wellness. Further, to be examined more deliberately by each campus is the appropriate role for all professionals, and who, specifically, should be involved with various wellness issues faced by students.

What does the professional literature say about preparation for wellness issues? Currently, a global assessment of wellness preparation for higher education professionals is not found. What is found are results from localized preparation activity. For example, with suicide prevention focusing on resident advisors, Pasco, Wallack, Sartin, and Dayton (2012) examined the impact of experiential exercises on communication skills. Indelicato, Mirsu-Paun, and Griffin (2011) also looked at suicide prevention on a single campus. Attention to exercise was addressed by Racette et al. (2014), and attention to wellness courses in the general undergraduate curriculum was examined by Kulinna, Warfield, Jonaitis, Dean, and Corbin (2010). Graduate programs in student affairs are examined by Silver and Jackman (2014), Bair, Haworth, and Sandfort (2004), Lee and Helm (2013), and Renn and Jessup-Anger (2008). Kuk, Cobb, and Forrest (2008) reviewed competencies of entry-level practitioners, and Roberts (2007) also cited professional development methods. While these studies, among others, are helpful, they do not address the requisite questions cited in this introduction. That is, while some research suggests that professionals believe their own preparedness is less than what is needed for various wellness issues, the documentation about ways in which this preparation takes place is lacking.

Development of Professional Skills

Blending students' identified wellness issues with professionals' (and students') aspiration for maximizing students' well-being and success provides a clear foundation for more substantive and significant attention to addressing these wellness issues. Further impetus is provided with the uncertainty about the nature and source of professional preparedness to address these issues. That is, it is unclear what, specifically, is being taught and learned at graduate preparation programs regarding the range of wellness issues. Further, it is unclear, from any documentation, what is being done for in-service or other professional preparation for student services, faculty, and staff as they prepare to anticipate and respond to and most effectively and efficiently address many of these wellness issues. It is within this context that the compilation of scientific grounding and recommendations is prepared.

Within the student affairs arena, the Council for the Advancement of Standards in Higher Education has long held professional standards for higher education, with 43 distinct topic areas, ranging from academic advising to health promotion, and from campus activities to student conduct. These CAS Standards (2012) provide a rich and substantive foundation for quality services for students; guidelines and assessment protocols are identified clearly, and student affairs practitioners can examine ways in which their academic preparation and ongoing in-service and professional development activities complement their skills to best address these standards. For faculty members, the American Association of University Professors (AAUP) has its "Policy Documents and Reports," known as the "Redbook." This document addresses numerous issues in the lives of faculty, including academic freedom, accreditation, research and teaching, and more. A chapter on students addresses three issues: rights and freedoms of students, graduate students, and intercollegiate athletics.

The important premise for this edited work is that numerous campus individuals, not just student affairs, and not just a specific office, should be involved with addressing students' wellness issues. Attention to wellness issues and concerns, from both a proactive and reactive perspective, is viewed as a shared responsibility. While specific areas of expertise are legitimately and appropriately housed within various arenas on campus, all professional staff have some responsibility, at some level, to contribute to the well-being of the students enrolled at the institution. That goes back to the origins of the institution and the varied mission statements found within institutions of higher education. Faculty have an important role, extending beyond the classroom; Umbach and Wawrzynski (2005) found students' learning and engagement enhanced when faculty members incorporated more active learning and collaborative interaction. While not harkening back to the days of *in loco parentis*, the responsibility for students' maximum development shouldered by higher education professionals is both substantive and appropriate.

An important perspective, for all professional staff, is to know as much as possible and as is reasonable, within the scope of professional responsibilities. Every person does not have to be an expert in all the areas; what is important is to know the basics, and to know with whom it is appropriate and timely to partner to achieve the overall goals, both for the institution and for the student.

Preparing for an Evolving Tomorrow

Appropriate for leadership with our institutions of higher education is attention to this range of wellness issues. These issues are documented, and are not going to disappear on their own. These issues affect the lives of our students, and they can ultimately affect the livelihood of our institutions of higher education, both individually and collectively. As Benjamin Franklin said, "By failing to prepare, you are preparing to fail."

In preparing for "tomorrow," several things may be on the horizon. One has to do with rating systems; various rating systems have existed for colleges and universities. The question is what serves as the basis for these assessments. Will it be cost? Job opportunities following graduation? Income levels 5, 10, and 20 years later? Preparation for professional advancement or public service? Will these include a measure of the quality of education, including student/faculty ratios, engagement with full-time faculty members, or exposure to world issues? Will they incorporate the diversity of the student population, or access for financially challenged individuals?

Another has to do with accreditation. Accrediting bodies have their criteria, covering a range of topics and issues. Different professional organizations have their own standards and guidelines, whether this relates to those affiliated with health services (the Joint Commission or the Accreditation Association for Ambulatory Health Care) or counseling centers (with the International Association of Counseling Services), or with implications for teaching faculty (with the American Association of University Professors) or the Association of Governing Boards for campus boards of trustees. Regional associations provide accreditation for the institution as a whole.

More recently, the U.S. Department of Education is preparing a rating system for colleges and universities. Considerations focus on measures of value as well as access. What the final assessment criteria and process will become is not determined at this point.

The rationale for highlighting this is for college professionals, particularly those in leadership positions, to contextualize wellness issues within these discussions. Ultimately, student success, however defined, will be part of any of these, and wellness is a clear part of student success.

This can start with, but not necessarily be limited to, the following three elements:

1. What are the college's key attributes and areas of emphasis, as determined by its mission statement, its history, its constituencies, and its values?
2. What criteria are important to the various constituencies served by the institution? These include students, alumni, faculty and staff, community members, parents, and others?
3. What standards are specified by various accrediting bodies, associations, and rating systems?

The campus leadership will blend and organize these various factors, to determine the specific direction and areas of focus for the college or university. The question is how attention to the range of wellness issues can contribute to as well as detract from the accomplishment of the institution's goals and direction. More specifically, what are elements affiliated with students' lives, and the wellness aspects of their lives, that can play a part in the attainment of the institution's mission and desired outcomes?

For example, if one of the institutional goals is having students, on average, complete their program of studies within a specified time period, what might contribute to this? Certainly, quality study and exam skills will be important. Time management, sound academic advising, and good physical health will all be parts of this. Conversely, what might interfere with students' attainment of graduation in a timely way? Alcohol abuse and prescription and illicit drug abuse serve as obvious distractors to academic progress. Problematic relationships, unhealthy sexual decision-making, and poor sleep patterns can also contribute to this. Technology can be a factor, helping students to work smarter, more efficiently, and more effectively; however, it can also be a disinhibitor to academic success, particularly if students are involved with a type of technology addiction or distraction.

In order for institutions of higher education to do better with meeting their own objectives and maximize the attainment of their own missions, it is vital that they identify factors that contribute to their climate and their success. Similarly, it is important that institutional leaders identify what detractors or challenges exist to their ultimate attainment.

Mills (2000) offers some astute perspectives, helpful to the journey regarding wellness within the context of our institutions of higher education.

We can examine trends in an effort to answer the question "where are we going?"—and that is what social scientists are often trying to do. In doing so, we are trying to study history rather than to retreat into it, to pay attention to contemporary trends without being "merely journalistic," to gauge the future of these trends without being merely prophetic. All this is hard to do. We must remember that we are dealing with historical materials; that they do change very rapidly; that there are countertrends. And we have always to balance the immediacy of the knife-edge present with the generality needed to bring out the meaning of specific trends for the period as a whole. But above all, the social scientist is trying to see the several major trends together—structurally, rather than as happenings in a scatter of milieux, adding up to nothing new, in fact not adding up at all. This is the aim that lends to the study of trends its relevance to the understanding of a period, and which demands full and adroit use of the materials of history.

(p. 153)

Mills further states, "I think we must accept the point that we must often study history in order to get rid of it. . . . Rather than 'explain' something as 'a persistence from the past,' we ought to ask, 'why has it persisted?'" (p. 154). For campus leaders' discussions of wellness issues, the challenge then becomes one of clearly defining the issues and determining appropriate strategies for moving forward.

Making a Difference: What Campuses Can Do

The context of this introduction is that if college personnel, whether student affairs professionals, campus administrators, or faculty, don't address these issues in some meaningful ways, then it is not unreasonable to expect them to persist or get worse. Or, if campus efforts to address these issues are ineffective, the consequence is that the behavior continues unabated. If the decision is to be silent on the issue, with no boundaries or restraining messages or clear support of positive behavior heard by students, the consequence is that students will likely continue in their current patterns and find the same concerns. The result will be unnecessary and preventable problems, with numerous negative consequences; further, our students will not maximize their potential, and our institutional reputations will be challenged.

To address wellness issues, the following 13 approaches are offered as an initial outline for campus-based efforts:

1. *Start with a positive, hopeful attitude.* Realize that wellness incorporates issues that have been part of higher education and young people for years. These can be much better managed if they are properly defined and articulated. These issues are manageable, and many of the associated problems are preventable.
2. *Gather local information about the needs and issues.* This may include perceptions that students have about various wellness issues and resources. Build upon the national NCHA data, and localize it with similar and locally appropriate data. This may include behavior patterns, attitudes, perceptions, and concerns.
3. *Realize that most students, most of the time, make healthy decisions.* Address areas of concern, which may be higher for certain groups, and may ebb and flow from one year to the next. Identify current and emerging areas of need, based on where risky behaviors or attitudes and other areas of concern or gaps exist.
4. *Build a reasonable plan.* It's important to address identified needs, and take into account existing resources, both on and off the campus. It is important that the program be both idealistic and realistic. By clearly specifying and articulating needs and plans, the resources will be more likely to be put into place.
5. *Be comprehensive.* Incorporate a wide range of strategies within the specified plan; include policies and procedures, training and education, public awareness and support services, and individual and environmental approaches.
6. *View this as a shared responsibility.* All areas of the campus community should be involved, rather than having a "silo" approach or specialists only. Faculty members can support and set standards, police and security can educate,

student government can sponsor events, clubs and teams can set guidelines, alumni and community members can volunteer, and campus presidents and provosts can be vocal. It is not a single office's role or specialist's responsibility to "do it all"; campus professionals can serve as "first responders" for various wellness issues.

7. *Incorporate grounded strategies.* Use evidence-based and/or theory-guided approaches to achieve specified goals and objectives. To rely on what has been done historically or what "feels good" is not appropriate. Use current evidence-based strategies to bolster the campus effort. Use grounded approaches from an individual and environmental perspective.

8. *Utilize appropriate metrics.* These should address both long-term and shorter-range objectives. While it is helpful to measure specific patterns, it is also important to assess the impact of campus efforts in the short run, such as the effects on perceptions, behaviors, attitudes, knowledge, skills, campus approaches, viability of campus services, knowledge, and perceptions of existing and needed support services.

9. *Remain honest.* Share what you know and what you don't know, as all too often students' information and grounding on this topic are quite limited and/or misguided. Acknowledge where the research is inconclusive or evolving. Share where controversies exist, and engage in constructive dialog about these issues.

10. *Address underlying causes.* With the aim of moving toward a more naturalistic approach to preventing and responding to problems and issues faced by students, start with the framework of emotional, social, cognitive, and physical reasons, as well as the larger environmental construct within which they live. Explore ways of best addressing these issues on the campus and within the surrounding community.

11. *Provide a supportive environment.* Emphasize a campus setting in which students, faculty, staff, and others can grow and prosper. Identify ways in which the campus, through its policies, procedures, resources, setting, services, and personnel, addresses the issues of living and learning in as complete and appropriate way as possible.

12. *Continue to learn.* The field of wellness issues continues to evolve as new issues make their way into the campuses and society as a whole. Student needs and questions also evolve, as do the scientific underpinnings of various approaches. It is vital that campus professionals continue to stay abreast of these needs, questions, and strategies.

13. *Provide substantive leadership.* It is vital that campus leaders be involved with and supportive of the campus effort. This includes statements by the president, chancellor, and/or provost, and more active involvement by the chief student affairs officer, whether through convening a task force or oversight group, or providing probing questions about how well the issues of wellness are addressed. Leaders from various academic, student services, and other offices and units should ensure that appropriate attention is provided to this issue; this suggests being visible on and outspoken about this.

Conclusion

Almost one-half century ago, Brubacher and Rudy (1968) said, "American higher education has by no means even yet arrived at an equilibrium. It remains in a state of dynamic evolution, much like the culture which surrounds it and sustains it. To be sure, the main themes of democracy and responsiveness to change stand out in bold relief for all to see. . . . The true American University lies in the future" (p. 406). Similarly, Sanford cited the important role of institutions of higher education with issues such as this, noted at the start of this chapter. Such is the case for wellness issues for higher education. This is the case for individual students, for the professionals serving them, and for the institutions of higher education within which all exist.

The challenges and opportunities abound. Based on the current state of affairs, numerous needs exist. However, things are changing quickly, much more so than in the fast-changing world described by Alvin Toffler (1970) in *Future Shock* decades ago. Professionals in the higher education setting are, and will continue, transforming the institution of higher education. Faculty, student affairs professionals, and other college professionals will continue to promote the safety and welfare of students; these have been and will continue to be central to their professional positions. Beyond this, however, the opportunity—the mandate—exists to promote the health and well-being of students. The challenge is one of promoting wellness with individuals and with the environment of the campus. It is vital that each professional identify ways, appropriate to his or her roles and responsibilities, to touch students to help students maximize their potential. Encourage students to use the resources that are available; help identify new resources that both address and anticipate new and emerging needs among the students. Take stock of the current campus culture—is it truly pro-wellness? How is this demonstrated? How is this articulated? How is this measured?

The results will show themselves in the years and decades to come. At that point, we will know how our commitment has been implemented and articulated, and what difference it has made with our students. Undoubtedly, attention to wellness issues will take new forms. But the impact will, within our vision, be one of stronger and healthier institutions and individuals.

References

American Association of University Professors. (2014). *AAUP policy documents and reports* (11th ed.). Baltimore: Johns Hopkins University Press.

American College Health Association [ACHA]. (2014). National College Health Assessment. Spring 2014 Reference group executive summary. Hanover, MD. Retrieved from http://www.acha-ncha. org/reports_ACHA-NCHAII.html

Anderson, D., & Gadaleto, A. (2012). The College Alcohol Survey 1979-2012: The national longitudinal survey on alcohol, tobacco, other drug and violence issues at institutions of higher education. Unpublished research findings. Fairfax, VA: George Mason University. Retrieved from www. caph.gmu.edu

Anderson, D., & Kretovics, M. (2013, March). *Substance abuse and wellness: How well do we prepare our staff?* Paper presented at the Annual Convention of the American College Personnel Association, Las Vegas.

Bair, C. R., Haworth, J. G., & Sandfort, M. (2004). Doctoral student learning and development: A shared responsibility. *Journal of Student Affairs Research and Practice, 41*(4), 1277–1295.

Brubacher, J. S., & Rudy, W. (1968). *Higher education in transition: A history of American colleges and universities.* New York, NY: Harper & Row.

Council for the Advancement of Standards in Higher Education. (2012). *CAS professional standards for higher education* (8th ed.). Washington, DC: Author.

Eagan, K., Lozano, J. B., Hurtado, S., & Case, M. H. (2013). *The American freshman: National norms, fall 2013.* Los Angeles, CA: Higher Education Research Institute.

Higher Education Research Institute. (2014). *HERI research brief, December: Findings from the 2014 College Senior Survey.* Los Angeles, CA: Author.

Indelicato, N. A., Mirsu-Paun, A., & Griffin, W. D. (2011). Outcomes of a suicide prevention gatekeeper training on a university campus. *Journal of College Student Development, 52*(3), 350–361.

Johnston, L. D., O'Malley, P. M., Bachman, J. G., & Schulenberg, J. E. (2012). *Monitoring the Future national survey results on drug use, 1975–2011: Vol. 2. College students and adults ages 19–50.* Ann Arbor: Institute for Social Research, University of Michigan.

Kuk, L., Cobb, B., & Forrest, C. S. (2008). Perceptions of competencies of entry-level practitioners in student affairs. *Journal of Student Affairs Research and Practice, 44*(4), 1061–1088.

Kulinna, P. H., Warfield, W. W., Jonaitis, S., Dean, M., & Corbin, C. (2010). The progression and characteristics of conceptually based fitness/wellness courses at American universities and colleges. *Journal of American College Health, 58*(2), 127–131.

Lee, J. J., & Helm, M. (2013). Student affairs capitalism and early-career student affairs professionals. *Journal of Student Affairs Research and Practice, 50*(3), 290–307.

Mills, C. W. (2000). *The sociological imagination.* Oxford: Oxford University Press.

Pasco, S., Wallack, C., Sartin, R. M., & Dayton, R. (2012). The impact of experiential exercises on communication and relational skills in a suicide prevention gatekeeper-training program for college resident advisors. *Journal of American College Health, 60*(2), 134–140.

Powers, S. K., & Dodd, S. L. (2003). *Total fitness and wellness.* San Francisco, CA: Pearson Education.

Racette, S. B., Inman, C. L., Clark, B. R., Royer, N. K., Steger-May, K., & Deusinger, S. S. (2014). Exercise and cardiometabolic risk factors in graduate students: A longitudinal, observational study. *Journal of American College Health, 62*(1), 47–56.

Renn, K., & Jessup-Anger, E. R. (2008). Preparing new professionals: Lessons for graduate preparation program from the National Study of New Professionals in Student Affairs. *Journal of College Student Development, 49*(4), 319–335.

Roberts, D. M. (2007). Preferred methods of professional development in student affairs. *Journal of Student Affairs Research and Practice, 44*(3), 959–975.

Sanford, N. (Ed.). (1962). *The American college: A psychological and social interpretation of the higher learning.* New York, NY: Wiley.

Seligman, M. E. P. (2008). Positive health. *Applied Psychology, 57*(S1), 3–18.

Silver, B. R., & Jakeman, R. C. (2014). Understanding intent to leave the field: A study of student affairs master's students' career plans. *Journal of Student Affairs Research and Practice, 51*(2), 170–182.

Toffler, A. (1970). *Future shock.* New York, NY: Random House.

Umbach, P. D., & Wawrzynski, M. R. (2005). Faculty do matter: The role of college faculty in student learning and engagement. *Research in Higher Education, 46*(2), 153–184.

World Health Organization. (1946). Preamble to the constitution of the World Health Organization. *Official Records of the World Health Organization, 2,* 100.

World Health Organization. (1948). The universal declaration of human rights, Article 1. National Center for Education Statistics (NCES).

Section 1
Emotional Wellness

Stress Manage ...nt
#Too Blessed to Be Stressed
CONSTANCE S. BOEHM AND LANCE C. KENNEDY-PHILLIPS

Introduction

Stress is discussed on college campuses every day and in many different ways. Faculty members murmur that they are stressed and unable to handle the demands of research, teaching, and service. Parents are concerned about stress of their sons and daughters and trust that the university will support their students and help them resolve their stressors. University student affairs staff struggle to balance the demands of their jobs and often work 50–60 hours a week, leading to them feeling stressed and burned out. Our students tell us that they are more stressed than they have ever been; that they drink and smoke to relieve stress; and that we need to do something to help them handle their stress.

One can't pick up a copy of a higher education journal without some reference highlighting mental health issues, many of these being stress-related. College students are not sleeping enough, are increasingly misusing prescription drugs, continue to engage in high-risk drinking, take out higher amounts of student loans, work more hours and more often work off campus, and are constantly connected to social media. Stress on our college campuses is at new highs, with student affairs and other professional administrators contemplating new ways to help students manage this stress.

The National College Health Assessment (NCHA), a national research survey organized by the American College Health Association, provides data about college student habits, behaviors, and perceptions about the most prevalent health issues. The NCHA reference group executive summary for 2013 lists that 28.5% of students reported stress affected their individual academic performance over the last 12 months. Stress was the highest rated factor, when compared with 29 other factors, including anxiety, sleep, homesickness, and depression. Individual academic performance was defined as received a lower grade in a course; received an incomplete or dropped the course; or experienced a significant disruption in thesis, dissertation, research, or practicum work. In addition, 57% of females rated their overall level of stress as more than average or tremendous over the last 12 months, compared to 43% of males who rated their stress the same (American College Health Association, 2013, p. 5).

Student affairs areas offer a variety of programs and services designed to help students manage their stress through departments such as Counseling and Consultation Service, Career Services, Student Wellness Centers, Student Health Services, and Recreational Sports, among others. In particular, campuses rely heavily on counseling centers for support in dealing with students' stressors and providing services to reduce the negative stressors for students. Unfortunately, campus counseling centers have long wait times and struggle to keep up with the demands (Farrell, 2008). Some centers have offered online counseling, online self-help brochures, and extensive website information to expand and enhance their services to meet the demands. This effort is led by the University of Florida's Therapist Assisted Online (TAO) initiative that delivered encouraging results with its pilot program, which included weekly video consultations with therapists (O'Neil, 2014).

In addition, such programs as *Let's Talk* at University of Wisconsin-Madison and Wellness Coaching at the Ohio State University assist with the demands at college counseling centers by supplementing their services. *Let's Talk* helps students with specific problems and is offered at various outreach locations on a walk-in basis, where students can get an idea of what more formal counseling may be like (University of Wisconsin–Madison, 2013). Wellness coaching is a free one-on-one and group service that provides opportunities for students to better understand the life they want to be living, both now and in the future. It is strength-based, encourages positive reflection, and suggests strategies to overcome students' challenges (Ohio State University, 2014).

Other campuses are increasing numbers of counseling staff, forming crisis teams, expanding outreach services, and bringing therapy dogs into their waiting room areas to help students relax. Three-quarters of the counseling centers offer stress reduction programs (Altschuler & Skorton, 2013). These programs focus on reducing stress during finals and the benefits of staying fit, of eating healthy, and of maintaining social connections to assist with stress management. Many centers provide students with mindfulness programming, stress reduction technique workshops, and online relaxation tapes.

Addressing college student stress is not just the responsibility of counseling centers. A number of resources on campus and online can assist with identifying stressors, with creative outreach activities, and with helping students manage their stressors. Recreational sports departments increase and promote fitness classes, campus dining services highlight healthy food options, faculty direct students to relaxation resources, and financial coaches help students budget their money. A number of online resources both locally and nationally provide stress assessments, brochures, videos, phone applications, and other stress reduction resources, some of which are highlighted in this chapter's resource section.

Campuses are held more and more accountable for the student learning experience and for student success after college. Stress affects the academic experience, and if students are not able to effectively deal with stress, it is the responsibility of the university to put the appropriate mechanisms in place to assist students in developing successful coping skills. Those areas providing services must have an outcomes orientation with clearly defined objectives when developing these services to help students cope with stress. There are many valuable ways to assess and address stress on a college campus. These sound assessment methods, as discussed later in this chapter, can provide the evidence needed to document the issues of stress and guide practices. By examining specific populations and their stressors, this chapter describes college student stress, supports ways to assess stress, and provides examples of best practices.

Defining Stress

Stress of today's college students is transforming our college campuses as it continues to rise and show itself in many ways. The wellness of our students is impacted in negative and positive ways through the manner in which students deal with their stressors. Stress has an impact on the way student affairs staffs provide services and what services are provided as expectations of parents and students change with regard to the role of the institution in helping students manage their daily lives. Parents and students expect their institution to teach students how to become healthy, productive adults, not just how to earn a living. College student stress is impacting this path for students.

The World Health Organization defines health as "the state of complete physical, mental, and social well-being and not merely the absence of disease or infirmity" (World Health Organization, 1948, p. 1). "It is the ability of each individual to successfully participate in the developmental tasks appropriate for their age; accomplish those tasks to the best of their ability; and to be resilient in the face of the stressors and challenges" (Ohio Adolescent Health Partnership, 2013, p. 7).

On our college campuses, students are experiencing lifestyle diseases, such as depression, anxiety, alcohol and drug abuse, and obesity, and these are often enhanced by stress. The belief that there is a relationship between stress and disease has been discussed for several decades. In fact, in a recent study researchers found such illnesses as the common cold linked to stress (Carnegie Mellon University, 2012). Another study showed that perfectionism among college students affected blood pressure, especially when they experienced stressful situations like tests (Albert, Rice, & Caffee, 2014). College students experience such stressors as multiple demands on their time and highly competitive academic programs, as described ahead by a first-year student.

I am not able to enter my academic program of choice on entrance to college, but I have to apply and compete for a spot in the highly selective academic program, special education. This program requires applicants to have additional work or volunteer experience in this field of study in order to be considered for this program. I am working for a family off campus who has a 13-year-old boy with autism and coaching. I am learning a great deal by working with the family and coaching, but it requires me to work an average of 30 hours/week along with managing my classwork, daily activities, and family and friend commitments.

First-year student, June 2014

Elements in any campus culture that harm community members' well-being in turn also harm the learning and teaching environment. In fact, many studies indicate strong correlations between health and academic performance, student retention, and satisfaction levels (Felsten & Wilcox, 1992; Pritchard & Wilson, 2003, p. 24). Research specifically indicates that social adaptation, physical fitness, and emotional stability can contribute to whether a student remains in school (Astin, 1999). Stress of college students impacts students at all levels, and the entire campus has a role to help students address stress, provide resources, and offer support.

One important factor to consider when researching stress is to explore which sources of stress are beneficial and which sources are detrimental. Stress is most often thought of as being negative to a student's well-being. Negative stressors include such things as too many commitments outside of class, relationship difficulties, overspending on credit cards, extreme homesickness, student loan expenses, final exams, death of a family member or friend, noise in the residence halls, and health issues. Some types of stress are positive for students, including being elected to a leadership position, starting a new romantic relationship, or landing a new job. Positive stressors help students stay motivated, feel good about their accomplishments, and enjoy life.

College administrators and faculty members strive to help students balance their stressors, both negative and positive, and take steps toward a healthier, happier, successful life. As advisors, mentors, disciplinarians, teachers, and supervisors, college staff and faculty do all they can to guide students and provide resources to students to help them effectively manage. An example of a campus that does this in an innovative manner is Georgetown University, where they integrate student health and wellness issues, including stress management discussions, into the curriculum (Olson & Riley, 2009).

Students' reactions to stress include psychological and physical responses, such as the inability to sleep or sleeping too much, loss of appetite or increase in appetite, acting out, drinking too much, smoking, overspending, or procrastination. Some students respond to stress in cognitive ways by keeping it bottled up and not talking about it or even recognizing it. One student described the way she responded to grade stress.

> I didn't want to tell my parents that I got a B in a class. I continued to dwell and worry about it. I had struggled with disordered eating in high school, and I felt these same issues returning. I also started cutting again. I felt like I was losing control and sought ways to be in control. I hid it by continually wearing long-sleeved shirts and loose-fitting clothes. I visited the gym at least daily and worked hard each day. If I missed a day, I worried and became upset and disappointed in myself.
>
> Anonymous student, September 2014

Stress and Today's Expanded College Student Population

Today's college students are diverse along with the stressors that they experience. According to the National Center for Education Statistics, 30% of university undergraduates are over the age of 24 and 40% of these students are part-time (Baum, 2010). In 2012–2013, more international students attended colleges and universities than ever before, at nearly 820,000 (Haynie, 2013). Students who are veterans make up only 3% of our college undergraduate population currently, but this number continues to rise (Sander, 2012). Another student population that is being recognized on college campuses with particular stressors is students in recovery from alcohol and other drugs (Perron et al., 2011).

In this chapter we explore in some detail: (1) the traditional-aged college student (18–24 years old), (2) the nontraditional-aged student (25–64 years old), (3) the international student, (4) the student who is a veteran, and (5) the student in recovery from alcohol and other drug addiction. Each of these different groups of students formulates different expectations and needs about their college experiences. These expectations influence their satisfaction and well-being while in college. Several factors influence their college experience, including academics, finances, social life, health, parents, and peers. If students' goals and self-determined academic targets are not met, they become dissatisfied and frustrated with their path through their college years. Without the necessary coping skills, this can lead to stress, restlessness, and obstacles to completion of their degrees (Murff, 2006).

Traditional-Aged Students: Millennial

Today's traditional-aged students were born prior to 2000. Their parents were baby boomers or Generation Xers, similar to many of the student affairs and other professional staff who currently engage with these students. The Millennial students are tech-savvy, feel special, and grew up with trophies for every activity, not just those they won. They enjoy working in teams because they grew up playing soccer, baseball, lacrosse, basketball, and any other sport offered in their community. This "connected generation" of students faces constant demands for their attention, from texts to tweets to Instagram. They say that their life is on their phone: pictures, contacts, homework, and more.

More of these students than students before them have mental health issues and were able to succeed academically in high school and move into higher education (M. Sharma, personal communication, September 25, 2014). They experienced terrorist attacks and campus shooting incidents and therefore come to college more concerned about safety on campus. They are the first generation of humans to live shorter lives than their parents, often due to risky behaviors and high stress (Belluck, 2005).

Traditional-aged college students want it all: a great social life, a great place to live, great grades, and a great job after college. Expectations like these lead to a great amount of stress. In fact, more than half of college students reported above average or tremendous stress levels in the spring 2012 American College Health

Association National College Health Assessment undergraduate summary, and 30% of students said it had a negative impact on their academic performance (American College Health Association, 2012).

A third-year student at a small private institution shared his thoughts about being a 20- year-old in college today.

> It's crappy how much stress we are under. College is supposed to be a time of learning more about oneself and growing as a person. Instead we try to balance grades, working, clubs, social interaction, sleep, etc. All the while being told there are no jobs, along with how awful our generation is as we are getting outperformed by students from other countries.
>
> Third-year student, May 2014

Millennial students focus on what's good for them, sometimes not acknowledging how it may affect anyone else. Often they were not really challenged in high school and didn't really have to study to get good grades. Their parents were there for them and often sheltered them from failure and gave them clear rules on how to succeed.

When coming to college, parents continue to be very connected. The average number of times parents and their students exchange texts per day is 7–8, with some texting as much as 20 times per day (J. Adams-Gaston, personal communication, August 5, 2014). Parents continue to be very engaged in their kids' lives by influencing or maybe even picking the courses that they take, where they live, and with whom they hang out. Parents are advisers and advocates.

Millennial students are perfectionistic, leaving high school with above 4.0 grade point averages and sometimes never even experiencing any grade other than an A. When met with a heavy course load during their first year of college and competing with classmates who are also perfectionists, some students pull all-nighters, use study aids to stay up, and end up being devastated by a less than perfect score. Some quickly conclude that they will not get a job if they don't have all A's all the time. They may base their personal worth on their grades.

Not only are students perfectionistic about their academic lives but also they are discontent in their social lives if they aren't the most popular on the floor or in their group. Sometimes millennial students are not where they feel they should be in their peer group and try new behaviors and habits to get to that position. If they are not invited to be part of their selected group, they feel that they have failed. They may submit to peer pressure in order to fit in and to be recognized. They are also concerned about never finding a mate and getting married. They worry about spending their lives alone.

Millennial students grew up hearing about school shootings, sexual violence, hate crimes, and other campus crime. These events are hanging in their mind every day. Frequent notices about campus incidents of sexual violence make the headlines nearly every week and are posted on campus at various locations, keeping this in front of students as constant reminders. Campus safety issues continue to be one of the most highly discussed worries for students on our campuses. In fact, at the Ohio State University, safety issues have been at the top of the student government leaders' concern for the last 10 years.

Homesickness may impede students' first weeks on campus and create great stress for them. Residence hall staffs see some of these students crying, not wanting to go to class, going home every weekend, and not fitting in on their floors. This could be addressed by helping students connect to their new place of residence even before they arrived. Phone calls or letters from upper-class students welcoming new students to the hall help students feel connected. Mentoring programs involving either upper-class students or faculty and staff also help students connect.

Checklist of Strategies for Traditional Aged Students

☐ Financial coaching opportunities
☐ Time management workshops
☐ Budgeting workshops
☐ Successful sleep tips
☐ Meditation classes

Nontraditional Students

The number of nontraditional students, including those who are over 24 years old, do not live on campus, work full-time, have families, and go to school part-time, is growing and greatly impacting our college student populations. Thirty-eight percent of those enrolled in higher education are over the age of 25, and one-fourth are over the age of 30 (Hess, 2011). Nontraditional students struggle with comparing themselves with most traditional students, who have more free time, who do not have the same financial struggles, and who do not have the conflict between education and other life obligations, like a family and work. A 30-year-old female, first-time college student at a large, public institution highlights her struggles ahead.

I am very blessed to have the opportunity to come to college. I have learned so much about the world around me and have met many amazing people. Going to college is like taking a free sociology class but with no grade attached. The most challenging thing that I face as a nontraditional student is not to compare my progress with others. I am learning that I may not always be at the same pace as someone who has been in school for the last 15 years of their life.

30-something third-year student, July 2014

Stressors of these students often revolve around time management, course selection, and resource identification. These students return to school after several years or start school for the first time. They may be interested in a different career or in enhancing their current career. When comparing themselves to traditional students they often do not feel as tech-savvy, as up-to-date on available resources, or as adaptable as recent graduates (E. Zehr, personal communication, September 1, 2014). They have a limited amount of time and energy to complete projects and connect to others in the classroom due to their commitments at home and/or at work.

Overwhelmingly, nontraditional students are challenged to comprehend and use the resources on campus, to manage their family and work commitments along with attending classes, and to maneuver online assignments and tests. Their time on campus is limited, and often they are challenged to be able to find the time or even the resources like computers and printers to complete some of their assignments. Their additional commitments challenge them to relate to the traditional-aged student, who is concerned about looking good, dating, and going out on the weekend, as well as doing well in class. They don't really understand the "study hard, party hard" mentality.

As the number of nontraditional students grows, student affairs staff and other professionals must recognize the stressors of these older students and their different needs. Adult students can bring a variety of life perspectives and experiences to the college student population. Campus professionals should assess if their programming and classroom structure are inclusive for the older student. Does the programming consider students' work and family responsibilities? Could older students be brought into the discussion and share their own experiences with the younger students?

Student affairs professional competencies, in particular, should be reframed to include working with the older, nontraditional students. These students have had different experiences and may be sensitive to a younger student affairs staff giving advice. Student affairs staff, as well as faculty and other staff, should be sensitive to the students' life experiences and exhibit active listening. Student affairs staff should explore the students' out-of-classroom, off-campus commitments, and work with these students from this perspective (Nunez, Stewart, & Harper, 2014).

Specifically, campus leadership should consider such resources as lactation rooms and lounges for nontraditional students between classes. Also offering cheap child care options for parents while they are in class would be valuable to this population. Online coaching and advising can assist nontraditional students when these resources are accessible from their homes.

Checklist of Strategies for Nontraditional Students

☐ Online resources that are offered 24/7
☐ Faculty recognize the special needs of these students; time constraints and family and work commitments

☐ In-person sessions on all the resources or provide online resource menu
☐ Goal-oriented sessions specifically for these students
☐ Events like career fairs held when they can attend without missing work or family commitments

International Students

Universities are looking to undergraduate and graduate international students to expand their global reach and to help domestic students learn and understand about the world. International students are coming to campuses in the United States to extend their education and develop their careers. In order to attend a university in the United States, they leave their families and friends, with little preparation for the cultural differences they will face, as expressed in the description from an international student on the Ohio State University campus. International students are challenged to be able to work on or off campus, have high tuition worries, and are challenged by basic needs of housing, food, and transportation. They may face racial, religious, and ethnic discrimination. International students often come to U.S. campuses without really understanding or speaking the language very well. They have to be able to learn the language well enough to be understood for such aspects as asking for directions and when responding in class.

Being homesick is one of the biggest stressors for me. School work is another big thing. I am an arts major, which to many American students is not that hard compared with STEM majors. However, as an international student, I have to put in double efforts to understand cultural contexts in many of my classes or school work. I have to do a large amount of research on American history and pop culture. So being in this major stresses me out a lot.

Another thing I noticed among my fellow international students is how they make friends with American students. Many of my international student friends complain to me that they find it hard to make friends with Americans because OSU is so big and they are kind of hanging around with people from their own country. It is far different from what we would have expected before we came here to study. I know this makes many people feel stressed too.

International student, July 2014

International students do not understand the college student culture, from the party scene to relationships to tobacco-free campuses. They seek to experience campus life as explained and demonstrated by domestic students. They go to parties with their friends and drink as the domestic students do. Stressed out from drinking too much and not understanding the consequences of this behavior, international students often will not seek guidance or assistance because of the stigma placed on getting help in their culture. Their culture supports independence and taking care of oneself without the need for help (C. Huang, personal communication, May 11, 2014).

In addition, international students also struggle with knowing where to go for assistance when they are struggling emotionally or academically. Support services have expanded exponentially, but the mechanisms of referral and advertisement have not kept pace. International students may keep to themselves and become more isolated and disconnected from others because of their lack of acknowledgment that they need help and lack of knowledge of available resources.

International students also want to please their parents and do not want them to know if they are struggling. They also want to get good grades. Their parents have paid a lot of money for them to attend a university in the United States and are expecting great grades and success in every way. They also want to complete their degree as quickly as possible and follow the plan outlined for them as they entered their program. They may feel committed to follow through with their choice of major regardless of whether they feel it is the best fit for them.

The Ohio State University Student Advocacy Center frequently works with students, including international students, who are experiencing stress that is impacting their academic success. In fact, in recent years, they have seen an increase in international students utilizing their services. A good example of one of these interactions occurred this past academic year when a student from China came to them, as described ahead.

An international student was majoring in business but was not performing well. She shared that her family had experienced some financial hardship and that she was not sure whether they could continue to pay her fees. Because international students are not eligible for federal financial aid, there are not many options. We made her aware of the possibility of a private loan, but in recent years the requirements placed on international students in order to be accepted for private loans have also become more stringent. This left few options for this student.

As we talked more, the student shared that she was not doing well partly because of the financial stressors, but also because she did not enjoy business and wanted to change her major. She did not want to disappoint her parents, who wanted her to major in business, because of the many sacrifices they made to send her to the United States for school. This student, like many others, was dealing with so many external pressures that were impacting her ability to focus on just being a student.

Director of Student Advocacy, August 2014

Checklist of Strategies for International Students

☐ Early orientation sessions that discuss being homesick
☐ American culture workshops, including pop culture
☐ Alcohol and other drug workshops woven into their orientation
☐ International students share their experiences with other students
☐ Mentoring programs with American students
☐ Special student affairs office that provides specialized services, including social activities

Students Who Are Veterans

Students who are veterans are charged to take care of each other and depend on each other to accomplish their mission while in the military. They are accustomed to working and living together. Instead, in the university classroom, most undergraduates are focused on themselves and concerned about themselves and their academic outcomes. Students who are veterans are challenged to connect with these nonveteran students in the classroom. Veterans are not used to trusting others who are not veterans. A female veteran shares her experiences ahead.

After being in the military it can be difficult to relate to other students in some aspects. For example, I may stress a little about an upcoming exam, but unlike many of my fellow students, I would never go into full "freak out" mode. An exam just doesn't seem like that big of a deal when you've had mortars and rockets launched at you. In another instance, the military teaches you to rely on the person next to you—your mission won't succeed unless all soldiers contribute. Conversely, some of my fellow students are so competitive that they won't share their notes, much less see my cohort as a team. They act as though I am actively trying to sabotage their chances of graduating *magna cum laude*, when in reality I just want to graduate.

Student who is a veteran, May 2014

Students who are not veterans often see the veterans' experiences as fascinating, and conversations can be awkward. Sometimes students ask inappropriate questions about being in combat. Very few current students have interacted with anyone in the military, and they are curious to learn about it.

Students who are veterans may feel out of place and have trouble relaxing and concentrating. They may be concerned about what they have missed while they were deployed and may feel behind academically and socially compared to other students their own age. They may be confused with the change in environments and not know how to deal with the very different routine. They may get impatient with how laid-back some professors and students may be about responding. They may also be anxious about being redeployed and leaving their course work once again.

Veterans face a variety of stressors on a college campus and respond in a variety of ways: shutting down, excessive use of alcohol, becoming a loner, or even leaving college. Veterans can experience post-traumatic stress disorder (PTSD) after being in combat. They can return with hearing and vision loss, missing limbs, and traumatic brain injuries. They may struggle to keep up because they can't concentrate and can't find resources to help. They are not used to having to search for resources, such as counseling, health services, or physical activity opportunities, but instead are accustomed to being given clear instructions about where to go for targeted, specific assistance and resources.

Many institutions have addressed the needs of this growing population by engaging veterans in the planning of their services to help themselves and other veterans adjust to life in and out of the classroom. Many are hiring staff to work specifically with veterans, including counselors who help the veterans connect to Veterans Affairs and other resources. Florida State University holds a special class for veterans that allows them to meet other veterans and that addresses their specific concerns; it also offers veterans the opportunity to defer certain fees until their veteran benefits are processed (Florida State University, 2014).

Checklist of Strategies for Students Who Are Veterans

☐ Engage veterans in the planning of activities specifically for them
☐ Develop mentoring programs among veterans
☐ Provide an area for veterans to hang out and connect with one another
☐ Engage with Veterans Affairs on campus
☐ Provide special housing

Students in Recovery

A recent trend on college campuses is recognizing students in recovery from alcohol and other drugs and their particular challenges and stressors. As one student in recovery said on a panel to student life staff at the Ohio State University, "I walk home using routes that are really out of the way for me but where I do not have to pass the bars and smell the alcohol" (Stephanie, personal communication, September 17, 2013). Every football Saturday, they are surrounded by the smell of alcohol and students talking about tailgating and what they are going to do after the game. This is stressful for students in recovery, who are seeking sober activities and sober friends. It is difficult for them to feel a part of a community that appears to have no understanding or consideration for what they must do to remain healthy and productive.

Students in recovery also grapple with the stigma of being in recovery. Students often think that only movie stars or criminals are in recovery. It is not talked about, and when other students find out, they stop being friends with the student in recovery because they do not want to be seen with them. Students in recovery are not able to share their past experiences with other students because they are concerned about being excluded from the group of friends. They tend to spend weekends by themselves and sneak off to meetings in order to maintain their sobriety. They often lie about where they are going to avoid telling friends. It is very lonely and a real struggle for students in recovery.

Students in recovery may receive support from programs such as Alcoholics Anonymous or Narcotics Anonymous, but these sources of support may not effectively identify with the specific stressors and experiences of being a student on a college campus (Perron et al., p. 52). Students in recovery may not feel connected to the campus as they may lack the connections with other students and faculty in their classes because they feel as if they don't fit in.

These struggles are in addition to the trials and challenges that students not in recovery face. Students in recovery often do not have the support of family and friends because family and friends do not understand or do not know this about the student. Students in recovery have amazing time management skills in order to be successful, as they have to manage going to classes, working, and making sure they have time to attend support groups and connect with sponsors or other people in recovery. As mentioned ahead in a quote from a student in recovery, they have additional stressors.

As a student in recovery, I experience a lot of the same stressors as most students in a campus setting. Such stressors as balancing academic and professional pursuits, participating in student organizations, and getting enough sleep are all part of my life. The most important part of handling stress and being a student in addiction recovery is practicing self-care. Eating a proper diet, getting any form of exercise, and finding a time to grow my spirituality are the most important aspects in combating stress. It is a never-ending journey of adapting and seeking balance.

Anonymous student, April 2014

Checklist of Strategies for Students Who Are in Recovery

☐ Provide an area for students in recovery where they can hang out, connect with one another, access counseling
☐ Provide special housing
☐ Provide special wellness programming
☐ Plan sober tailgates

Services for Stressed-Out Students

When working with college students and addressing their stress, it is clear that one size does not fit all! In this chapter we specifically addressed groups within our college student populations on which campuses have recently focused more attention and resources. These groups are growing and changing the scope and culture of our campuses. In addition to the differences of traditional, nontraditional, international, students who are veterans, and students in recovery, there are other specific groups of college students that face other stressors. For example, numerous studies have found that women experience stress at a higher rate and respond in different ways to stress, especially financial stress, than men. Women tend to seek social support when stressed and talk about the stressors with others. Men are more likely to withdraw and not seek help (Reisberg, 2000).

Other populations on college campuses that experience stress from different sources and in different ways include the lesbian, gay, bisexual, and transgender (LGBT) community, first-generation students, student-athletes, and students of color. A supportive campus climate that helps all students thrive is important on a college campus. Such a campus also enacts policies, programs, and practices that work to enhance the experience for all students.

Student affairs and other college professional staff are committed to eliminating barriers to student success; helping students develop their skills in leadership, teamwork, decision-making, communications, and problem-solving; creating a climate of support and appreciation for all; and collaborating with academic units to integrate classroom and co-curricular activities to provide a meaningful and cohesive total learning experience. They also provide opportunities for students to interact with faculty, staff, and other students, allowing them to tap into the university's far-reaching network of diverse resources and perspectives in ways that will enrich and transform their lives.

Most important in working with college students is recognizing that every student is unique. The services, programs, and support structures need to be broad, deep, and designed to be responsive to the evolving needs of students. Students arrive on campus with different expectations of what the college experience will offer them. From summer orientation to their first night in the residence hall to their first class, students monitor their surroundings, their peers, their professors, and the university staff who support them. They evaluate those around them to make sure that they fit in and will be able to succeed on the campus.

As college professionals, we need to choose our words wisely from the very first contact with students. For example, telling students at orientation that they are the smartest class yet to arrive on our campus may add to students' stress about keeping up with that expectation. Instead, if we congratulate them on being accepted to the institution and applaud the efforts that they have made to get to this point, it assures and supports them that they have made a good choice. They will leave the session feeling comfortable and confident among their peers and continue connecting with others because of such a positive experience and feeling good about being a part of the institution (T. Gibbs, personal communication, September 18, 2014).

Understanding the Developmental Needs of Students

Student affairs faculty and other college staff strive to understand student developmental theory and to be able to examine the important issues students face as their lives progress, such as how to define themselves, their relationships with others, and what to do with their lives. This will assist college professionals in predicting some of the stressors of students and concentrating on ways to help them address the stressors. The goal is to help students successfully manage their stress so as not to delay their progress.

Students need to be able to identify their stressors, and then they should be able to address the stress in healthy ways; these include exercise, talking to friends or family, engaging in relaxation techniques, or seeking assistance to address the stress. Students should be aware of which risk factors they have and identify ways to protect themselves against these risk factors. Our role as college professionals is to assist students in identifying their stressors and then provide the guidance and resources to help them address the stress in positive ways and protect themselves from the negative stressors that may overwhelm them and impede their progress. In order to do this, faculty and staff members need to recognize the changing college-student populations and the differences in the intensity of the stressors that today's students face. We must take time to listen to our students, engage with them as many different types of students, connect them to their communities, and learn from them what they need while using our knowledge and backgrounds to provide the best services. We must incorporate the best available research evidence into the design of all our interventions, programming, and policies.

We believe that the college experience can be a pivotal time for establishing, maintaining, and enhancing lasting healthy behaviors. Our goal is to provide students with innovative, creative wellness services while also recognizing that our highly competitive academic environments are changing and becoming more and more challenging. We explore technology and social media resources, hoping to meet the students where they are developmentally. In order to do this most effectively, we must assess the changing needs of our students, assess the impact of our services, and continually be open to changing and updating our efforts.

Assessing Stress in College Students

For wellness services to be successful, departments must have an outcomes orientation when developing programs and services to help students better anticipate and cope with stress. There are many valuable ways to assess stress on a college campus. The following section gives an overview of assessment, methods for assessing stress levels on a college campus, and a best practice example.

The accountability movement has become an important consideration for all levels of management in American higher education. On college and university campuses across the country, there is a growing need for a shared responsibility for student learning and success. Historically, faculty members were charged with "learning" and student affairs practitioners were charged with planning fun activities to keep the students busy when they weren't in class or studying.

That's not the world in which we're living anymore. Student learning takes place at the intersection of three factors: the curricular environment, the co-curricular environment, and the student's motivation. It is important for students to share responsibility for their learning and success. Colleges and universities must be able to demonstrate that student learning occurs at this intersection and that all actors—academic affairs divisions, student affairs divisions, and students—are contributing to the learning process. When put in the context of student stress, if students are not able to effectively deal with stress, it is the responsibility of the college and division to put the appropriate mechanism in place to assist them in developing coping skills.

Internal and external constituents demand results backed by clear and convincing evidence. Parents, legislators, employers, and students want assurances that the higher education environment will be a pathway to employment upon graduation. They want to believe the university is providing students with the skills they need to be successful in their career pursuits and as citizens in a global society. Although some of the skills needed are related to academic disciplines, others (e.g., ability to deal with stress) are often learned and practiced outside of the classroom in the programs and services provided by student affairs professionals. Specifically, sound assessment methods can provide the evidence needed to document the issues of stress on a college campus. This evidence can lead to securing more resources to support student programs around this issue.

Student affairs professionals entered the assessment scene in the early to mid-1990s, and at that time the dimensions of assessment in student affairs included assessing student needs, satisfaction, campus environments, student cultures, program and service outcomes, and organizational performance comparisons (Upcraft & Schuh, 1996). Toward the late-1990s Student Affairs Administrators in Higher Education (the national organization referred to as NASPA) put forward a new statement to define good practice in the profession that defined student affairs professionals as educators responsible for engaging students in active learning (NASPA, 1998). This definition of good practice expanded the dimensions of student affairs assessment to include student learning.

The ultimate purpose of assessment is to improve practice. Walvoord (2004) identifies three commonly accepted steps to assessment: (1) identify the outcome, (2) gather evidence, and (3) use information for improvement. With this in mind, institutional research practitioners can play an important role by assisting in the gathering of evidence. The data from an effective assessment can be used to support institutional scorecards (often maintained by institutional research offices), university-wide strategic indicators, and Facebook sections geared toward the co-curricular activities of the students. For data to have an impact on improving practice it must be collected in a methodologically sound fashion. Even data used for action research purposes should follow the basic guidelines of data collection, such as those of a quantitative, qualitative, or mixed method (each outlined in other sections of this chapter). Poor data collection will lead to poorly informed decisions, which in turn can lead to misguided improvement of practice.

Developing Outcomes

While it is important to ground our practice in multiple outcomes, it is also important to make sure that the assessment of those outcomes is done to the highest standards of rigor and sound methods. To truly address the issues of stress on campus, the institution must understand the needs of the students and develop programs that address those needs. Those programs should be grounded and include sound and measurable outcomes. Outcomes can be learning, developmental, or operational, depending on the activity, audience, and desired result.

Learning outcomes focus on the direct learning that students should gain by attending our programming, living in our residence halls, or being a part of a student organization. An example would be the following: "As a result of living within Residence Life, students will learn strategies for dealing with college stress, including: (1) exploring and clarifying their feelings; (2) identifying and taking control of their thoughts; and (3) getting support by communicating their thoughts to someone they trust."

Similarly, developmental outcomes delineate the growth that students should attain as a result of our efforts. An example of a developmental outcome may be: "As a result of participation in summer orientation programming, students will be able to successfully navigate campus resources."

Finally, operational outcomes provide the third leg to our stool. While it may be ideal to focus on student growth and learning, our offices must also focus on procedural tasks that are important to our daily work. An example here is: "As a result of new admit procedures for the Counseling Center, student wait time will be reduced by 50%." Clearly, creating an optimal student environment is a goal of any campus. However, in order to get there, we must focus on segments of our daily work and how each can contribute to the ultimate goal.

Methods to Assess Stress on Campus

All data sources are considered when measuring levels of stress on a college campus. Quantitative data are collected through intake forms, budget documents, and surveys. Qualitative data are collected through focus groups, interviews, written documents, and professional observation. Practitioners struggle with the appropriate methodology for conducting assessment of student stress. In what circumstances should we use a quantitative methodology versus a qualitative methodology? When should we use both?

Quantitative methods are recommended if departments are attempting to use a descriptive, comparative, or correlative approach to collect assessment data (McMillan, 2000). Descriptive research includes studies that provide information about frequency or amount of time spent during a particular activity. Comparative studies examine differences between groups on particular variable specifics of types of stress or the behaviors that result from stress. Correlative studies, on the other hand, investigate the relationship between two or more variables, such as between an activity of the department and the reduction of student stress.

Because of its exploratory nature, qualitative research is a popular methodology because campuses want to have a deeper understanding of the factors that contribute to student stress. Departments use focus groups, document analysis, and professional observation to answer questions regarding departments' impact on student learning.

The data from mixed methods research provide a rich source for measuring the environment. Departments combine qualitative and quantitative paradigms into a mixed research methods approach. According to Johnson and Onwuegbuzie, "The goal of mixed methods research is to maximize the strengths and minimize the weaknesses of [qualitative and quantitative methods] in a single research study" (2004, p. 15). For example, a department implemented a mixed methods approach to understanding student stress by using the results of a survey instrument such as the NCHA II to develop questions for focus group interviews.

Conclusion

If an organization is going to understand student stress in the context of a college campus, it must be committed to being an outcomes-focused, evidence-driven organization. To truly understand stress, an organization must:

- Be committed. For any culture of evidence to be sustained and successful, it needs executive support and it needs ownership from all levels of the division.
- Be connected. A strong and sustained culture of evidence is connected to the larger university mission and goals.
- Be consistent. Assessment and evidence gathering must become part of the routine institutional and divisional management process.
- Be communicative. Without transparent, clear, and frequent communication, a sustained and strong culture of evidence is not possible to develop or implement. With these components in place, an organization can have a strong and deep understanding of stress on a college campus.

While compiling the information for this chapter, the authors reviewed many resources, including talking with professionals and students from across the country about the activities that they implement on their campuses to help students address stress. The authors found several initiatives and activities that were promising in helping students better deal with stresses. These are listed in the checklists and in the specific examples from institutions.

Campus coalitions address high-risk alcohol use and abuse on college campuses. Student affairs staff could establish similar coalitions or advisory boards to address college student stress. Highly competitive academic institutions foster higher levels of stress among faculty, staff, and students. Faculty, staff, and students from a variety of different areas across campus could work together to develop a comprehensive plan. In order to change a culture on campus, a widespread plan and efforts should be in place, just like in alcohol abuse prevention efforts.

Unfortunately, the authors were unable to discover much research indicating if the initiatives actually reduced the stress of college students. In order to better meet the needs of students, more creative projects to address stress should be identified and the impact of initiatives followed longitudinally to gauge impact. Also, as indicated in the study by Heckman, Lim, and Montalto (2014), researchers should explore factors that impact financial stress as well as interventions that assist college students in addressing this stress (p. 36). In addition to financial stress, other stressors such as social pressures, parental pressure, safety concerns, and other wellness concerns like sleep should be further studied to guide campus professionals in enhancing and expanding stress reduction efforts for the campus.

References

Albert, P., Rice, K., & Caffee, L. (2014). Perfectionism affects blood pressure in response to repeated exposure to stress. *Stress and Health.* doi:10.1002/smi.2591

Altschuler, G., & Skorton, D. (2013, November 23). How college health centers help students succeed. *Forbes.* Retrieved from http://www.forbes.com

American College Health Association. (2012). *National College Health Assessment II: Ohio State University executive summary, spring 2012.* Hanover, MD: American College Health Association.

American College Health Association. (2013). *National College Health Assessment II: Ohio State University executive summary, spring 2013.* Hanover, MD: American College Health Association.

Astin, A. (1999). Student involvement: A developmental theory for higher education. *Journal of College Student Development, 40*(5), 518–529.

Baum, S. (2010, August 22). As students change, colleges must follow. *Chronicle of Higher Education: Almanac of Higher Education.* Retrieved from http://chronicle.com

Belluck, P. (2005, March 17). Children's life expectancy being cut short by obesity. *New York Times.* Retrieved from http://www.nytimes.com

Carnegie Mellon University. (2012, April 2). How stress influences disease: Study reveals inflammation as the culprit. *ScienceDaily.* Retrieved from www.sciencedaily.com/releases/2012/04/120402162546.htm

Farrell, E. (2008, February 29). Counseling centers lack resources to help troubled students. *Chronicle of Higher Education.* Retrieved from http://chronicle.com

Felsten, G., & Wilcox, K. (1992). Influences of stress and situation-specific mastery beliefs and satisfaction with social support on well-being and academic performance. *Psychology Reports, 70*(1), 291–303.

Florida State University. (2014). Accolades. Retrieved from http://veterans.fsu.edu/about-us/accolades

Haynie, D. (2013, November 11). U.S. sees record number of international college students. *U.S. News and World Report: Education.* Retrieved from http://www.usnews.com

Heckman, S., Lim, H., & Montalto, C. (2014). Factors related to financial stress among college students. *Journal of Financial Therapy, 5*(1), 19–39. doi:10.4148/1944-9771.1063

Hess, F. (2011, September). Old school: College's most important trend is the rise of the adult student. Retrieved from http://www.theatlantic.com/business/archive/2011/09/old-school-colleges-most-important-trend-is-the-rise-of-the-adult-student/245823/

Johnson R. B., & Onwuegbuzie, A. J. (2004, October). Mixed methods research: A research paradigms whose time has come. *Educational Researcher, 33*(7), 14–26.

McMillan, J. H. (2000). *Educational research: Fundamentals for the consumer* (4th ed.). White Plains, NY: Addison Wesley Longman.

Murff, S. H. (2006, February 6). The impact of stress on academic success in college students. Retrieved from http://www.redorbit.com

NASPA. (1998). Principles of good practice in student affairs. Retrieved from https://www.naspa.org/images/uploads/main/Principles_of_Good_Practice_in_Student_Affairs.pdf

Nunez, H., Stewart, J., & Harper, M. (2014). Professional competencies in the framework of nontraditional student work: Reframing for a "new traditional" world. In *The Annual Knowledge Community Conference publication*. Washington, DC: NASPA.

Ohio Adolescent Health Partnership. (2013). *Promoting and improving the health of Ohio adolescents: Strategic plan 2013–2020*. Columbus, OH: State Adolescent Health Resource Center.

Ohio State University. (2014). Wellness coaching. Retrieved from http://swc.osu.edu/about-us/wellness-coaching

Olson, T.A., & Riley, J.B. (2009). In practice: Weaving the campus safety net by integrating student health issues into the curriculum. *About Campus, 14*, 27–29. doi:10.1002/abc.286

O'Neil, M. (2014, January 13). Campus psychological counseling goes online for students at university of Florida. *Chronicle of Education*. Retrieved from http://chronicle.com/

Perron, B.E., Grahovac, I.D., Uppal, J.S., Granillo, T.M., Shuter, J., & Porer, C.A. (2011). Supporting students in recovery on college campuses: Opportunities for student affairs professionals. *Journal of Student Affairs Research and Practice, 48*(1), 47–64. doi:10.2202/1949–6605.6226

Pritchard, M., & Wilson, G. (2003). Using emotional and social factors to predict student success. *Journal of College Student Development, 44*(1), 18–28.

Reisberg, L. (2000, January 28). Student stress is rising, especially among women. *Chronicle of Higher Education*. Retrieved from http://chronicle.com

Sander, L. (2012, March 11). Out of uniform: At half a million and counting, veterans cash in on post-9/11 GI bill. *Chronicle of Higher Education*. Retrieved from http://chronicle.com

University of Wisconsin–Madison. (2013). Let's talk. Retrieved from http://www.uhs.wisc.edu/services/counseling/lets-talk

Upcraft, M. L., & Schuh, J. H. (1996). *Assessment in student affairs: A guide for practitioners*. San Francisco, CA: Jossey-Bass.

Walvoord, B. E. (2004). *Assessment clear and simple: A practical guide for institutions, departments, and general education*. San Francisco, CA: Jossey-Bass.

World Health Organization. (1948). *Constitution of the World Health Organization*. Retrieved from http://apps.who.int/gb/bd/PDF/bd47/EN/constitution-en.pdf?ua=1

3

Mental Health

Creating and Cultivating a Campus Community That Supports Mental Health

DORI S. HUTCHINSON

Introduction

Higher education in the United States serves as a critical gateway for young adults as it provides opportunities to build the intellectual and interpersonal skills and to obtain the necessary credentials for roles in the workforce and in our communities. It is also a critical time in the development of a young adult's sense of self, purpose, and meaning in life. Both traditional students and nontraditional students, undergraduates and graduate students, are invited to and select our campuses to achieve their educational and vocational goals. Yet their academic goals represent just one aspect of their personhood, and these goals are highly influenced by many factors. Our students' mental health is an essential component of their overall wellness and is inextricably linked to their overall success on our campuses. The research has shown that there is a strong connection between mental health and academic success during college (Eisenberg, Golberstein, & Hunt, 2009). For many of these young adults, their college or university becomes their primary community as they live, learn, play, and work in our campus environments. Their capacity to be successful will have lifelong consequences for their employment, income, and health (Douce & Keeling, 2014). While the emphasis of this time of life is often on the academic and social domains of young adults, the role of developing positive mental health as a foundation for academic success, personal development, and adult resiliency cannot and should not be overlooked on our campuses.

This chapter highlights the critical importance of student mental health and resiliency as a necessary component of the higher education experience. The challenges that both our students and our institutions of higher education face to support the development of positive mental health on campuses will be discussed. Strategies for campuses to build a culture of caring and engage all the stakeholders to feel empowered to respond to mental health challenges will be reviewed.

Our Students and Their Mental Health

Much has been written about the current students on our campuses, Generation Y—or the millennials, as they are often referred to by others. Born between 1982 and 2002, they are described as self-centered, competitive, accomplished, and entitled. They are portrayed as highly optimistic, excessively scheduled, driven toward perfection, yet more miserable than ever before (Twenge, 2006). This generation has been raised on feeling good before doing good. Their self-esteem and individual success have been placed first at all costs, and have been the core goals of our parenting. They are also the first generation raised on social networking, many living their emotional and social lives online, spending less time than past generations on the face-to-face experiences of engaging in real-time relationships. But the costs are emerging. As college students, this generation is living in a time of "soaring expectations and crushing realities" (Twenge, 2006, p. 2). They have been raised to believe every dream is attainable and that they have an untenable right to this achievement. Yet, they are not prepared to deal with discovering that dreams don't always come true. They lack emotional resilience. Resilience, a key component of well-being, is the ability to recognize, face, and overcome challenges as well as to grow as a result of these challenges (Douce & Keeling, 2014). A lack of resilience can be a major impediment to successful learning. Students are more depressed, lonelier, and more anxious and more have thought about suicide than any other generation of students before them (American College Health Association, 2014). Studies have clearly found that mental health problems have a very strong and negative impact on academic performance, retention, and graduation rates (Eisenberg, Golberstein, & Hunt, 2009; Kitzrow, 2003). GPAs go down, students underperform, and some will leave school when they are experiencing serious mental health conditions.

Higher education is not only an important time of intellectual development but also a very important developmental phase of young adulthood. Students in college must learn to integrate their academic lives with their social development; this, in turn, is influenced by the student's demographics, goals, capacity to persist, and motivations (Tinto, 1993). It is, as importantly, a time when young adults must learn to adapt to stressful environmental demands and to think about building a self (Deresiewicz, 2014). College is a time when young adults begin to understand the essence of their mind-body-soul connection and what that means to their uniqueness. There is also strong evidence that academic and social integration and well-being impact college retention (Douce & Keeling, 2014; Pascarella & Terenzini, 2005).

This time of adaptation and discovery is not an easy journey; it never has been, and it is certainly is not easy now. But the college experience of today is not the same as it was a decade or 20 or 30 years ago, making this passage more fraught for the increasing numbers of students with mental health challenges who are on our campuses. And they are on our campuses. Recent prevalence rates of mental health issues on residential and community campuses are as high as 37% (Eisenberg & Lipson, 2014). The complexity of these mental health disorders on campus is increasing in number and severity as well (American College Health Association, 2014). Significant numbers of students are living with depression and anxiety disorders and substance use disorders, and trying to balance academic, work, family, and extracurricular demands. This rate has clearly been influenced by the impact of historic legislation, including Section 504 of the Rehabilitation Act of 1973 and the Americans With Disabilities Act (ADA) of 1990, which embodies our educational system's commitment to the inclusion of all people in our higher education institutions. It was at this time in the early 1990s that Stone and Archer (1990, p. 543) noted increasing numbers of students with serious psychological issues on campuses. In addition, the improved medications and more effective mental health treatments and interventions have helped to make college a possibility for young adults and people with serious mental health conditions (Collins & Mowbray, 2005). Add to this the fact that most lifetime mental health conditions have an onset before or during the traditional college ages of 18–24 (Kessler, Chiu, Demler, & Walters, 2005). The most common mental health problems at any type of university or college are depression, anxiety, co-occurring substance problems, eating disorders, suicidal ideation, and self-injury (Eisenberg & Lipson, 2014).

What do mental health problems look like in terms of student functioning? They include academic struggles and failure, excessive absences from classes and obligations, excessive substance use, loneliness and isolation, social and interpersonal difficulties with others on campus, changes in self-care and lack of self-care, extreme risky behaviors, inability to tolerate frustration and normal stressors in college, inability to regulate emotions, hopelessness and despair (Chung & Klein, 2007; Eisenberg, Golberstein, & Gollust, 2007). While all students may exhibit one or more of these functional behaviors at some time, students who are distressed and at risk will often exhibit one or more of these indicators concurrently. Further, there is often community concern for these students even if they are not seeking or receiving mental health services. Many campuses have begun to implement weekly meetings to discuss students of concern; these meetings include the campus police, Dean of Students office, judicial affairs, student health services, and faculty, with a purpose of monitoring the behavior and consequences that these young adults experience. In addition, concern by students for other students in distress is rated as one of the top factors impacting their academic performance (American College Health Association, 2013).

The intense emphasis on career preparation at the expense of all else and the significant financial burden that students and families assume to achieve a higher education are, no doubt, another factor in the mental health distress experienced by so many of our students. An alarming 15% of graduate students and 18% of undergraduate students have seriously considered attempting suicide in their lifetimes. Between 40% and 50% of these same students report multiple episodes of serious suicidal thoughts, which suggests prior experience with suicidal ideation (Drum, Browson, Denmark, & Smith, 2009). A national college health assessment found that 23.3% of students "felt very sad," and 14.8% stated they "felt so depressed that it was difficult to function" at least once in the prior 12 months. Suicide has become a public health problem on our campuses and is now the second leading cause of death in college-aged youth (SPRC, 2004). Risk factors for suicide are complex and multidetermined, including not only mental or emotional problems but also alcohol and drug abuse, acute psychosocial stressors, difficulty accessing mental health resources, and availability of lethal means. These factors are also interrelated, as alcohol and drugs increase the risk of depression and worsen depression outcomes (Murphy, Barnett, & Colby, 2006). This troubling statistic speaks to the importance of the promotion of mental health as an asset and suicide prevention widely emphasized on our campuses so that our students can flourish as adults.

Academics, work, financial issues, family, and relationship problems are the major sources of student distress we see on our campuses. Community college students face different pressures that contribute to their mental health problems, most notably financial pressures, family obligations, and housing insecurities (Eisenberg & Lipson, 2014). Of note is that in times of distress, 67% of college students will turn to each other for help instead of an adult or provider on campus (American College Health Association, 2012). Adding to their distress is the fact, according to research, that this generation is 40% lower in empathy than their counterparts from 20–30 years ago (Konrath, O'Brien, & Hsing, 2011). This empathy "deficit" was also highlighted in interviews conducted by Christian Smith, a sociologist whose book on the spiritual lives of young adults argues that millennials feel no sense of obligation or collective responsibility to help others in distress (Smith & Snell, 2009).

Add to this lack of individual empathy the fact that society still finds mental health a taboo and frightening condition. Students feel great shame, and schools are concerned with risk and liability. It is a mix that results in reticence to seek help and reticence to support programs and policies that are mental health–friendly. In fact, only approximately a third of students on college campuses will seek help when they need it (Eisenberg, Hunt, & Speer, 2012). A recent article highlighted that many schools are taking a hard line toward students with serious mental health conditions who seek services, strongly encouraging or requiring them to take medical leaves (Kincade, 2014). These types of policies and procedures can actually backfire as students become more reluctant to seek help for fear of academic dismissal or removal from campuses. Thus a culture of higher education that is increasingly less empathetic, more competitive, and more expensive and has more on the line for students in terms of career decisions and jobs may also be a factor in the increase of distress and mental health conditions on our campuses (Smith & Snell, 2009).

What other factors may be influencing the development of a generation of young adults who are so accomplished in terms of their academic, athletic, and social lives, but lacking in emotional resilience and empathy for each other? The fact that they have been raised during a time of enormous change in how we communicate may play a role. For example, today's college students have been raised on electronic devices, such as computers, iPads, and smartphones. Applications for every aspect of life are just a touch or swipe away. There are even applications to let students know where their friends are on campus, an irony not lost on many faculty and staff when students are constantly looking at their screens instead of at the community around them. For these students, change is fast, constant, and another part of life to be managed. We are just beginning to understand the interplay between social media use and mental health. While there are certainly many positive benefits of social media, this technology does provide constant electronic "connectedness" that may, in fact, prevent people from developing the emotional skills they need to navigate the realities of life's disappointments. Several recent

Social Skills development

research studies have found an association between decreased subjective well-being and self-esteem and increased distress (Chen & Lee, 2013; Kross, Verduyn, Demiralp, Park, & Lee, 2013). Social media, such as Facebook, Snapchat, Twitter, and Instagram, provide a "functional buffer" that makes it easier to ignore others' pain and even inflict pain without experiencing the immediate emotional consequences (Kornath, O'Brien, & Hsing, 2011). It is hard to develop empathy when you are constantly plugged in and buffered. It is easy to believe that everyone else is living a charmed life when all one sees are posted pictures and comments about the highlights of life. It is easy to minimize distress and dismiss despair online for anyone, including students, faculty, and staff. The research has explored reasons for these detrimental effects, which include information overload, modeling of high-risk behaviors, and Internet addiction (Chen & Lee, 2013; Christakis, Moreno, Jelenchick, Myaing, & Zhou, 2011).

Others suggest that the lenient parenting styles and helicopter/snowplow parenting that has been a hallmark of our current students' lives have resulted in this generation's lack of coping skills. The reluctance of parents to discipline, the anxious quest to give their children every opportunity to succeed at everything, and the lack of life skills teaching imparted by parents surely are also factors in the delayed development of stress hardiness (Twenge, 2006). Parents feel entitled to their involvement in their young adult children's lives because of the high price of a college education. They continue to intervene, manage, direct, and advise through daily texting and calls that, in many instances, curtail the development of emotional resilience in their child. Universities and colleges find students are often plagued by "toxic levels of fear, anxiety, depression, emptiness, aimlessness and isolation" (Deresiewicz, 2014, p. 3). Deresiewicz (2014) suggests that today's college students, especially those who have been accepted to the more elite institutions of higher education, are terrified at the prospect of mediocrity. Parents and schools place such emphasis on the pursuit of success and perfection that they have "manufactured" students for success, and as a result, these students are lacking in a "self." Deresiewicz suggests that all these pressures to succeed have developed a generation of young people who are smart, talented, and driven, yet are anxious, timid, and lost, and feel a sense of lacking meaning. Others have suggested the increasing divide between the haves and the have-nots, as well as the frightening amounts of debt, may make it harder for college students to cope, as well as understand and have empathy for the challenges faced by others (Kahlenberg, 2011).

These issues influence our students' lives every single day and are integral to their academic and social well-being. This is reflected in the staggering increase in university and campus counseling centers' appointments and demand for services that has continued to grow (Blacklock, Benson, Johnson, & Bloomberg, 2003). And these are the students willing to seek help. It is well known that at-risk college students often do not make appointments at a university's health services. Stigma represents a significant barrier to seeking treatment, along with embarrassment about their needs, lack of awareness of services, and a misperception of the benefits of seeking help (Golberstein, Eisenberg, & Gollust, 2008). The growing diversity on campuses also highlights the role of stigma, shame, and lack of education about mental health, which will be addressed later, that faculty, staff, and students have about mental illness and distress. Efforts to promote mental health and prevent suicide must respond to the needs of each campus's culture and its student population. Commuter students, older students, international students, minority students, and gay, lesbian, bisexual, transgendered, and questioning students face particular challenges that can increase their potential for distress and refusal to seek help (JED Foundation & EDC, 2011; Suicide Prevention Resource Center, 2004). Cultural sensitivity and competency in college mental health services often require additional staffing resources and training to ensure that those students' needs are met.

The Role of Universities and Colleges

Higher education programs and institutions are placing increased focus on student grade point averages, retention rates, and return on investment with tuition and job placement rates. Higher education is a business. Thus, it is not surprising that administrators, faculty, staff, and providers on campuses across the country are increasingly challenged and stressed, in terms of sufficient resources, to meet students' mental health needs. Due to highly visible tragedies on campuses over the last decade, mental health and mental illnesses are increasingly seen as risk and liability issues, not as the foundation for adult flourishing and resiliency. Risky behaviors, academic troubles, social challenges, and mental health crises require thought, time, attention, and resources on our campuses. They can bring unwanted public attention to campuses that is perceived as bad for business and college rankings. As a result of this overload, many campuses and universities have embraced the model of community outplacement and disclaiming responsibility for students' mental health problems due to lack of resources (Mowbray et al., 2006). There are spoken tensions between the academic mission of higher education and its role in the provision of mental health care. There exist difficult dilemmas between mission, budget, and resources of higher education institutions (Hunt, Watkins, & Eisenberg, 2012). Higher education institutions do have significant challenges in meeting their missions.

Many institutions are asking if they have moral, clinical, or fiscal obligations to meet the mental health needs of the students on their campuses. Some universities have developed return from leave policies for students who leave for mental health reasons that require documentation of mental fitness for the rigors of academia. These types of conditions (one institution requires a full-time job for six months) can be difficult to meet if students are in treatment, thus elongating their leaves. More universities are creating mental health policies that demand robust functioning to remain and to return, causing students (and their families) with mental health issues to feel increasingly frustrated, discouraged, and outraged (Kincade, 2014). In many respects, these types of policies and procedures end up being a loss for both students and universities. Students do not graduate, and universities lose tuition as well as the opportunity to have a positive impact on a person's life. Another perspective suggests that if we can provide preventive programs and services, our universities may offer an age-appropriate and promising venue for prevention and treatment of mental health, while meeting our mission of setting students on a path to success, community involvement, and well-being (Barber, 2012; Hunt et al., 2012).

Most colleges and universities provide access to mental health treatment services on their campuses or to community mental health services through a referral system. Medication, talk therapy, and therapeutic and support groups are often the minimal offerings for students who present with needs. Antidepressant and anxiety medications can help alleviate distressing symptoms, cognitive-behavioral strategies can teach coping skills, and therapeutic groups can provide peer support and mutual learning of wellness strategies. The good news is that these services can be very effective if young people are connected to supports and have access to a variety of treatments (JED Foundation & EDC, 2011). Distressing symptoms can be reduced or eliminated and thus lessen the risks to students' ability to thrive on campus. Yet students are reluctant to seek help, and many of our students who are struggling are not being seen. Despite this fact, the growing consensus is that treatment alone is an insufficient strategy if we are to meet our students' mental health needs so they can flourish on our campuses (JED Foundation & EDC, 2011). College mental health services need to go beyond simply treating students and expand their efforts *to prevent* mental health problems from arising and promoting the mental health of all students. Mental health is essential for not only academic success but also a healthy adult life.

Achieving Mental Health on Our Campuses

A public health approach is recommended as a critical strategy for all types of campuses to use to address the social, emotional, financial, academic, and environmental factors that play a role in student mental health (Davidson & Locke, 2010). Multiple strategies should be used to promote comprehensive, prevention-focused, targeted, and collaborative mental health plans for the campus or university (JED Foundation & EDC, 2011). Many campuses, in their anxiety to do something, provide gatekeeper trainings for faculty and staff, have bystander trainings for students, have crisis protocols, and provide brief treatment services. While helpful, these efforts do not constitute a comprehensive strategy for mental health; they represent some of the many approaches that should be employed.

Seek Administration Support

A key strategy is to gain administrative support. The support of university leadership is critical for funding to support targeted programs and interventions, as well as for helping shift stigma, prejudice, and discrimination toward students with mental health issues. When leadership allocates funding to create sustainable programs, positions, and services, the message to students, families, faculty, and staff is that mental health is a valued priority. Without administrative support, it can be very difficult to promote mental health on any campus (DeJong, 2007). Suggestions to engage upper-level support include using data from the campus to highlight the number of students using mental health services, the number of students engaged in risky behaviors (alcohol, illegal substances, sexual assaults), and the number of students involved in judicial affairs that are linked to substance use and campus violence. Further, it is important to highlight any negative mental health events, such as campus suicides or local incidents. These incidents are expressions of mental health distress. Organizations such as the American Foundation for Suicide Prevention offer media protocols for responsible and sensitive reporting of suicide for institutions to use. Administrators appear willing to fund mental health initiatives if they believe it will avert a crisis on their campus or if it will reduce the number of public incidents that bring negative attention to their colleges and universities (Hunt et al., 2012).

Use data to make an economic case for mental health, as money talks. Administrators are concerned about attrition and tuition dollars. Nationally, it has been found that as many as 86% of students with mental health disorders dropped out of college without completing their degree (Kessler, Foster, Saunders, & Stang, 1995). This is twice as high as the rate of students without mental health conditions and represents an enormous economic loss in tuition dollars, not to mention the economic loss of future earnings for these students. Utilizing activism and advocacy with the campus administration by student groups, families, and faculty is a powerful way to sway the university leadership to the view that mental health matters. The dynamic between data and activism has emerged as a primary factor for increased financial support for mental health (Hunt et al., 2012).

Build Capacity Through Collaboration

Engaging all stakeholders on campus in the conversation about mental health is also a critical strategy. The mental health of our students cannot be the sole responsibility of the counseling center, as every single person and department on our campuses are affected. It is important to create a mental health task force or roundtable group that invites a representative from every single office and department on the campus; include student leaders, police, the dean's office, residential life, athletics, campus ministries, judicial affairs, international and minority student offices, the career office, the office of disability services, the student support office, and faculty. Large or small, this strategy works very well to de-silo communication across the campus about students of concern and provides an opportunity to talk about mental health concerns and potential programs and services. This communication strategy can take the form of weekly meetings about students of concern with key stakeholders or annual gatherings to develop mental health programming goals. Consider creating a campus team that identifies and monitors students of concern. The JED Foundation, in collaboration with Higher Education Mental Health Alliance, has created an excellent resource, "Balancing Safety and Support on Campus: A Guide for Campus Teams" (2012), that outlines the steps to guide a campus team that has the responsibility of identifying and monitoring students of concern in such a way that they can receive the support and treatment they need.

At Boston University, a mental health roundtable and Students of Concern Team were established in 2008. The mental health roundtable meets once a year to discuss mental health issues and programs on campus. Since its inception, many mental health initiatives have come from the roundtable, including a much improved website, university-wide collaboration for National Depression Screening Day, training exercises for mental health events and disasters that well prepared Boston University for the marathon bombing in 2013, and better coordination among all offices charged with student well-being. The Students of Concern Team meets weekly with diverse stakeholders on campus to discuss students who are demonstrating behaviors that are of concern and that may require treatment and intervention.

Create a Vision of Mental Health: Engage in Strategic Planning

Many colleges and universities are reactive when it comes to mental health; in other words, they react to a crisis with a new policy, initiative, or task force, instead of engaging in a strategic, proactive planning process for the mental health of their students. An excellent example of this type of behavior is how campuses and universities around the country are reacting to the issues of sexual assault and alcohol use on their campuses. Most campuses respond to these issues and events one at a time, as they happen, without connecting them as reflective of overall student mental health. A more comprehensive approach to consider is to engage in a strategic planning process for the mental health of all students. Consider asking how much time, effort, and funding are spent on reacting to mental health and behavioral issues on campus that might be better spent on proactive planning and implementation of programs that support student wellness and success. The use of a social ecological framework addresses mental health needs on an individual level, program level, environmental level, and policy level (DeJong & Langford, 2002). This means that the student, the campus culture, the services available, and the policies shape health and safety behaviors. See mental health challenges as learning problems, as they impact learning and success (Douce & Keeling, 2014).

An example of this is a campus-wide wellness office that works in collaboration with all stakeholders and provides a wide variety of programming, training, and initiatives that addresses all the mental health issues on campus. It means placing value on students' mental health as it relates to their academic and social success. It means ensuring that there are enough staff and requisite expertise to develop and implement programming on sexual violence, understanding depression and anxiety, eating disorders, screening events, bystander trainings for *all types* of negative and risky behavior, suicide prevention strategies, substance use education and monitoring, and similar issues. A centralized office can provide faculty, staff, and student gatekeeper and bystander trainings on a wide array of issues, and life skills training to promote resiliency and mental health to *all* students. A centralized *mental health* (not mental illness) resource on campus also helps keep the conversation going on campus about mental health with all stakeholders. Campus professionals, faculty, staff, and students need to be talking openly about depression, anxiety, mental illnesses, suicide, and how to seek help on our campuses. We contribute to the shame, stigma, and myths of mental illness when we do not acknowledge that our students struggle with these issues and when our students die from these issues. Silence about mental health issues is deadly to our campuses, as we have learned from the many tragic events at our colleges and universities over the last decade (Van Brunt, 2012).

Mental health strategic planning is a proactive and responsive rather than reactive strategy. Strategic planning for mental health will also create a culture shift on the campus where mental health is seen as a valued aspect of student, staff, and faculty wellness and essential to the mission of the college or university. Consider strategic programming where all incoming freshmen not only learn study skills or take a required freshman writing course but also are inoculated against stress and build empathy with required wellness programming that builds student skills, rather than just awareness and knowledge. First-year programs that promote mental wellness skills will help to decrease the stigma of seeking help, improve academic performance, and create healthy conversations about the role of mental health in adult life.

Create a Caring Community

Most campuses and universities offer student health services that include mental health treatment. And for those that do not, linkages to community services are provided. Mental health treatment on campuses may include talk therapy and medication. Both of these types of evidenced-based interventions require licensed clinicians and insurance coverage. Despite these resources, many colleges and universities are struggling to meet the mental health needs of so many students in distress; thus there exists the need to provide services that not only treat distress but also *prevent* levels of distress that have an impact on academic and social functioning.

While all these resources are critical components in creating a caring culture, what is most needed when students are in distress is an empathetic person who witnesses their distress and shares their concern for the student. This person can be a student, staff, or faculty person. Many people may be reluctant to reach out to someone in distress because they feel it is none of their business or it is not their job to tackle. Others feel they don't know what to say in that moment or that they might say something that makes the situation worse. Creating a caring community means that all campus personnel are willing to recognize distress, respond with empathy toward that person, and then support that person in getting the help he or she needs. This does not mean that faculty, staff, and students are expected to or should take on the role of a clinician, but it does mean extending ourselves, human to human, to those students we feel are suffering. Creating a caring community rests upon the principle that we view mental and behavioral health as a critical component of well-being for all students and desire to have a campus culture and learning environment that support healthy minds (Douce & Keeling, 2014).

There are often academic, behavioral, and physical indicators that demonstrate that students are struggling in our classrooms and campuses. These indicators are all about change in the student's well-being (Karr, 2009). Students in distress demonstrate a marked change in their academic performance. They miss classes, exams, and deadlines. They may turn in work that is extremely disorganized and not reflective of their past work. Their written and artistic expressions may express disturbing thoughts, feelings, and images. We all wonder what the threshold is for taking action. Use your professional experience as teachers, coaches, and administrators as well as your intuition that something is not right. It is okay to let a student know you are concerned about his or her academic well-being. This is our most powerful tool in creating a caring culture: communicating our concern about one another. Even if students reassure you that they are okay, they now know you care about them enough to notice. If your concern is high, share your concern with not only the student but also his or her academic advisor, dean, or the mental health team. Behavioral indicators often include direct statements of despair and hopelessness, excessive crying, extremes in risky behavior (alcohol, drugs, and sex), isolation and withdrawal, and excessive anxiety and anger. Physical indicators include extreme weight loss or weight gain, change in their hygiene habits, deterioration in appearance, being visibly under the influence of substances, too little or too much sleep, and disorganized speech. Again, it is not only okay but also important to let the student know you are concerned about him or her. Ask the student how you might help. Offer to accompany the student to resources on campus that can help. Affirm the universal difficulty in seeking help. And then offer to help the student seek help with the message that "no one does it alone" and "we all struggle at one time or another." Always let another person know you are worried about a student.

Extreme concern for a student's safety and well-being always supersedes confidentiality. Empathy requires attending to these indicators in our students and sharing our concern. We are not dismissing the problem or trying to fix their problems when we are empathetic. We are not doing someone else's job. Instead we are reflecting back to the student what we see in their academics, behavior, and physical health that worries us, and letting them know we care about them. Creating a caring community also requires sharing our concern with others about students and referring them to resources that can help. When we all collectively watch out for our students and each other, it helps create a culture on our campuses that helps prevent tragic events and promotes overall mental health for everyone.

Use a Resiliency Framework

There is growing evidence that a resiliency framework for college mental health services will help students develop academic and emotional resilience, resulting in better retention and graduation rates (Hartley, 2013). Resilience is the capacity to face and overcome adversity. Rather than focusing solely on risks, increasing resilience through provision of distress tolerance skills, coping skills, active problem-solving skills, wellness skills, and academic persistence skills holds great promise to increase students' success and happiness. In a resiliency framework, students who can persist when things are difficult, who can make a plan and execute it, and who feel a sense of control, as well as have social network on campus, are the students who succeed (Hartley, 2013). All these factors work together in a cumulative effect (i.e., the more success a student has in meeting his or her challenges, the more resilient she or he becomes); this makes an effective argument for the essential delivery of resiliency promotion services that will support the academic success of students. Consider offering resilient interventions that improve students' ability to compete in a demanding postsecondary environment. Offering groups that focus on enhancing a student's interpersonal and academic strengths, rather than groups that are problem-focused, has been shown to be more successful (Luther, Cicchetti, & Becker, 2000). Consider groups or classes that develop the skills related to resilience (such as learned optimism and humor), mindfulness, meditation, affirmation and appraisal skills, cognitive flexibility (including acceptance and reframing), personal meaning (including spirituality and altruism), building social networks or capital, and active coping skills (including exercise) (Southwick, Vythilingam, & Charney, 2005). These types of groups appeal to students more than Coping With Depression groups or Illness Management groups because they focus on life skills, are strengths-oriented, and have an educational and future focus.

Engage Students as Peers and Voices of Mental Health

We need to create caring communities on our campus so that everyone shares in the responsibility of mental health. We know that students prefer to seek support from their peers rather than adults when they are distressed and challenged by a mental health condition. In fact, two-thirds of college students will turn to one another when in distress instead of an adult on campus (American College Health Association, 2012). One very viable and inexpensive way to create a caring community is to train students as gatekeepers of their campus mental health. The Student Support Network (SSN) training developed through a federal campus suicide prevention grant by Worcester Polytechnic Institute is an evidence-based training listed in the best practices registry of the Suicide Prevention Resource Center, and teaches students to respond with empathy to distress in their peers and then refer and accompany peers to resources on campus that can help (Morse, 2014). This six-hour training has been successfully implemented at a wide variety of universities and colleges and helps students do what they are already doing—listening and observing distress—but with more effectiveness. It empowers students to resist the human urge to dismiss or diminish the emotional pain of a peer, and reflect back with empathy what they are hearing. Students are then educated about mental health problems that young adults experience, including suicide, and resources on their campus available to help. Once trained, their only obligation is to be listening and talking about the importance of mental health in the fraternities and sororities, in the clubs, on the fields, and in the residence halls. This gatekeeper training builds a broad safety network from the ground up—where it is needed most. In addition, this gatekeeper training has been successfully adapted for staff and faculty. There are many gatekeeper trainings, and many are online courses. Gatekeeper training and bystander training are, ultimately, about human beings helping human beings. It is about stepping in, being present, and deeply listening. While smartphone applications can be incredibly helpful tools, and online courses may reach a lot of people with efficiency, these types of gatekeeper trainings are incredibly powerful and effective when done in person. This format allows for questions, sharing, and skills practice.

Empower Faculty and Staff

Talking about student mental health concerns is still difficult for many faculty and staff. Many don't know how to start the conversation; even with gatekeeper training, many faculty and staff are so uncomfortable that they resort to silence. In a very emotional and compelling editorial in the *Chronicle of Higher Education*, titled "The Suddenly Empty Chair" (2012), Marguerite Choi, a faculty member at a large university, writes of this silence, her painful experience with a student suicide, and how inextricably mental health is tied to our roles on campus.

> These young adults are not out of our realm of caring for their emotional, as well as intellectual, best interests. We are not here merely to disseminate information. We expect our students to care for themselves and each other; that expectation should be held for faculty and staff, as well. Geoffrey's death has taught me that my friendship, honesty, and compassion must extend far beyond the boundaries of my classroom. I care for my students. And they deserve to know that.

Faculty and staff want to talk about mental health and how to start the conversation with any student. They want permission to talk to those students about whom they are concerned without worrying about breaching some boundary. One large university tackled this issue by having wellness staff attend every single staff and faculty monthly meeting and presenting on the mental health of their students. They went to the dean's office, residential life, athletic meetings, chaplain meetings, and faculty meetings. In a brief hour, they shared the power of asking, "How can I help?" and stating, "I am worried about you." Wellness staff shared campus resources on which faculty and staff could call and reach out to when concerned. This simple type of training made adults feel more confident and relieved that they had been empowered to talk about mental health.

Conclusion

We live in a world where one in four Americans is diagnosed with a mental health condition. Despite the prevalence of these life challenges across the life span, our society at large is ashamed, frightened, overwhelmed, and risk-averse when it comes to mental health. We also live in a time when postsecondary education is a viewed as a primary route to career advancement and economic self-sufficiency. And we live in a time when obtaining a postsecondary degree comes with many costs; there are financial pressures, academic and social pressures, and family pressures, to name the major ones. Yet, these are our students and they are on our campuses, commuting, living, learning, playing, and struggling. Colleges and universities are challenged in how to best meet their mental health needs and even wonder if they should be obligated to meet their mental health needs. Some schools have gone to great lengths to support the mental health of their students, while other colleges have made public disclaimers and written policies to ensure that student mental health is relegated to community resources. But mental health matters. And it matters on our campuses. There is a strong evidence base that documents the important connection of positive mental health to academic and social success. Positive mental health is an asset for students, laying an important foundation for adult resiliency, career advancement, and wellness. Mental health is not a priority in most budget proposals at universities. It is very challenging for mental health programs to compete for resources on campuses, perhaps because mental health is difficult to quantify and there is so much aversion to talking about mental health. There is an urgent need to educate administrators, boards of trustees, faculty, staff, and students about mental health and its relationship to higher education outcomes. Mental health problems and all the events linked to distressed mental health—substance abuse, suicide, sexual assaults, and attrition—are all considered bad business. There is double the risk of departure among students with significant mental health problems. The best return on investment of making mental health priority in our environments of higher education is the fact that suffering is reduced and student wellness and academic functioning improve. These outcomes are necessary to support our mission of educating young adults so they can work, contribute, and live full lives in our communities. Keep the conversation going on the campus about mental health. Everyone's mental health, including that of our students, matters.

References

American College Health Association. (2012). *National College Health Assessment II: Reference group executive summary, spring 2012.* Hanover, MD: Author.
American College Health Association. (2013). *National College Health Assessment II: Reference group executive summary, fall 2013.* Hanover, MD: Author.
American College Health Association. (2014). American College Health Association–National College Health Assessment II: Reference Group Executive Summary, Spring 2014. Hanover, MD: Author.
Barber, P. (2012, September). College students with disabilities: What factors influence successful degree completion? A case study. In *Disability and work: Research report.* Retrieved from http://www.heldrich.rutgers.edu/sites/default/files/products/uploads/College_Students_Disabilities_Report.pdf
Blacklock, B., Benson, B., Johnson, D., & Bloomberg, L. (2003). *Needs assessment project: Exploring barriers and opportunities for college students with psychiatric disabilities.* Unpublished manuscript, University of Minnesota.
Chen, W., & Lee, K. (2013). Sharing, liking, commenting, and distressed? The pathway between Facebook interaction and psychological distress. *Cyberpsychology, Behavior, and Social Networking, 16*(10), 728–734.

Choi, M. (2012, April 22). The suddenly empty chair. *Chronicle of Higher Education.* Retrieved from http://chronicle.com/search/?contextId=5&searchQueryString=The+suddenly+empty+chair&facetName=content&facetValue=article&facetCaption=Article

Christakis, D., Moreno, M., Jelenchick, L., Myaing, M., & Zhou, C. (2011). Problematic Internet usage in US college students: A pilot study. *BMC Medicine, 9,* 77.

Chung, H., & Klein, M. (2007, June). Improving identification and treatment of depression in college health. *Aetna Student Health Spectrum,* 13–19.

Collins, M. E., & Mowbray, C. T. (2005). Higher education and psychiatric disabilities: National Survey of Campus Disability Services. *American Journal of Orthopsychiatry, 75*(2), 304–315.

Davidson, L., & Locke, J. H. (2010). Using a public health approach to address student mental health. In J. Kay & V. Schwartz (Eds.), *Mental health care in the college community* (pp. 267–288). Hoboken, NJ: John Wiley & Sons.

DeJong, W. (2007). *Experiences in effective prevention: The U.S. Department of Education's alcohol and other drug prevention models on college campuses grants.* Washington, DC: U.S. Department of Education, Office of Safe and Drug-Free Schools, Higher Education Center for Alcohol and Other Drug Abuse and Violence Prevention.

DeJong, W., & Langford, L. (2002). A typology for campus-based alcohol prevention: Moving toward environmental management strategies [Supplemental material]. *Journal of Studies on Alcohol, 14,* 140–141.

Deresiewicz, W. (2014, July 21). Don't send your kid to the ivy league. *New Republic.*

Douce, L., & Keeling, R. (2014). *A strategic primer on college student mental health.* Washington, DC: American Council on Education.

Drum, D., Browson, C., Denmark, A., & Smith, S. (2009). New data on the nature of suicidal crises in college students: Shifting the paradigm. *Professional Psychology: Research and Practice, 40*(3), 213–222.

Eisenberg, D., Golberstein, E., & Gollust, S. E. (2007). Help-seeking and access to mental health care in a university student population. *Medical Care, 45*(7), 594–601.

Eisenberg, D., Golberstein, E., & Hunt, J. (2009). Mental health and academic success in college. *B.E. Journal of Economic Analysis & Policy, 9*(1), Article 40.

Eisenberg, D., Hunt, J., & Speer, N. (2012). Help seeking for mental health on college campuses: Review of evidence and next steps for research and practice. *Harvard Review of Psychiatry, 4,* 222–232.

Eisenberg, D., & Lipson, S. (2014, March 13). *Data from the healthy minds network: The economic case for mental health services.* Paper presented at the Depression on College Campuses Conference, University of Michigan, Ann Arbor.

Golberstein, E., Eisenberg, D. & Gollust, S. (2008). Perceived stigma and mental health care seeking. *Psychiatric Services, 59*(7), 392–399.

Hartley, M. T. (2013). Investigating the relationship of resilience to academic persistence in college students with mental health issues. *Rehabilitation Counseling Bulletin, 56*(4), 240–250.

Hunt, J., Watkins, D., & Eisenberg, D. (2012). How do college campuses make decisions about allocating resources for student mental health? Findings from key participant interviews at 10 campuses. *Journal of College Student Development, 53*(6), 850–866.

JED Foundation and Education Development Center. (2011). *Balancing safety and support on campus: A guide for campus teams.* New York, NY: Author.

JED Foundation Campus MHAP and Education Development Center. (2011). *The guide to campus mental health action planning.* New York, NY: Author.

Kahlenberg, R. (2011, August 9). Should we teach empathy in college? *Chronicle of Higher Education.* Retrieved from http://chronicle.com/blogs/innovations/should-we-teach-empathy-in-college/30044

Karr, K. (2009). *Recognizing and responding to students in distress: A faculty handbook.* Retrieved from http://dos.cornell.edu/dos/cms/upload/Total-Book-2.pdf

Kessler, R., Chiu, W., Demler, O., & Walters, E. (2005). Prevalence, severity and comorbidity of twelve-month DSM-IV disorders in the national comorbidity survey replication (NCS-R). *Archives of General Psychiatry, 62*(6), 617–627.

Kessler, R. C., Foster, C. L., Saunders, W. B., & Stang, P. E. (1995). Social consequences of psychiatric disorders, I: Educational attainment. *American Journal of Psychiatry, 152*(7), 1026–1032.

Kinkade, T. (2014, October 14). Using college mental health services can lead to students getting removed from campus. *Huffington Post.* Retrieved from http://www.huffingtonpost.com/news/college-mental-health

Kitzrow, M. (2003). The mental health needs of today's college students: Challenges and recommendations. *NASPA Journal, 41*(1), 167–181.

Konrath, S. H., O'Brien, E. H., & Hsing, C. (2011). Changes in dispositional empathy in American college students over time: A meta-analysis. *Personality, Social Psychology Review, 15*(2), 180–198.

Kross, E., Verduyn, P., Demiralp, E., Park, J., & Lee, D. S. (2013). Facebook use predicts declines in subjective well-being in young adults. *PLoS ONE, 8*(8), e69841. doi:10.1371/journal.pone.0069841

Luthar, S, Cicchetti, D., & Becker, B. (2000). The construct of resilience: A critical evaluation and guidelines for future work. *Child Development, 71*(3), 542–562.

Morse, C. (2014, March 12). *Students supporting students on college campuses: Fostering healthy connections.* Paper presented at the Depression on College Campuses Conference, University of Michigan, Ann Arbor.

Mowbray, C., Megiveren, D., Mandiberg, J., Strauss, S., Stein, C., Collins, K., . . . Lett, R. (2006). Campus mental health services: Recommendations for change. *American Journal of Orthopsychiatry, 76*(2), 226–247.

Murphy, J. G., Barnett, N. P., & Colby, S. M. (2006). Alcohol-related and alcohol-free activity participation and enjoyment among college students: Behavioral theories of choice analysis. *Experimental and Clinical Psychopharmacology, 14*, 339–349.

Pascarella, E. T., & Terenzini, P. T. (2005). *How college affects students: Vol. 2. A third decade of research.* San Francisco, CA: Jossey-Bass.

Smith, C., & Snell, P. (2009). *Souls in transition: The religious and spiritual lives of emerging adults.* New York, NY: Oxford University Press.

Southwick, S., Vythilingam, M., & Charney, D. (2005). The psychobiology of depression and resilience to stress: Implications for prevention and treatment. *Annual Review of Clinical Psychology, 1*, 255–291.

Stone, G., & Archer, J. (1990). College and university counseling centers in the 1990s: Challenges and limits. *Counseling Psychologist, 18*, 539–607.

Suicide Prevention Resource Center [SPRC]. (2004). *Promoting mental health and preventing suicide in college and university settings.* Newton, MA: Education Development Center.

Tinto, V. (1993). *Leaving college: Rethinking the causes and cures of student attrition.* (2nd ed.). Chicago, IL: University of Chicago Press.

Twenge, J. M. (2006). *Generation me: Why today's young Americans are more confident, assertive, entitled— And more miserable than ever before.* New York, NY: Free Press.

Van Brunt, B. (2012). *Ending campus violence: New approaches to prevention.* New York, NY: Routledge.

4

Technology
The Challenging Role Technology Plays in the Lives of College Students

KEVIN KRUGER

The use of all types of information technology and the Internet is virtually universal for teens, college students, and adults. The widespread use of technology by all sectors of our society is increasing so quickly that most published research data is already behind and outdated, given the rapidly shifting technology environment. While more established social networking sites, such as Facebook and Twitter, seem to be constants, new applications are developed weekly, and historically teen and adolescent technology patterns are notoriously fickle and can change from year to year.

As such, this chapter will say very little about specific technologies, except where individual research references a specific technology (Facebook and Twitter), but will attempt instead to examine the general effects technology and social networking sites have on health, wellness, and student learning for college students. As expected, there are ample examples of both positive and negative outcomes associated with the use of technology among college students; it is the intent of this chapter to identify key issues for educators in the design of programs, services, and learning opportunities that maximize the beneficial and reduce the harmful outcomes associated with technology and Internet use.

Teen and Young Adult Technology Use

Research on college and young adult use of technology is still relatively sparse. Since the behaviors and habits of teens and their use of technology will carry over to their college years, both teen and college-age research will be reviewed in this chapter. In addition, given that technology changes so rapidly, more recent studies are more useful in understanding effects on mental health, even if the research was primarily on pre-college experiences.

It is clear that both teen and college student use of social networking sites (SNS) has increased significantly over the past five years. Social networking refers to the array of websites, applications, and services that are used to "support collaboration, community building, participation, and sharing" (Junco, Heiberger, & Loken, 2011, p. 1).

In their most recent survey of teen Internet use, the Pew Center's Internet and American Life Project found that 94% of teens (12–17) use the Internet and 81% use social media (Madden et al., 2013). Facebook is by far the most widely used social networking platform; 93% of teens report using Facebook and have, on average, 450 friends on Facebook. Twitter and Instagram are well behind, but show signs of more widespread adoption. In just one year, the Pew Center found teen use of Twitter more than doubled from 12% in 2011 to 26% in 2012 (Madden et al., 2013). Teens who use sites other than Facebook report more disillusionment with Facebook and increasingly are migrating their use to other sites, such as Twitter, Instagram, and Snapchat. "In focus groups, many teens expressed waning enthusiasm for Facebook. They dislike the increasing number of adults on the site, get annoyed when their Facebook friends share inane details, and are drained by the 'drama' that they described as happening frequently on the site" (Madden et al., 2013, p. 7).

Teen use of social media has undergone meaningful changes in recent years. They share more and seem to be more open to sharing personal information on social networking sites. "Teens are increasingly sharing personal information on social media sites, a trend that is likely driven by the evolution of the platforms teens use as well as changing norms around sharing. For the five different types of personal information that we measured in both 2006 and 2012, each is significantly more likely to be shared by teen social media users on the profile they use most often.

- 91% post a photo of themselves, up from 79% in 2006.
- 71% post their school name, up from 49%.
- 71% post the city or town where they live, up from 61%.
- 53% post their email address, up from 29%.
- 20% post their cell phone number, up from 2%."

(Madden et al., 2013, p. 3)

Not surprisingly, the research on the use of technology and social media by college students looks a lot like the teen research referenced earlier. Art Levine and Diane Dean (2012), in their book *Generation on a Tightrope*, discovered this in their new research on college students. When asked to identify the most important components of their lives, the number one key element in the lives of college students was their digital culture. Surprisingly digital culture was ahead of both the economy and 9/11. The students who are enrolled in college now are all "digital natives" (Levine & Dean, 2012). Today's college students use social networking to continue relationships with previous friends and explore new relationships (Pempek, Yermolayeva, & Calvert, 2009; Wang, Chen, & Liang, 2011). These SNS sites also play an important role in identity development and the students' expression of who they are (Pempek et al., 2009). In an innovative study that monitored actual technology use, rather than self-reported data, Junco (2013) found that Facebook, MS Word, Learning Management Systems (LMS), Skype, and email were the most popular uses of technology by students. When time was used as the measure, this same study found that "social networking was the most popular computer activity" (Junco, 2014, p. 75). Other studies have supported Facebook as the most popular SNS among college students, with daily usage averaging between 80 and

120 minutes per day (Ellison, Steinfeld, & Lampe, 2011; Junco, 2012; Kalpidou, Costin, & Morris, 2011). Most current research has found that students' use of SNS is a constant in the lives of students, even when controlling for race, ethnicity, and gender. However, some research has found differences not in the amount of time devoted to social networking but in the types of activities that make up this time. For instance, Junco (2013) found that African American students, when using Facebook, were less likely to tag photos and explore friends' pages. This same research also found that students from a lower socioeconomic status were less likely to use Facebook for communicating, connecting, and sharing with others— which are the purposes for which Facebook was created (Junco, 2013). Although these differences concerning race and SES may not seem significant, they relate to overall social capital and can put these students at a disadvantage in both their social and academic worlds. If students of color and students from lower socio-economic status do not have the experience or technology competency to use all of the social aspects of SNS, this may create an impediment to engagement and social connection to their peers. As Junco (2013) stated, "Failure to connect in these ways could deprive students of the benefits of participation on such sites, such as increased social capital, improved social integration, opportunities for peer-to-peer learning, and improving the technological and communication skills valued in today's workplace" (p. 2335).

It is clear in 2014 that Internet usage and engagement in social networking are virtually ubiquitous. It is important for educators both within and outside the classroom to understand the positive outcomes associated with this involvement with technology and to equally understand the potential harm that can come from a lack of balance in the time allocated to technology use. The next sections in this chapter will explore both of these dimensions in more depth.

Internet Use and Mental Health

It is well documented that depression is a serious mental health concern for college students. The Centers for Disease Control and Prevention estimate that almost 10% of adults suffer from a depressive disorder. It is even higher for college students. In their annual survey of college student health, the American College Health Association (2014) estimated that as many as 30% of college students "felt so depressed that it was difficult to function" (p. 14).

A key question is to understand any linkages or associations between technology use and mental health issues. It is important to acknowledge that not all technology and Internet usage has a positive effect on learning, student success, relationships, or mental health. There is ample evidence that in some cases excessive technology usage can be associated with a range of mental health issues. In a survey of 200 volunteers, one research study found a linkage between patterns of Internet usage and depression. In this study they found "peer-to-peer file sharing, heavy emailing and chatting online, and a tendency to quickly switch between multiple websites and other online resources all predict a greater propensity to experience symptoms of depression" (Ward & Valdesolo, 2012, para. 5). These studies do not suggest causality, but provide important markers for mental health and student affairs professionals to explore in their work with students who are experiencing depression.

Although Internet addiction has not been formally recognized by the American Psychological Association in the most recent *Diagnostic and Statistical Manual of Mental Health Disorders (DSM-V)*, many mental health professionals do recognize this as an actual mental health disorder. Internet addiction shares the same characteristics of addiction. A person who experiences Internet addiction will develop a "preoccupation with the internet or internet gaming, withdrawal symptoms when the substance (internet) is no longer available, tolerance (the need to spend more and more time on the internet to achieve the same 'high'), loss of other interests, unsuccessful attempts to quit, and use of the internet to improve or escape dysphoric mood" (Walton, 2012, para. 2). Internet addiction may create significant barriers to student success. Constant texting, hyper-gaming, and excessive use of social networking, often into the early morning hours for college students, can result in serious consequences, such as depression, social isolation, and the deterioration of relationships (Kriger, 2014).

Other studies have reinforced these findings. In a study of college student Internet use and addictive behaviors, between 5% and 10% of Internet users appeared to show a form of web dependency; subsequent brain imaging studies revealed that compulsive Internet users have similar brain reward pathways as those who have a drug addiction (Fulps, 2013). This is further evidence that Internet addiction and compulsion may be an important focus for mental health professionals on campus.

The amount of time devoted to nonacademic technology can obviously detract from the time needed for academic success. In addition, the connections between Internet addiction and other mental health issues make this an important issue for both faculty and college administrators. One challenge will be how to identify students who go beyond normal, healthy technology usage to technology usage that affects their mental health or time devoted to be successful academically. Virtually all students use the Internet, and increasingly most college classes involve access to the Internet. It will be challenging to distinguish heavy Internet users from those who are exhibiting addictive behavior. When involvement in technology begins to detract from interacting with people in "live" settings or when normal interpersonal development is inhibited, referrals to counseling or psychological services will be important. In those cases, helping students manage their Internet usage should be the focus of any psychological intervention. Research on effective treatment strategies is currently incomplete. Some early studies have suggested that Internet addiction might be treated in similar ways as other impulse control and addictive behaviors, using motivational interviewing and cognitive and behavior therapies (Khazaal et al., 2012; Walton, 2012). Acknowledgment of the problem, self-observation, time management, and development of offline activities have been used successfully as part of cognitive behavioral therapy (Khazaal et al., 2012).

There is additional evidence that Internet addiction can result in more aggressive behaviors among adolescents. In a study of over 9,000 adolescents, researchers studied the relationship between Internet addiction and aggressive behavior, controlling for a set of other variables, including violent television watching, depression, self-esteem, and family functioning. The results demonstrated that adolescents with Internet addiction were more likely to exhibit aggressive behaviors in the previous year (Ko, Yen, Liu, Huang, & Yen, 2009). Although the focus of this research is on young adults in junior and high school, it further suggests that educational, prevention, and treatment efforts to address Internet addiction are important for college students.

Technology and Interpersonal Communication

One of the more important developmental experiences for college students—particularly those in the 18–24 demographic—is the development of interpersonal and intrapersonal competence (Keeling, 2004). The challenges of developing interpersonal competence in a world dominated by social networking and the Internet seem almost self-evident. There is a shift in the ways people communicate and a preference for mediated communication using social networking and instant messaging over face-to-face interaction (Keller, 2013). Interestingly, some researchers suggest that this preference for mediated communication may actually be *increasing* social interaction, even as we move away from face-to-face interaction (Keller, 2013). But as this form of communication increases, it is important to understand the need to develop face-to-face interpersonal relationship skills for "digital natives," those traditional-aged college students who were born after the widespread use of technology. Heavy users of social media may experience more superficial social connections and relationships, and the nature of social media relationships may lack the diversity of perspectives that are possible in face-to-face connections (Keller, 2013). Therefore, college educators would be well served to train staff to identify signs of Internet addiction and to develop programmatic alternatives that promote in-person, face-to-face social interaction that can serve as a balance and distraction to online activities.

Social Networking and Engagement

The importance of engagement as a key variable in student success is well documented in the literature of higher education. Intentional and purposeful engagement is linked to a wide set of positive student learning outcomes, such as critical thinking, interpersonal development, degree progress, and individual student development (Kuh, 2009). Kuh additionally described the importance of both in-class (academic) and out-of-class (co-curricular) engagement as critical to student success. As a result of years of research on engagement, colleges and universities have been deliberate in creating opportunities for high-impact practices that maximize opportunities for engagement. In *How College Affects Students*, the case for this institutional effort is stated clearly: "Because individual effort and involvement are the critical determinants of impact, institutions should focus on the ways they can shape their academic, interpersonal, and extracurricular offerings to encourage student engagement" (Pascarella & Terenzini, 2005, p. 602).

Given the importance of engagement, there are two critical questions related to technology and engagement:

- In what ways can student use of social networking and other technologies contribute to overall engagement?
- In what ways does student use of social networking and other technologies inhibit or lessen opportunities for intentional engagement?

In the last few years, research is emerging that supports the premise that social networking has a positive effect on the engagement process for college students (Haeger, Wang, & BrckaLorenz, 2014; Junco, 2011; Junco, Heiberger, & Loken, 2011; Valenzuela, Park, & Kee, 2009). It appears that participation in social networking sites, such as Facebook, Twitter, Instagram, and others, creates a forum for students to connect socially and "provides students with wider access to diverse social support networks and shortens the distance between students, faculty and staff within the college community" (Haeger et al., 2014, p. 4).

In a study of 19,000 students at 42 institutions who participated in the National Survey of Student Engagement (NSSE), researchers found that using social media to interact with staff and administrators had a positive effect on the quality of those relationships (Haeger et al., 2014). In this same study, students who, using social media, interacted with their peers about either academic or social issues reported a positive effect on the quality of those peer relationships (Haeger et al., 2014). One additional finding from this research was of particular interest in examining the differential effect and use of social media by first-generation college students. This relates specifically to concerns about the "digital divide" that exists among college students. Supporting this concern, these researchers found that first-generation students were not using social media in the same way as other students and were not making the same kinds of connections with faculty, staff, and peers. This identifies a clear challenge for our work with first-generation students. "Without conscious effort to make sure traditionally disadvantaged students are also connected through social media, this technology does not bridge the gap in social capital development in college" (Haeger et al., 2014, p. 8).

Other studies have supported the relationship between technology use and engagement. For instance, Chen, Guidry, and Lambert (2009) used experimental questions from the NSSE to study the relationship between technology usage in classrooms and measures of engagement. Their research found that students who used the Internet and other online technology scored higher on engagement measures and were also more likely "to make use of deep learning approaches like higher order thinking, reflective learning, and integrative learning in their study" (Chen et al., 2009, p. 19). In another study, Junco et al. (2011) specifically examined the effect of encouraging Twitter use for educationally relevant purposes on student engagement. Basing their work on previous engagement research, Junco et al. focused their research on the use of Twitter for the following class activities:

- Class discussions
- A low-stress way to ask questions

- Book discussions
- Class reminders
- Class and event reminders
- Providing academic and personal support
- Helping students connect with each other and with instructors
- Organizing service learning projects
- Organizing study groups

The results of the research found that using Twitter in educationally relevant ways had a positive effect on student engagement, grades, faculty-student interaction, cooperation among students, and active learning. This is one of the first studies examining the effect of Twitter usage in the classroom and provides evidence that "using Twitter in educationally relevant ways can increase student engagement and improve grades, and thus, that social media can be used as an educational tool to help students reach desired college outcomes" (Junco et al., 2011, p. 12).

Valenzuela et al. (2009) focused on Facebook use as a variable in affecting a wide range of social capital variables, including civic participation, political engagement, life satisfaction, and social trust. Their research found a positive and significant relationship between intensity of Facebook use and the acquisition of these social capital variables. As stated by Valenzuela et al., "These findings do not support the popular view that heavy Facebook users are more isolated and less connected than occasional users" (p. 893). In another study, Gray, Vitak, Easton, and Ellison (2013) also found a relationship between Facebook and another set of positive college outcomes. Their research focused on two key Facebook variables: the number of Facebook friends and students' engagement in collaborative behaviors with classmates using Facebook. In their study at a large, private institution, they found a positive relationship between these two Facebook variables and social support, social adjustment, and persistence (Gray et al., 2013). The first year of college, particularly at a large institution, can present challenges to social integration for many students. This research suggests that Facebook may be a useful tool in helping students connect with each other, ease their transition from high school, and connect with fellow students who are in the same classes. This social integration can play an important role in the persistence of first-year students. As noted earlier, this may be particularly important for first-generation students, who have less social capital upon entering and who often experience degree completion challenges. While social integration is important to first-generation students, it is also important for other segments of the student population whose previous life experiences may create barriers to success. International students, military veterans, and foster youth are examples of other subgroups who will benefit from the social integration process.

The previous studies all demonstrated the positive effect of two commercial social networking sites, Twitter and Facebook. DeAndrea, Ellison, LaRose, Steinfield, and Fiore (2011) conducted similar research using a noncommercial, campus-based social networking site that allowed students to connect with each other prior to and during their matriculation at the institution. While conducted only at a single institution, they did find that activity on the campus-based social network site was a significant predictor of interacting with faculty outside the classroom, getting helpful information from staff, and connecting with a diverse group of students (DeAndrea et al., 2011). The authors suggest that access to a network of information creates a sense of self efficacy or social capital and that "simply having access to a student-focused online community may have helped students believe that they would be able to reach other students who could provide help" (DeAndrea et al., 2011, p. 5).

Kalpidou et al. (2011), in their study of the relationship between Facebook use and psychological well-being, found differential effects between lower-class and upper-class students. "The first-year students who had a lot of Facebook friends experienced lower academic and emotional adjustment, while upper-class students with many Facebook friends reported high social adjustment and attachment to the institution" (Kalpidou et al., 2011, p. 188). Their research provides a cautionary tale for the use of social networking during the first year. Particularly for students who are introverted or who are struggling with the social adjustment to college, higher amounts of time spent on social networking may detract from psychological well-being and increase isolation. For upper-class students, who already have established social networks, social networking seems to be positively linked to their overall emotional and total college adjustment (Kalpidou et al., 2011). Another study examined the role social networking might play in social integration for students living off campus as compared to students living on campus (Dorum, Bartle, & Pennington, 2010). As might be expected, students living on campus who used social networking had a higher sense of belonging than reported by off-campus students. However, more importantly, this study found that engagement in social networking increased the sense of belonging for those off-campus students (Dorum et al., 2010). This suggests that student affairs might create intentional strategies to connect off-campus students through SNS to increase their social integration and sense of connection to the institution.

In summary, it seems clear that social networking can supplement face-to-face interaction in creating intentional and meaningful engagement and is an important tool for both faculty and staff in their efforts to increase engagement of their students in and out of the classroom. College staff might consider creating Facebook groups that connect marginalized subgroups or scheduled synchronous Twitter chats (often called "tweet-ups") to encourage students to engage with each other on current and contemporary issues. Faculty might also consider ways to use SNS as a way to increase dialogue between students and also to expand faculty-student interaction.

Technology and Mental Health

Beyond the linkages of technology and social networking to engagement, social integration, development of social capital, and persistence referenced earlier, there is conflicting evidence about the use of social networking and the linkage to both positive and negative mental health. In the early days of the Internet, there was some evidence that technology and Internet usage was linked to depression, lone-liness, and a reduction in social involvement and psychological well-being (Kraut et al., 1998). Even this early research was revisited in later years and revealed that the negative effects had largely dissipated and that use of Internet technolo-gies actually had positive results for communication, social involvement, and well-being (Kraut et al., 2008). But, like many studies that have examined the rela-tionship between the use of technology and positive mental health outcomes, the results can be complex. In the research referenced earlier, while finding a positive connection to well-being, this effect was greatest for individuals who already had some level of social capital—namely, extroverts. For introverts, they experienced much less social involvement and well-being as a result of their technology use.

Teens largely report very positive experiences with technology. Results from the Internet and American Life Project support this overall positive experience. "In broad measures of online experience, teens are considerably more likely to report positive experiences than negative ones" (Madden et al., 2013, p. 12). This same research found that teens' online experiences helped them in making friends and feeling closer to others; 52% of teens reported an online experience that made them feel good about themselves, and 33% said that they felt closer to another person as a result of their online experience (Madden et al., 2013).

Other research finds conflicting results between social networking and positive mental health. For example, Gonzalez and Hancock (2009) examined the role of Facebook on a person's reported self-esteem. They found that participants who updated and viewed their profiles and actively edited their personal information on Facebook reported greater self-esteem and became more self-aware. This active use of Facebook enhanced self-esteem rather than diminished it (Gonzalez & Hancock, 2009). In another study conducted by the University of Gothenburg in Sweden, 1,000 participants (18–73 years old) were surveyed to determine if there was a relationship between Facebook use and self-esteem. The amount of time spent using Facebook was quite significant; the average user reported using Face-book 75 minutes per day and logging in over six times/day, and 70% of respondents logged into Facebook every time they started or accessed their computer ("Swe-den's Largest," 2012). Perhaps most troubling were their findings that 26% felt "ill at ease" if they did not log in to Facebook and that women who used Facebook felt less happy and content with their lives (University of Gothenburg, 2012). This addresses the addictive nature of Facebook and the concern that users may feel they are missing something if they are not regularly connected.

Other research identified similar and related themes—often, increased use of social networking sites has a negative effect on self-esteem. The findings range from increases in eating disorders among women (Mabe, Forney, & Keel, 2014) to increases in requests for cosmetic surgery due to patients being more self-aware of looks in social media (American Academy of Facial Plastic and Reconstructive Surgery, 2014). What seems to be a common theme is almost counterintuitive: "In theory, the social networking website Facebook could be great for people with low self-esteem. Sharing is important for improving friendships. But in practice, peo-ple with low self-esteem seem to behave counterproductively, bombarding their friends with negative tidbits about their lives and making themselves less likeable" (Association for Psychological Science, 2012, para. 1).

Social networking sites such as Facebook can have a positive association with self-esteem and other measures of self-efficacy. However, the research suggests that the most positive effects are among those who already have significant social capital, who are extroverts, and who are not already struggling with psychosocial issues in college. The use of social networking is heavily nuanced. Students are very self-aware of their social networking use and also can identify the negative consequences of overengagement. Even strategies to reduce social networking should be carefully considered, as the removal of social networking can also have a negative effect on the psychological well-being of students (JED Foundation, 2010). It is critical for counselors, mental health providers, and campus faculty and staff to be aware of the negative consequences for many who are active users of social networking sites and also understand the important role social networking plays in the lives of students. It may be important in the training for all paraprofessional and professional staff who have "frontline" responsibilities to understand both the symptoms of excessive Internet use and the positive ways in which online social connections can expand healthy relationships. Student involvement in social networking should not immediately be discounted as "less than" face-to-face interactions, nor should social networking be ignored as an area of potential abuse.

As student use of technology continues to increase, it is also revealing unexpected connections to mental health. In a study of over 2,000 students from 40 campuses, the JED Foundation (2010) found that social networking sites were often used by students to talk about psychological issues, such as depression, stress, and suicide. Their study found that almost 70% of students had read something online that was interpreted as a cry for help or a need for emotional support. The JED Foundation study found that about half of the students who had read a "cry for help" post would call the student who expressed the issue and/or respond privately to the student, using the same social networking channel (JED Foundation, 2010). This research is a call for action to encourage more students to respond to perceived psychological distress expressed through social networking. Since only 10% of respondents would inform a faculty or staff member, this also is an area that might be further encouraged.

Cyberbullying and Cyberstalking

When 18-year-old Rutgers University student Tyler Clementi jumped off the George Washington Bridge in September 2010, after discovering his roommate had streamed a romantic encounter with him and another man over the Internet, it sparked a national debate about the prevalence of cyberbullying and cyberstalking on college campuses. The Tyler Clementi case, as well as other high-profile cyberbullying and cyberstalking cases, exposed a dangerous dimension of the exploding world of social networking among college students. Cyberbullying is defined by the Cyberbullying Research Center as online behavior in which someone repeatedly harasses, mistreats, or makes fun of another person online or while using cell phones or other electronic devices. Cyberstalking, which often has state laws that define it, has many similarities to cyberbullying. The National Institute of Justice defines cyberstalking as the use of technology to stalk victims and involves behavior that "involves the pursuit, harassment, or contact of others in an unsolicited fashion initially via the Internet and e-mail. . . . Cyberstalkers may use information acquired online to further intimidate, harass, and threaten their victim via courier mail, phone calls, and physically appearing at a residence or work place" (National Institute of Justice, 2007).

Teens and college students have unwanted, threatening, or harassing online encounters at rates that are disturbingly high. The Cyberbullying Research Center, in a review of research from 2004 to 2010, found that around 20% of students (10–18 years old) had experienced cyberbullying (Hinduja & Patchin, 2010). In this same study, 13% of students reported experiencing mean or hurtful comments or having rumors spread about them in the last 30 days (Hinduja & Patchin, 2010). Even in the seemingly harmless world of online gaming, teens are experiencing negative behavior by others in the gaming community. "Nearly two-thirds (63%) of teens who play games report seeing or hearing 'people being mean and overly aggressive while playing,' and 49% report seeing or hearing 'people being hateful, racist, or sexist' while playing" (Lenhart et al., 2008, p. iv). On a more positive note, these authors also found that students will often "police" themselves and confront offensive and hurtful comments, using what is commonly known as "bystander intervention." Almost 75% reported that other players will ask the aggressor to stop their offending behavior, and 85% reported seeing other players being helpful when aggressive behavior is present. "This active bystander intervention might be something that can be encouraged more widely, among college students" (Lenhart et al., 2008, p. iv).

Research on college students suggests that the problem of cyberstalking and cyberbullying continues throughout the college years. In one study, "almost half of a sample of undergraduate and graduate students who responded to an advertisement asking them if they had been 'stalked online or via text message or any other type of technology' met the legal criteria for cyberstalking victimization" (Hensler-McGinnis, 2008, p. 138). Hensler-McGinnis (2008) also found that victims of cyberstalking often experience psychological issues that affect academic progress and performance, suggesting that colleges should "be better prepared to assess and address the educational/career impact of cyberstalking victimization" and to educate students and broader campus communities about the crime of cyberstalking (p. 164). Other, more recent research finds similar rates of cyberstalking. In their sample of almost 1,000 students from a Midwest college, Reyns, Henson, and Fisher (2012) found that just over 40% of students had an experience of cyberstalking at some point in their lives. They also found that, consistent with previous stalking research, "a higher percentage of females were victimized than males for all types of pursuit behaviors, except threats of violence. Nearly a third, 32.1%, of males experienced cyberstalking victimization, whereas 46.3% of females were cyberstalked" (Reyns et al., 2012, p. 13). This gender difference has been reported in other research as well. In a study of teens from 15 to 18, 38% of girls reported having experienced cyberbullying, compared to 26% of boys (Lenhart, 2007).

Cyberbullying and cyberstalking, as in the case of Tyler Clementi and others, can have devastating effects on the mental health of the victims of this form of harassment. The disturbances in the life of students can range from somewhat trivial frustration to more serious psychological and life problems (Tokunaga, 2010). The psychological reactions that victims experience vary according to the length and severity of the harassment but often include a noticeable drop in academic performance, affective disorders, a range of psychological issues, and problems in family relations (Juvoven & Gross, 2008; Tokunaga, 2010).

Conclusion

Given the widespread use of technology, the amount of time spent online, and the important role that technology, social networking sites, and the Internet play in the lives of college students, it is important to understand the potential for both positive and negative effects on the mental health and psychological wellness of college students. Research on the intersection between technology use and college student mental health and wellness is still fairly young. A review of the literature reveals the need for more research on the many dimensions of this relationship.

However, several themes emerge as we begin to understand this important area. College administrators, faculty, and staff should be aware of the key issues related to technology use by college students:

- The use of technology and social networking, in particular, is increasing year after year in overall percentages and the amount of time spent. The perceived role of social media is also increasing year after year.
- Access to broadband Internet and access to technology are affected by the socioeconomic status of students when they enter college. There is a tangible "digital divide," and college faculty and staff need to focus on increasing the technology competence for low-income, first-generation students in particular. Many of the students do not have the social capital necessary to take full advantage of the positive effects of online technologies.
- High amounts of technology usage among college students may be problematic for those who already have psychological issues or low socioeconomic status. Significant time spent on the Internet, gaming, and social networking can increase symptoms of depression as well as loneliness and isolation for some students. Faculty and staff should understand the negative effects of technology for these students and make appropriate referrals to mental health professionals when observed.
- Internet addiction is a serious mental health disorder. Counseling, health, and wellness centers should include Internet addiction in their prevention and educational programs and clinical practices.
- Cyberbullying and cyberstalking are experienced by many students. Prevention and reporting information should be widely available to students, and all faculty and staff should be aware of the harmful effects these behaviors can have on student success and degree progress.

• Intentional use of social networking in and beyond the classroom can be an effective educational tool that can create meaningful engagement experiences for students. While more research needs to be conducted in this area, it seems clear that social networking is an important tool that can provide opportunities to expand social and interpersonal development, community development, intercultural dialogue, and peer-to-peer and faculty-staff interaction.

In the end, while being wary of the negative consequences of the overuse of technology and the negative effects on health and well-being, college educators should more importantly focus on the ways in which technology will become the centerpiece of the tomorrow's college learning experience. "The future of higher education is more than a digital replica of yesterday's campus or even today's classroom. The building blocks of our future higher education institutions are physical and virtual; they are human and technological. By combining these capabilities—the best of both the traditional (the campus) and the digital (computing), we can build colleges and universities that are designed to engage" (Oblinger, 2014).

References

American Academy of Facial Plastic and Reconstructive Surgery. (2014). Selfie trend increases demand for facial plastic surgery [Press release]. Retrieved from http://www.aafprs.org/media/press_release/20140311.html

American College Health Association. (2014). *National College Health Assessment: Reference group executive summary 2013*. Retrieved from http://www.acha-ncha.org/docs/ACHA-NCHA-II_ReferenceGroup_ExecutiveSummary_Fall2013.pdf

Association for Psychological Science. (2012). Facebook is not such a good thing for those with low self-esteem [Press Release]. Retrieved from http://www.psychologicalscience.org/index.php/news/releases/facebook-is-not-such-a-good-thing-for-those-with-low-self-esteem.html

Chen, D.P., Guidry, K.R., & Lambert, A. D. (2009, April). *Engaging online learners: A quantitative study of postsecondary student engagement in the online learning environment*. Paper presented at the meeting of American Educational Research Association, San Diego, CA.

DeAndrea, D. C., Ellison, N.B., LaRose, R., Steinfield, C., & Fiore, A. (2011). Serious social media: On the use of social media for improving students' adjustment to college. *Internet and Higher Education, 15*(1), 15–23. doi:10.1016/j.iheduc.2011.05.009

Dorum, K., Bartle, C., & Pennington, M. (2010). The effect of online social networking on facilitating sense of belonging among university students living off campus. *Proceedings of World Conference on Educational Multimedia, Hypermedia and Telecommunications 2010* (pp. 529–535). Chesapeake, VA: Association for the Advancement of Computing in Education.

Ellison, N.B., Steinfield, C., & Lampe, C. (2011). Connection strategies: Social capital implications of Facebook-enabled communication practices. *New Media & Society, 13*(6), 873–892. doi:10.1177/1461444810385389

Fulps, L. (2013, December 18). College students' heavy internet use shares symptoms of addiction. *ScienceDaily*. Retrieved from http://www.sciencedaily.com/releases/2013/12/131218095408.htm

Gonzalez, A.L., & Hancock, J.T. (2009). Mirror, mirror on my Facebook wall: Effects of exposure to Facebook on self-esteem. *Cyberpsychology, Behavior, and Social Networking, 14*(1–2), 79–83. doi:10.1089/cyber.2009.0411

Gray, R., Vitak, J., Easton, E.W., & Ellison, N.B. (2013). Examining social adjustment to college in the age of social media: Factors influencing successful transitions and persistence. *Computers & Education, 67*, 193–207. doi:10.1016/j.compedu.2013.02.021

Haeger, H., Wang, R., & BrckaLorenz, A. (2014, April). *Bridge or barrier: The impact of social media on engagement for first-generation college students.* Paper presented at the meeting of American Educational Research Association, Philadelphia, PA.

Hensler-McGinnis, N. F. (2008). *Cyberstalking victimization: Impact and coping responses in a national university sample* (Doctoral dissertation). Retrieved from ProQuest Dissertations and Theses database. (UMI No. 3307936)

Hinduja, S., & Patchin, J. (2010). Cyberbullying victimization. Retrieved from http://cyberbullying.us/blog/wp-content/uploads/2013/07/2010_victimization.jpg

JED Foundation. (2010). Associated Press study examines college students' mental health and relationships with technology [Press release]. Retrieved from http://www.jedfoundation.org/press-room/press-releases/MTVu-AP-Study

Junco, R. (2011). The relationship between frequency of Facebook use, participation in Facebook activities, and student engagement. *Computers & Education, 58*(1), 162–171. doi:10.1016/j.compedu.2011.08.004

Junco, R. (2012). Too much face and not enough books: The relationship between multiple indices of Facebook use and academic performance. *Computers in Human Behavior, 28*(1), 187–198. doi:doi:10.1016/j.chb.2011.08.026

Junco, R. (2013). Inequalities in Facebook use. *Computers in Human Behavior, 29*(6), 2328–2336. doi:10.1016/j.chb.2013.05.005

Junco, R. (2014). iSpy: Seeing what students really do online. *Learning Media and Technology, 39*(1), 75–89. doi:10.1080/17439884.2013.771782

Junco, R., Heiberger, G., & Loken, E. (2011). The effect of Twitter on college student engagement and grades. *Journal of Computer Assisted Learning, 27*(2), 119–132. doi:10.1111/j.1365-2729.2010.00387.x

Juvoven, J., & Gross, E. F. (2008). Extending the school grounds?—Bullying experiences in cyberspace. *Journal of School Health, 78*(9), 496–505. doi:10.1111/j.1746-1561.2008.00335.x

Kalpidou, M., Costin, D., & Morris, J. (2011). The relationship between Facebook and the well-being of undergraduate college students. *Cyberpsychology, Behavior, & Social Networking, 14*(4), 183–189. doi:10.1089/cyber.2010.0061

Keeling, R. (Ed.). (2004). *Learning reconsidered: A campus-wide focus on the student experience.* Washington, DC: American College Personnel Association and National Association of Student Personnel Administrators.

Keller, M. (2013, May/June). Social media and interpersonal communication. *Social Work Today, 13*(3). Retrieved from http://www.socialworktoday.com/archive/051313p10.shtml

Khazaal, Y., Xirossavidou, C., Khan, R., Edel, Y., Zebouni, F., & Zullino, D. (2012). Cognitive-behavioral treatments for "Internet addiction." *Open Addiction Journal, 5*, 30–35. doi:10.2174/1874941001205010030

Ko, C., Yen, J., Liu, S., Huang, C., & Yen, C. (2009). The associations between aggressive behaviors and internet addiction and online activities in adolescents. *Journal of Adolescent Health, 44*(6), 598–605. doi:10.1016/j.jadohealth.2008.11.011

Kraut, R., Kiesler, S., Boneva, B., Cummings, J., Helgeson, V., & Crawford, A. (2008). Internet paradox revisited. *Journal of Social Issues, 58*(1), 49–74. doi:10.1111/1540-4560.00248

Kraut, R., Patterson, M., Lundmark, V., Kiesler, S., Mukophadhyay, T., & Scherlis, W. (1998). Internet paradox: A social technology that reduces social involvement and psychological well-being? *American Psychologist, 53*(9), 1017–1031. doi:10.1037/0003-066X.53.9.1017

Kriger, J. K. (2014). *Turned on and tuned out: A practical guide to understanding and managing tech dependence.* Bloomington, IN: WestBow Press.

Kuh, G. D. (2009). What student affairs professionals need to know about student engagement. *Journal of College Student Development, 50*(6), 683–706. doi:10.1353/csd.0.0099

Lenhart, A. (2007). Cyberbullying. Pew Research Center. Retrieved from http://www.pewinternet.org/2007/06/27/cyberbullying

Lenhart, A., Kahne, J., Middaugh, E., Macgill, A., Evans, C., & Vitak, J. (2008). *Teens, video games and civics.* Pew Research Center. Retrieved from http://www.pewinternet.org/~/media//Files/Reports/2008/PIP_Teens_Games_and_Civics_Report_FINAL.pdf.pdf

Levine, A., & Dean, D. R. (2012). *Generation on a tightrope: A portrait of today's college student.* San Francisco, CA: Jossey-Bass.

Mabe, A. G., Forney, K. J., & Keel, P. K. (2014). Do you "like" my photo? Facebook use maintains eating disorder risk. *International Journal of Eating Disorders, 47*(5), 516–523. doi:10.1002/eat.22254

Madden, M., Lenhart, A., Cortesi, S., Gasser, U., Duggan, M., Smith, A., & Beaton, M. (2013). Teens, social media, and privacy. Pew Research Center. Retrieved from website: http://www.pewinternet. org/2013/05/21/teens-social-media-and-privacy

National Institute of Justice. (2007). Stalking. Retrieved from http://www.nij.gov/topics/crime/stalking/ Pages/welcome.aspx#

Oblinger, D. (2014). Designing a future of digital engagement. *EDUCAUSE Review, 49*(5). Retrieved from http://www.educause.edu/ero/article/designing-future-digital-engagement

Pascarella, E. T., & Terenzini, P. T. (2005). *How college affects students.* San Francisco, CA: Jossey-Bass.

Pempek, T. A., Yermolayeva, Y. A., & Calvert, S. L. (2009). College students' social networking experiences on Facebook. *Journal of Applied Developmental Psychology, 30*(3), 227–238. doi:10.1016/j. appdev.2008.12.010

Reyns, B. W., Henson, B., & Fisher, B. S. (2012). Stalking in the twilight zone: Extent of cyberstalking victimization and offending among college students. *Deviant Behavior, 33*(1), 1–25. doi:10.10 80/01639625.2010.538364

Sweden's largest Facebook study: A survey of 1,000 Swedish Facebook users. (2012). [Web log post]. Retrieved from http://codify-heddi.blogspot.com/2012/04/sweden-largest-facebook-study-survey-of.html

Tokunaga, R. S. (2010). Following you home from school: A critical review and synthesis of research on cyberbullying victimization. *Computers in Human Behavior, 26*(3), 277–287. doi:10.1016/j. chb.2009.11.014

University of Gothenburg. (2012). Sweden's largest Facebook study: a survey of 1000 Swedish Facebook users [Press Release]. Retrieved from http://gri.gu.se/english/latest-news/news/d/sweden-s-largest-facebook-study--a-survey-of-1000-swedish-facebook-users.cid1073014

Valenzuela, S., Park, N., & Kee, K. F. (2009). Is there social capital in a social network site? Facebook use and college students' life satisfaction, trust, and participation. *Journal of Computer-Mediated Communication, 14*(4), 875–901. doi:10.1111/j.1083–6101.2009.01474.x

Walton, A. G. (2012, October). Internet addiction: The new mental health disorder? *Forbes.* Retrieved from http://www.forbes.com/sites/alicegwalton/2012/10/02/the-new-mental-health-disorder-internet-addiction/

Wang, Q., Chen, W., & Liang, Y. (2011). *The effects of social media on college students.* Unpublished manuscript, Johnson & Wales University, Providence, RI. Retrieved from http://scholarsarchive. jwu.edu/mba_student/5

Ward, A. F., & Valdesolo, P. (2012, August). What Internet habits say about mental health. *Scientific American.* Retrieved from http://www.scientificamerican.com/article/what-internet-habits-say-about-mental-health

Section 2
Social Wellness

5

Relationship Health
Helping Students Thrive as They Relate to Others

BRIDGET GUERNSEY RIORDAN

Introduction

Relationships take many forms and are often the key to a student's success in college. How he or she feels about himself or herself, family members, friends, advisors, and persons of all influence shapes the college student's experience. Professionals working in the higher education setting can have a major impact on how a student fosters, develops, and maintains these varied relationships. This chapter explores the multitude of relationships students have and how they impact the college experience. Attention is provided to some of the more common among the varied relationships an individual may experience: with oneself; with families; with peers, friends, and roommates; with significant others; and with faculty, staff, and community members. In addition, attention is provided to the role of the Internet, technology, and virtual relationships. For each of these types of relationships, specific recommendations are provided for how campus professionals, whether student affairs practitioners, faculty, staff, or others, can educate, promote, and guide students to develop healthy and meaningful relationships.

The Context of Relationships in Higher Education Settings

College communities provide a unique environment for students to grow, develop, and determine who they are in relation to others. The variety of settings colleges offer through residential living, classrooms, co-curricular activities, athletics/intramurals, student organizations, and spiritual life creates a multifaceted means for experiential learning and individual development. The college student environment represents a place where everyone is fairly intelligent, where each person has a considerable amount of free time, and where adult supervision is minimal. For traditional-aged college students, this level of independence makes the experience much different than what students experienced in high school.

Interspersed with this new environment is the development of new relationships. Part of a college's mission is to educate the "whole" student (not just the student's mind) with experiences and knowledge learned both inside and outside of the classroom. Through varied experiences, students mature and determine who they are as individuals and who they are based on their relationships with others. These relationships are often a key to a student's success or failure in college. Whether it is the support of a caring faculty member or the encouragement of a close friend, relationships impact the collegiate experience. In addition, today's college students have a multitude of relationships and experience them in a variety of ways. Whether through direct one-on-one interactions, living arrangements, group meetings, or social media, students engage with others like never before. And the complexity of these relationships has far-reaching implications for each student.

Research shows that learning can be enhanced by experiencing it with others. Learning connections are made through intellectually and emotionally connecting with peers, professors, and student affairs professionals. The purpose is to connect student learning experiences in ways that are both developmentally and intellectually coherent (Keeling & Hersh, 2011, p. 52). Student learning also is enhanced by discussion with others (Kuh, Douglas, Lund, & Ramin-Gyurnek, 1994). Students can hear other opinions, debate issues, and develop evolving attitudes and values that are influenced by exposure to broader perspectives. Also, by asking students to think about and interpret what they are learning and then discuss it with faculty, staff, and/or peers, they do not simply repeat previously learned information, as they may have done in high school; rather they analyze and make meaning of how learning has transformed them. As Keeling and Hersh (2011) reported, "Higher education is a preparation for life in a global society" (p. 54). A college education should develop a student's ability to understand oneself and take others' views into perspective. Student growth includes contextual education, which can happen through a range of experiences, interactions, and challenges to one's beliefs.

The relationship of self to others is a concept prominently discussed in student affairs research. Chickering and Reisser (1993) are among the researchers who noted the value of higher education as it promotes "interpersonal literacy competence." This competence prepares students by "knowing when and how to communicate what to whom in order to achieve specified goals" (Chickering & Reisser, 1993, p. 75). More specifically, it also prepares students to "express feelings appropriately, maintain group cooperation and support, and make commitments to others" (Chickering & Reisser, 1993, p. 16). All of these skills will be extremely valuable to students while in college and throughout their adult lives.

Through the development of interpersonal competence, relationships also can become more intimate and meaningful. Tolerance, empathy, compassion, and openness are among the traits that develop in mature relationships. Students can understand and appreciate others on an emotional level and not just an intellectual one. When individuals grow in their understanding of one another, they can become more intimate. With intimacy can come increased respect, honesty, sensitivity, and the ability to be vulnerable (Chickering & Reisser, 1993).

As students take on new and varied relationships, they also realize that people are individuals, with individual and complex experiences and histories. As they mature, students no longer base their opinions on stereotypes. They understand the value of each person. With this growth, students increase their interest in others and shift away from self-absorption. Empathy grows, and students realize the equal worth of all people. In an engaging college setting, students debate about what is meaningful in life. They discover that self-interest does not need to be at odds with concern for one another (Delbanco, 2012).

With the development of mature and contextual thinking and the increase in intimate relationships, students begin the transformation into complex thinkers with an understanding of individual differences and a better understanding of themselves. This introspective thinking is one of the markers of maturity and adulthood. Students learn through others. Relationships have a direct impact on a college student's life.

While through complex thinking and maturation the young adult may seem to be adequately prepared for adulthood, their biological brains may not. For traditional-aged college students (ages 18–22), the college years represent a key time in their brain development. With the onset of puberty, researchers have found that the brain continues to develop and may not be fully developed until well into the early twenties (Walker, 2008). Recent research shows that although adolescents can distinguish between risky and nonrisky behaviors, they underestimate the magnitude of the risk and may be prone to engaging in risky behaviors. Compared to adults, they simply do not perceive the potential for harm in risky activities (Walker, 2008). The impact this may have on the formation of relationships can be of interest. Does the still-developing brain cause individuals to take risks in their relationships? Do they have the mental capacity to adequately navigate the many nuances of complex relationships?

Influences on how relationships develop and evolve are numerous. Class, ethnicity, age, religion, gender, sexual identity, sexual orientation, and regional or cultural background are among the many factors that affect and shape relationships. In addition, various relationships require various skills and approaches. College students are at a key age for developing, fostering, and gaining a new understanding of these relationships.

Self and Self-Identity

Students' self-concepts—how they feel about themselves—shape every relationship they enter. Students' relationships with themselves determine how they perceive the world, and these self-concepts often reveal how the world perceives them. Students who are self-confident and willing to accept and understand personal failures and inadequacies can typically practice self-compassion and deflect self-criticism. They realize that life is full of risks and that every challenge may not be met with success. They accept disappointments and know that pain, frustration, and failure are opportunities for growth and development. On the other hand, students who lack confidence and revel in self-doubt often are self-critical and wary of trying new experiences and taking risks. Faced with the additional challenges of college life, these students may struggle to the point of failure even if they are academically prepared for college.

As outlined in Erickson's nine stages of psychosocial development, personality develops over an entire life span (Evans, Forney, Guido, Patton, & Renn, 2010). The college years are a significant period in a person's development. As emerging adolescents, Erikson described this period as "identity vs. identity confusion." Individuals are asking "Who am I?" while developing a coherent sense of self and ego-identity. Traditional college aged students are typically independent for the first time and have the opportunity to personally contemplate this question. "Who am I?" becomes a significant question for ongoing internal debate. The next phase, experienced in early adulthood, consists of intimacy versus isolation. Individuals should be able to reach out and connect with others in order to become intimate with someone and work toward a career. The transition from the identity phase to the connection phase is pivotal in a person's development; for college students, this transition often takes place during the college years.

In the process of discovering who they are, students face issues of racial, sexual, ethnic, religious, and cultural identity. Students have seen the world through their own identities and are now faced with interacting with many students with many different identities. Also, an increase in domestic and international adoptions brings a number of students to college who experienced typical living settings outside of their native cultures. In a college environment where learning and exploration are valued and encouraged, students will likely question and want to learn more about their own unique identities. College professionals must realize that simply recruiting a diverse student body will not result in cultural appreciations. Intentional discussion, educational programs, and meaningful interactions will promote students of diverse cultures understanding one another and comprehending their own identities.

International students will have a completely different view of what higher education is like based on how it is practiced in their native countries. Language barriers, new customs, and different social mores may prove frustrating and daunting for students new to the United States. Higher education has unique practices in each country. The differences in student-faculty relationships and how students experience friendships and family can be very confusing for international students. Americans tend to focus on sameness and closeness, which allows hierarchy to have less importance. However, other cultures focus on rights and responsibilities of relative age and believe a hierarchy will endure and ensure closeness (Tannen, 2011). Although well-meaning staff and faculty may recommend counseling as a means for talking out a problem, cultural barriers faced by international students may prevent them from seeking this useful resource. Feelings of isolation may be very strong, and students may choose to associate only with students of their own culture. Internal struggles for international students must be recognized and addressed in order for them to succeed as American college students.

Through these stages of growth and development, students should be able to stop depending on others to meet all of their emotional needs. Neff (2011) and Brown (2012) found that self-kindness/self-compassion contributes to a person's ability to adjust to his or her environment and forge healthy relationships. Expressing kindness, showing a sense of common humanity, and practicing mindfulness are basic components of self-care. When applied toward the suffering of others, they manifest as compassion. When applied toward oneself, they demonstrate self-appreciation (Neff, 2011).

Many students of modest means may try to disguise this fact by taking on debt in order to dress more extravagantly, eat at restaurants over their budgets, or buy accessories, such as iPads, designer bags, jewelry, or sportswear. "Fitting in" becomes very important to students. Fitting in often becomes more important to students than being valued for their individual traits. Standing out in the crowd may paralyze some students.

Students who do not fit the traditional mold of college students by age or residence (older students and nonresidential students) have to deal with additional challenges while attending college. Nonresidential students, commonly called "commuters," have to commute to college, often by car or mass transit. They may be balancing a college life and a family life. If so, expectations of family members may clash with responsibilities of academic studies. Their identities are not tied to where they live on campus or how they are adjusting to being out of high school. They may have graduated from high school years earlier and are only now able to work on their college education.

Students also are affected by how they feel in relationship to their bodies. In a world filled with media images of "hard" bodies, "sexy" bodies, and magazines named *Shape* and *Glamour*, students are surrounded with what is the "ideal" body. In order to have the "perfect" body, many students go to extremes with diet and exercise. The feeling that they aren't perfect enough can take over their lives and affect their ability to succeed in college.

With all of these self-identities is the reality that college can be a time for students to create a new record. They can decide to try new experiences, explore identities, and engage with others whom they may have never interacted with before. Getting students out of their comfort zones is a major opportunity for college faculty and staff. The ability to adapt to new surroundings, adjust their approach, and establish new norms will be useful to students throughout their adult lives. The opportunities are limitless, and the relationships formed will shape their college experiences.

Recommendations:

- Help students find or further develop their passions. Expose them to student organizations, sports, the arts, and/or interest groups early during their first semester. Help them discover what brings them joy.
- Provide mental health services free of charge to students. Make sure they know how to access these services through marketing and a website with updated information.
- Provide access to quality health care. This can be through the on-campus clinic or through a local clinic that accepts student health insurance and walk-in visits.
- Engage health education and promotion staff members with students as soon as they arrive to campus. Get students to discuss healthy lifestyles and how they can thrive in their new communities.
- Address body image issues with all students. One idea, whether as a program or in an academic course, is to discuss the unrealistic body examples in the media. Have students do a body assessment, noting what they like and what they don't like about their bodies. Have them determine what they can change and what they can't change—for example, hair color can be changed, while height can't

be changed. Help them understand the importance of accepting individual body characteristics and self-love.

- Expose students to student activist groups and support groups, such as sexual assault survivors or Alcoholics Anonymous, so they can be empowered to get involved and practice self-care and activism on issues of importance to them.
- Provide multiple means for serving the community through alternative break trips and regular service opportunities. Help students identify a passion, such as animal rescue or feeding the hungry, so they can grow their own levels of compassion for others.
- Offer opportunities for personal growth and reflection through topical discussion groups, religious observations, and student organizations.
- Provide opportunities for study abroad experiences, through either the academic classroom or service opportunities.
- Encourage students to assume leadership roles in student organizations. Not everyone can be the president, but most everyone has valuable skills and talents that can benefit a student group.
- Determine tangible student learning outcomes for regular student affairs programs and activities or classroom experiences, and assess them. Strive to constantly update and improve resources and services as needed by current student desires and trends.

Families

Family dynamics have an incredible influence on how students view others and how they develop relationships outside of the family. Whether an only child or one of multiple children, a student's relationship with his or her parents was the very first relationship ever established. Parental influence begins at birth, progresses through adolescence, and often continues into adult life.

Although the model of traditional parents—one father and one mother—was the norm in the 1950s, single-parent households in America have more than tripled since 1960. According to Marthur, Fu, and Hansen (2013), single mothers make up about one-quarter of U.S. households while single fathers make up another 6%. In addition, more and more children are being raised by someone other than their biological parents, and they are often referred to as custodial parents. This could be a grandparent, stepparent, or foster parent. Over the past 50 years, the definition of family has evolved to include these varieties of parental structures as well as varied sibling categories, such as only child, child of multiple birth, several siblings, youngest, oldest, or middle. The modern family of the new millennium means that current students may come from families that are more diverse and unique than ever before.

These differences and unique configurations in family structures give students a variety of experiences. These varied perspectives influence their lives, what roles and influences family members have over them, and how they interact with others.

Although characters and plots on television may seem to have families that work out all of their problems in 30 minutes, the dysfunctional family is commonly discussed and deconstructed in terms of challenging relationships. As defined by Kansas State University Counseling Services (n.d.), family dysfunction

> interferes with healthy family functioning. Most families have some periods of time where functioning is impaired by stressful circumstances (death in the family, a parent's serious illness, etc.). Healthy families tend to return to normal functioning after the crisis passes. In dysfunctional families, however, problems tend to be chronic and children do not consistently get their needs met. (n.p.)

It is important for students to know that family dysfunction can occur in many families and impact family members in various ways.

Parents who have been deficient in the support of their children can affect students in other ways. These children have typically been forced to take on adult responsibilities, such as child care, housework, and meal preparation. Their childhood may have been diminished by their parental inadequacies. As a result of dysfunctional parenting, students may need approval from others to feel good about themselves. They may have trouble expressing feelings or emotions. They may find it hard to trust others or maintain intimacy. They may have difficulty accepting responsibility or may try to take on too much responsibility.

Although many challenges of being raised in a dysfunctional family may have negative consequences, college may also serve as a refuge for these students. At college, they may develop a new support network and form relationships that act like a family. They may see others as independent and confident and use them as role models. Through sharing experiences with other students, they also may see that every family has imperfections. They can redirect and develop into the person they want to be and not the person they may have been forced to be due to family dynamics. For those students who continue to struggle with adjustment issues due to family dysfunction, campus resources will be essential for their success. Whether it is guidance from skilled counselors or influence from mentors, college relationships can help students work through difficult issues.

Another major factor in families that affects students is their relationships with siblings. As Tannen (2006) noted, sibling relationships can be both positive and negative. Lifelong comparisons can create competition that can help a student achieve or feel defeated. Students who have older siblings may have learned from the successes and failures of their brothers or sisters, while the oldest child in the family may have assumed leadership at an early age just by nature of birth order. Students who were raised as only children may have the positive impact of unshared attentions from their parents. On the other hand, they have not had the daily practice of negotiating everyday issues, such as sharing household items or deciding whose turn it is to walk the dog.

Family dynamics are typically very different for nontraditional-aged college students. They may be parents or may be caring for family members. For them family life often takes priority over college life. If the student is a parent with young children, child care may be a major issue. The challenge of finding affordable and convenient child care can adversely affect class attendance and participation. Balancing finances may force students to forgo a tuition payment in order to care for a child. Completing a degree may take many more academic terms than it would take for a nonparent. Also, group meetings, co-curricular activities, participation in student organizations, and other activities outside of class time may all suffer due to parenting responsibilities. Other students who are caregivers for family members may face the same issues. Efforts must be made by faculty and staff to understand the challenges faced by students who are also caregivers while trying to obtain a degree.

The college years may be the most significant time for self-discovery outside of the family unit. Although family pressures exist to either succeed academically or to not drift far from the family, students have a framework for independent thought. Through varied experiences and interactions as well as the multitude of resources present at college, students may find the most opportunities for in-depth discovery and development of their independent adult personalities.

Recommendations:

- Recognize that students bring various complexities within their family relationships to the college setting. Acknowledge that each family is unique and valuable. Use inclusive language, such as "family" and not just "parent," in all publications and social media sources.
- Realize that some students have not had siblings and may need to learn how to negotiate shared environments. Prepare to counsel and advise students on how to cope with the nuances of others.
- Maintain an updated and thorough website dedicated to information crucial to families. Include basic information, such as calendar, billing, residential, and food options, as well as family weekend information, scholarship applications, and student involvement opportunities.
- Educate families about how students are treated in the college setting with regard to confidential information, such as grades and conduct records. Inform them about the Family Educational Rights and Privacy Act (FERPA), the use of waivers to obtain confidential information, and the pros and cons of waiving privacy rights. Educate students and family members during orientation by providing a separate family track to address issues and take questions out of the range of the students' purview.
- Host webinars for families on various topics. Families can do a live view of information and ask questions of professionals during the webinar via phone or email. Professionals who are knowledgeable about specific issues, such as sorority/fraternity recruitment, housing assignments, co-curricular activities, or choosing a major, can share information and resources.
- Engage family members early on through mailings and electronic communications. Direct mail information may still be the best way to reach out to a generation that includes those who may not have embraced the Internet or have easy access to it.

- Provide information to students about accessible child care. Work with area agencies to see if they will offer a student discount. Work with the college/ university to investigate subsidized child care for undergraduate and graduate students.
- Host a family weekend that is inclusive of all families. Keep costs minimal or at no charge. Include activities for multiple generations. Allow the family to have a look into the student's collegiate life.
- Offer information about support groups for students struggling with various issues, such as Adult Children of Alcoholics (ACOA) or PFLAG (support group for families, allies, and people who are LGBTQ).

Friends, Peers, and Roommates

Part of the marketing of colleges today is the fact that students will meet and interact with a very new and varied group of peers. Astin (1993), a leading higher education expert and founding director of the Higher Education Research Institute at UCLA, found that students' peers had an extremely strong impact on their development while in college. He reported:

> Every aspect of the student's development—cognitive and affective, psychological and behavioral—is affected in some way by peer group characteristics, and usually by several peer characteristics. Generally, students tend to change their values, behavior, and academic plans in the direction of the dominant orientation of their peer group.
>
> (Astin, 1993, p. 363)

Students have a strong need to belong and feel accepted by their peers. They want to be a part of something bigger than themselves and feel a part of a bigger community. As Brown (2012) found, the desire to belong is primal and people may go to great lengths to fit in and seek approval. They often miss the fact that by "fitting in" they are not being fully accepted for their individual qualities. They may compromise their beliefs or values in order to not cause friction within a larger group. Unfortunately, they may lose their own uniqueness and those traits that make them a notable person. Nonetheless, a college setting typically provides students the first opportunity to branch out on their own and set a new course.

Involvement in student organizations, athletics, and other co-curricular activities often allows students to develop relationships with students of different ages in varied settings with a multigenerational experience. This can be very valuable to both first-year and upper-class students.

Sorority and fraternity members have long touted the benefits of peer and alumni mentoring within their organizations. Formed based on common interests and values, Greek letter organizations are often criticized for promoting a culture of alcohol abuse (Riordan & Dana, 1998) and hazing (Hennessy & Huson, 1998). As they combat these issues, they traditionally offer opportunities for new members to participate in activities with older students and alumni. The ability to offer strong role models and hours of community service work is attractive to many students looking for a smaller community within a large college community. A balance has to be struck between overdue peer influence that may be detrimental and positive peer influence that can be affirming and supportive.

College athletes also have the chance to formally engage with students of different classes. Depending on the sport and intensity of the athletic program, student-athletes can offer one another support, a team environment, and a structured schedule within a typically unstructured college setting. Although much has been reported about top college athletes who put their sport above their academic achievement, institutions who promote a strong academic program can set the tone for balance between the intercollegiate sport and classroom requirements. Teammate interactions and upper-class coaching can do a great deal to help a student learn about the institution and adjust to the complex life of college student and athlete.

One of the most significant opportunities for peer relationships happens with on-campus living and roommate assignments. Pascarella and Terenzini (2005) reported that living on campus had the most significant impact on a student's college experience. One of the most significant relationships resulting from that experience is the relationship between college roommates. For those students choosing to live in on-campus residential units, the college roommate experience is often fraught with expectations and frequently different than most students imagined. Students come with perceptions and ideals about how connected they may be to their roommates, how they may share new experiences, and how the roommate may help them navigate this new community. Since many students arrive to college without ever having shared a bedroom, the idea of sharing a 200-square-foot room 24 hours a day and seven days a week may be frightening and foreign. With varied preferences and habits in sleeping, eating, music, studying, and personal hygiene, adjusting to a new roommate can be extremely difficult.

Anthropology professor Rebekah Nathan looked at the college roommate experience by immersing herself as a student at her own university. Without revealing that she was an anthropologist, Nathan lived among first-year students at University of Northern Arizona and enrolled as a full-time student. She not only lived the residential experience but also studied it. She found that most college students believed the college experience was about "fun," "friendships," "partying," and "late night talks" (Nathan, 2005, p. 103). When students don't automatically encounter this, they may become disillusioned and believe they don't fit in or aren't having the college experience that is ideal. Nathan also found that traditional-aged college students wanted activities in groups or at least with one other person. Seldom did a student go to an activity alone. They preferred to attend with a companion, rather than walk into a room solo.

Part of the college education must be to show students how to peacefully coexist and respect one another. Although roommates or classmates do not always have to be friends, they must seek to understand and be civil to one another.

Recommendations:

- Provide multiple opportunities for social interactions. Through orientation groups, residence halls, student organizations, and classroom projects and discussions, ensure that students make connections and have a way to find others who share their interests and passions.

- Sponsor discussion groups about diversity so that students have an opportunity to discuss difference in a safe and supportive environment.
- Consider a roommate matching program so students can select roommates based on shared information.
- Offer theme residence halls as options for students who want to live with students who share the same passions and interests. Some popular themes may include citizenship, sustainability, and leadership.
- Provide areas in the residential unit for studying, cooking, relaxing, and recreation. A study lounge can allow for group studying outside of individual rooms as well as the independent, undisturbed study time that some students crave. A kitchen can promote community building with baking, cooking, and sharing food in a home-like environment. A TV lounge can be the place where students gather to watch favorite television shows, movies, or sporting events. Recreation areas, such as rooms with Ping-Pong tables, pool tables, or card tables, can help students relax while doing something fun and enjoyable.
- Offer programming that capitalizes on this shared space, such as a cooking demonstration, Super Bowl watching party, or organized study groups.
- Ensure a social media presence with housing information and as a means to promote the positive experiences in on-campus residences. Include a page on frequently asked questions (FAQ) that gives updated and detailed information on housing applications and processes.
- Consider the advantages of a multigenerational living experience that allows upper-class students mentoring opportunities with first-year students. If residence halls aren't part of the campus culture, consider matching mentors by major or common interest.
- Explore academic opportunities, whether specific courses, assignments, readings, projects, guest lectures, internships, or related activities that help students understand and engage in issues surrounding diversity, cultural competence, and understanding of differences. Some of these courses and activities may already exist, and could be promoted more widely; they may also be instituted as new courses or approaches. Further, guest lecturers could incorporate this emphasis for regular courses or in lieu of canceling a class session.
- Offer professional development opportunities to enrich staff members' understanding of a range of cultural relationship issues, whether from an international perspective or other background differences.

Significant Others

Whether referred to as a partner, significant other, girlfriend/boyfriend, hookup date, spouse, or a variation of titles, relationships between students that are romantic or revolve around sexual attraction provide an opportunity for personal growth and exploration during the college years. In today's college setting, relationships can occur between males and females, males and males, and females and females. Due to the accelerated pace of a college environment, an individual's relationships can change and evolve rather dramatically in a short period of time.

Over the past few decades, college dating has evolved from traditional dating, in which a man asked a woman for a one-on-one event-based experience (dinner and a movie or a sporting event), into a variety of possibilities. Most common is "group dating," in which groups enter into a safer and less intimate situation. Confusion may arise over whether group members are just friends or something more, but the safety lies in the low-risk feeling of the group (Tannen, 2011).

Most prevalent talk of intimate relationships among college students over the past decade has centered on the "hookup culture." Characterized by spontaneous, commitment-free (and often alcohol-fueled) romantic flings, "hooking up" is a popular means for experiencing short-term impersonal sexual relationships. As college students yearn to fit in with their peers, many believe that hooking up is the mainstream culture and that sex without feelings is the norm. Although hooking up may appear to be the behavior of most students, a large number of students are not looking for casual sex or a "friends with benefits" relationship (Levine & Cureton, 1998).

With regard to nontraditional-aged students, often their entry or return to college may be due to a change in their relationship status. Couples split up, and one or both may pursue additional education for long-term stability. Others may have a partner who is able to support them as they explore a college education. In these situations, the significant other has had direct influence over the educational status of the student. Managing that relationship, especially if there are other factors involved, such as shared children, will have a significant impact on students' co-curricular life.

With gender identity and expression a developmental aspect of many students during their college years, students may be contemplating their sexual identity. Gone are family or childhood community cultures, which have dictated a rigid conformity. In a completely new environment, students may look beyond traditional gender roles. Various identity theories exist related to sexual identity, including those researched by Broida, Cass, and D'Angelo (Pascarella & Terenzini, 2005). From identity confusion to identity comparison, identity tolerance, identity acceptance, and identity pride, students may experience all of these stages during the college years. Where they are in these stages will have an impact on the relationships they have. As they are questioning their own identities, they may question how they were raised by their families, how their peers treat them, and how they pursue intimate relationships. As they progress through the stages, they will need the support of their peers and staff within the college community.

Relationships with intimate partners can provide a great deal of support to students. Having personal support and affirmation can build confidence. On the other hand, some students find partners who may be controlling and manipulative. If the student is not prepared to sever the relationship, resulting consequences can be treacherous. Relationship violence can be as covert as threatening text messages or emails, or it can be overt, such as stalking, physical, violence, or sexual abuse. Students must be guided on how to address these behaviors and where to obtain appropriate resources. Part of the guidance must be to help students learn the importance of self-respect and how it is crucial to a loving relationship.

Significant others, partners, spouses, and others who share close, intimate relationships with students will engage with them in deeply personal ways. The scope of these interactions will have a significant impact on the choices students make during their college careers. Having healthy relationships will aid students as they move forward with their college education.

Recommendations:

- Enlist experts, such as health education staff or faculty in psychology or sociology, to lead discussion groups on how to have healthy relationships.
- Provide sexual health education that includes health issues for all individuals. Target various populations, such as the lesbian, gay, bisexual, transgender, and queer (LGBTQ) community, to ensure sexual and relationship health is discussed among all populations of the college community.
- Encourage student organizations to be open in their events, such as dances and "date" parties, so that a "date" doesn't have to be a traditional heterosexual couple, but can include same-sex partners and friends.
- Early in a student's transition, provide numerous social opportunities where students can meet and interact with a variety of students.
- Offer casual group interactions through specialized interests, such as knitting clubs, card games, and drop-in coffee houses.
- Provide structured activities, such as intramural sports, outdoor activities, a cappella groups, dance groups, and other special interest activities.
- For those students more comfortable with one-on-one interaction, provide upper-class mentors in residence halls or sorted by college major. Allow upper-class students to help one another and serve as role models to new students.
- Provide numerous opportunities for dialogue on topics such as dating, diversity, adjusting to college life, and hookup culture.
- Offer LGBTQ resources and information. Support groups, discussion groups, and seminars can help students understand and explore issues of sexuality.
- Promote counseling services and/or support groups for survivors of relationship violence. Help students understand how to help a peer or loved one in an abusive relationship.
- Educate staff on Title IX compliance regarding discrimination based on sex in education programs or activities that receive federal financial assistance. Enlist the Title IX compliance officer.

Faculty/Staff/Community Members

Faculty and staff at a college or university play a key role in the development of each student. Many students leave a home environment and move to a college setting away from family members and friends, who have been their major sphere of influence. The faculty and staff often represent their new families and are challenged with guiding and developing these emerging learners.

As Astin (1993) reported, "Next to the peer group, the faculty represents the most significant aspect of the student's undergraduate development" (p. 410). He found a positive association between academic achievement and hours per week student spent talking with faculty outside of the classroom. In addition, student retention improved when there was positive student-faculty interaction. Colleges often boast of student-faculty ratios that are low and promote higher interaction. Nonetheless, faculty members are stretched to teach in the classroom, perform research, obtain grants, publish, and serve the college community. In 1975 close to 60% of faculty members were full-time professors with tenure or on the "tenure track." In recent years that number has dropped to 35% (Delbanco, 2012). The result is more students are taught by part-time faculty, who may have little or no commitment and allegiance to the college community. Nonetheless, although faculty time is stretched, their time with students makes a significant contribution to the lives of their students.

Due to the complexity of student interpersonal relationships that may include the influence of social media, fractured family relationships, and mental health challenges, faculty, staff, and administrators may be significantly challenged by their work with students. However, with education and experience, they understand the value of establishing meaningful relationships with students and how they can have an impact upon the student experience. One example of this impact, concerning Emory University president James Laney, occurred after a racial issue emerged on campus in the early 1990s. Laney reflected:

> But it brought me out of a cloistered office into a situation where I had no choice but to talk with the students, the faculty, and the staff as an educator, and not just an administrator. It gave everybody in the community a chance to reassess how we want to relate to each other and what kind of community we want to be . . . to be more deliberate and not always just reactive. It has energized me to see us wrestling with our soul.
>
> (Laney, quoted in Loeb, 1994, p. 204)

Student affairs professionals, support staff, teaching assistants, and other university officials and administrators also interact with students on a daily basis in a variety of roles. Whether it is the hall director, administrative assistant in a student-centered office, or a student affairs staff member responsible for volunteer or leadership programs, staff members can have incredible influence over students. Serving as advisors, mentors, counselors, and role models, staff and administrators provide guidance and direction to students as they explore learning outside of the classroom. Of course, trying to handle every student's individual needs can be exhausting for staff. As Sandeen (2003) noted, "One of the realities of student affairs is knowing there will never be enough staff to meet all of the needs of the students" (p. 66). Staff members need to realize when they need outside resources, such as public safety officials or specialized counselors, to assist students with complex issues.

Outside of the traditional college experience, such as on-campus housing, classrooms, and the campus environment, students often develop relationships with individuals who have a part in their outside activities. These may include coworkers, spiritual advisors, or individuals they meet through volunteer or off-campus community experiences. These individuals may have a great deal of influence and impact on the daily lives of college students. Offering students opportunities to engage off campus allows them be a part of the greater community. Part-time jobs in local stores and restaurants as well as tutoring or babysitting allow students to meet others who may have an impact on their lives. In addition, service opportunities allow students to give back and help others. It may not be someone older or more educated who influences students. It can be the child they met through the Boys and Girls Club, the person they coached in Special Olympics, or the custodian who cleaned their study space. Seeing the bigger world through the eyes of a variety of individuals can open the minds of college students well beyond the wall of the campus.

Recommendations

- Educate faculty and staff on the value of their mentor roles. Provide clear policies on appropriate relationships between faculty, staff, and students. Promote the community-building advantages of assisting students outside of their academic requirements.
- Recruit faculty to serve as faculty-in-residence in on-campus residential units. This allows informal engagement and time for relationships to form between faculty and students outside of the classroom.
- Provide opportunities for student affairs staff who do not serve in live-in positions to engage with residential students in their living units. This can occur through short-term housing stays (Week with the Dean) or programs and activities held in residential units with student affairs staff (Cookies and Milk or Pancake Breakfast with the student affairs staff).
- Recruit faculty and staff to serve as advisors to student organizations. Encourage them to relate to students through common interests, such as political, religious, recreation, or environmental issues.
- Find opportunities for faculty or staff members to participate in study abroad experiences. Serving as advisor, teachers, and/or mentors, they can assist students as they grow and develop outside of their typical environments.
- Encourage faculty to serve on student affairs committees and task forces. Encourage staff to serve on university committees outside of their division. Encourage community members to develop their leadership skills and understanding of the college community through these experiences.
- Encourage faculty and staff to serve as role models by participating in college activities, using the college/university gym for exercise, and attending college programs and/or sporting events. Show support for what students do outside of the classroom. Bring families and/or significant others.

- Provide informal places on campus for faculty/student interactions. Close proximity to faculty offices and/or classroom space can allow for interactions to occur organically without planning or forethought.
- Use faculty and staff expertise when assisting students with various issues, concerns, and interests. For instance, involve health education faculty in health-related work, such as positive body image awareness.
- Work with faculty and staff to establish clear standards and expectations for students to know and understand what is expected of them in order to succeed. Within the classroom, rubrics should be used and explained so students understand how they will be graded. For co-curricular activities, students should understand the intended learning outcomes and how success will be measured.
- Offer opportunities for students to engage with others through internship and employment experiences.
- Promote access to religious/spiritual services and programs.
- Provide access to off-campus venues, such as shopping areas, restaurants, and area attractions, in order for students to fully engage in the neighboring community.
- Include lecturers and part-time faculty as well as all levels of staff as possible members and participants in student programs and activities. This includes custodians, administrators, assistants, and food service and maintenance workers.
- Bring religious and community leaders to campus for programs, talks, and discussion groups. Expose students to varied and opposing views. Engage them in opportunities to discuss these views with others.
- Enlist alumni to engage with students through mentoring programs, speaking engagements, and advising of student organizations.
- Clarify university policies, activities, and processes. Allow students to access information about the college through a website, phone application, social media, or other customer-friendly ways so that students have clear and updated information.

The Internet, Electronics, Virtual Relationships, and Technology

The use of technology is a daily part of the lives of college students. Looking up research on the Internet, emailing a question to a professor, or texting with a friend can make the daily tasks of college life more effective and efficient. Smartphones and iPads can be a student's best friend. While technology use can simplify many processes and interactions, Lloyd, Dean, and Cooper (2009) reported that it can be both supportive of and harmful to student success. Male students tend to use technology primarily for entertainment purposes, and female students tend to use it for social purposes. Video games, a primary form of technological entertainment, allow users to participate for hours at a time with people from all over the world. According to Good (2012), the interactive franchise "Call of Duty," done through Xbox and popular among high school and college males, has more than 40 million monthly active users. Aside from the time invested in varied technology uses, popular sites like Facebook and Instagram also can offer instant and personal insights into an individual's personal life.

The distractions caused by technological entertainment and use may have negative effects on student peer relationships, academic engagement, and overall health. Using technology for social purposes may have a negative impact on the academic performance of a student. Posting the most recent "selfie" on Facebook or checking the phone every time a text bling is heard may result in numerous interruptions to daily tasks and unreasonable distractions. A person's social media life may take precedence over his or her present company.

Beyond the typical technology activities, such as Xbox, phone texting, and email, students establish relationships with others through social media. Social media Internet sites, such as Facebook, Instagram, Twitter, Pinterest, and Foursquare, are currently among the platforms available to students to communicate with others without ever leaving the comfort of their rooms. These "virtual" relationships can be positive and/or negative, depending on the nature and use of the social media platform. While these platforms allow a person to establish a wide variety of relationships in a variety of mediums, these relationships are limited by the lack of direct and personal interaction. Students can harass one another through typed words that the world can see. In addition, with the onset of smartphones, users can have their virtual world constantly at their fingertips wherever they are.

Thousands of students believe in their virtual relationships. Today's students don't feel the need to directly talk to someone. They are more apt to text, send a Facebook message, communicate on Twitter, post a photo on Instagram, or choose some other form of social media for communication.

The cavalier use of social media and sharing of information makes for complicated social mores. Etiquette regarding social media usage is often personal and inconsistent. What one person believes to be oversharing another may believe shows transparency. Furthermore, technology use may keep students from having meaningful one-on-one interactions. Internet profiles may mask or distort real life. Often students may post their most favorable photos and put up an unrealistic profile to show the outside world that everything is great in their life. A Facebook profile may not reflect the actual life of the person who posts it. However, a person's popularity can be measured by how many "likes" his or her post gets.

Recommendations:

- Educate students regarding the reality of social media use. Explain the permanence of what is posted on the Internet or on electronic devices. Provide case studies to show how unintentional acts of fun, such as posting a nude photo online, are never "private" and potentially can be viewed by millions.
- Discuss the value of personal, face-to-face interactions where people can address issues together and communicate while seeing one another's facial expressions and reactions. Help students understand personal meaning and how to acknowledge the context in which information is received.

- Demonstrate how anyone can be behind the computer or mobile device. Help students understand that Internet relationships are not fully engaged relationships.
- Have students practice direct communication through mock interviews at the career center. Provide interview experience through applying for leadership roles.
- Encourage attendance at university events, such as cultural, music, or arts festivals, athletic events, or lectures. Help students understand that immersion in a culture has more meaning and lasting value than Internet relationships.
- Engage with students through social media as appropriate. Create Facebook pages for offices and activities.
- Consider how to personally engage with students on social media sites. If you "friend" students, determine how much personal information you are willing to share with them. Remember that you are a role model and need to keep all public information on a professional level.

Conclusion

Higher education professionals in general, and student affairs practitioners in particular, must remember that each student is unique and brings unique perspectives to college. That is one of the reasons student relationships are so complex. They are a compilation of past history mixed with the current context and blended with an engaging, educational environment. In addition, campus professionals must understand the value and significance of establishing a welcoming and open community.

How student affairs practitioners and other campus professionals choose to help students build healthy relationships may depend on how they and their institution build their own relationships with students. They may choose to act in place of the parents, commonly referred to as "in loco parentis," which was often the practice prior to the 1970s; this provides discipline, control, regulations, and, ultimately, power by the college over students. They may choose to be a bystander in the lives of their students and count on them to act independently, with the college solely offering information and resources. They may be facilitators and promote a shared governance approach by offering guidance, resources, and support, while allowing the students to make their own decisions and to be held accountable for their actions (Bickel & Lake, 1999). Or they may choose to relate to their students in a combination of ways. Each institution must determine what works best for its community.

Willimon and Naylor (1995) noted that a college or university is truly a community when the students, staff, and faculty are seriously concerned about each other's well-being. It is imperative that higher education professionals develop positive relationships with students and help them learn how to enhance and thrive in their own relationships. Through assessing student needs, providing valuable resources, and demonstrating care, student affairs professionals, faculty, and others can and must guide and influence student relationships. Through varied relationships students will often find their first job or internship, commit to a partner in a serious relationship, and develop into a mature and independent adult, capable of making meaningful and intelligent decisions. Enhanced by valuable relationships throughout college, students will become adults who are equipped to practice good health as well as to pursue successful endeavors at college and beyond. We owe this to them; they depend on us for this.

References

Astin, A. W. (1993). *What matters in college?: Four critical years revisited.* San Francisco, CA: Jossey-Bass.

Bickel, R. D., & Lake, P. F. (1999). *The rights and responsibilities of the modern university: Who assumes the risks of college life?* Durham, NC: Carolina Academic Press.

Brown, B. (2012). *Daring greatly: How the courage to be vulnerable transforms the way we live, love, parent, and lead.* New York, NY: Gotham Books.

Chickering, A., & Reisser, L. (1993). *Education and identity.* San Francisco, CA: Jossey-Bass.

Delbanço, A. (2012). *College: What it was, is, and should be.* Princeton, NJ: Princeton University Press.

Evans, N. J., Forney, D. S., Guido, F. M., Patton, L. D., & Renn, K. A. (2010). *Student development in college: Theory, research, and practice.* San Francisco, CA: Jossey-Bass.

Good, O. (2012, September 2). Call of Duty population explodes to 40 million users, half coming from Modern Warfare 3. Kotaku. Retrieved from http://kotaku.com/5883901/call-of-duty-population-explodes-to-40-million-users-half-coming-from-modern-warfare-3

Hennessy, N. J., & Huson, L. M. (1998). Legal issues and Greek organizations. In E. G. Whipple (Ed.), *New challenges for Greek letter organizations: Transforming fraternities and sororities into learning communities* (pp. 61–77). San Francisco, CA: Jossey-Bass.

Kansas State University Counseling Services. (n.d.). What is a Dysfunctional Family? Retrieved from http://www.k-state.edu/counseling/topics/relationships/dysfunc.html#whatisadysfunctionalfamily

Keeling, R., & Hersh, R. H. (2011). *We're losing our minds: Rethinking American higher education.* New York, NY: Palgrave Macmillan.

Kuh, G. D., Douglas, K. B., Lund, J. P., & Ramin-Gyurnek, J. (1994). *Student learning outside the classroom: Transcending artificial boundaries.* Washington, DC: Graduate School of Education and Human Development, George Washington University.

Levine, A., & Cureton, J. S. (1998). *When hope and fear collide: A portrait of today's college student.* San Francisco, CA: Jossey-Bass.

Lloyd, J. M., Dean, L. A., & Cooper, D. L. (2009). Students' technology use and its effects on peer relationships, academic involvement, and healthy lifestyles. *NASPA Journal, 46*(4), 695–708.

Loeb, P. R. (1994). *Generation at the crossroads: Apathy and action on the American campus.* New Brunswick, NJ: Rutgers University Press.

Marthur, A., Fu, H., & Hansen, P. (2013, September 3). The mysterious and alarming rise of single parenthood in America. *Atlantic.* Retrieved from http://www.theatlantic.com/business/archive/2013/09/the-mysterious-and-alarming-rise-of-single-parenthood-in-america/279203

Nathan, R. (2005). *My freshman year: What a professor learned by becoming a student.* Ithaca, NY: Cornell University Press.

Neff, K. (2011). *Self-compassion: Stop beating yourself up and leave insecurity behind.* New York, NY: William Morrow.

Pascarella, E. T., & Terenzini, P. T. (2005). *How college affects students: A third decade of research.* San Francisco, CA: Jossey-Bass.

Riordan, B. G., & Dana, R. Q. (1998). Greek letter organizations and alcohol: Problems, policies, and programs. In E. G. Whipple (Ed.), *New challenges for Greek letter organizations: Transforming fraternities and sororities into learning communities* (pp. 49–59). San Francisco, CA: Jossey-Bass.

Sandeen, A. (2003). *Enhancing student engagement on campus.* Lanham, MD: University Press of America.

Tannen, D. (2006). *You're wearing that?: Understanding mothers and daughters in conversation.* New York, NY: Ballantine Books.

Tannen, D. (2011). *That's not what I meant!: How conversational style makes or breaks your relations with others.* New York, NY: HarperCollins.

Walker, E. F. (2008). *Adolescent risk taking, brain development, and mental health.* Atlanta, GA: Emory University.

Willimon, W. H., & Naylor, T. H. (1995). *The abandoned generation: Rethinking higher education.* Grand Rapids, MI: Eerdmans.

6

Sexual Decision-Making
Everyone's Doing It, Right?

JOLEEN M. NEVERS AND HEATHER EASTMAN-MUELLER

Introduction

Sexuality and sexual decision-making are important aspects of college life. Understanding all aspects of decision-making is essential to maintaining healthy sexuality, regardless of whether a person chooses to remain sexually abstinent or chooses to be sexually active. According to the Centers for Disease Control and Prevention (CDC)/Health Resources and Services Administration Advisory Committee on HIV, Viral Hepatitis, and STD Prevention and Treatment (CHAC) (2012),

> Sexual health is a state of well-being in relationship to sexuality across the life span that involves physical, emotional, mental, social and spiritual dimensions. Sexual health is an intrinsic element of human health and is based on positive, equitable, and respectful approaches to sexuality, relationship and reproduction, that is free of coercion, fear, discrimination, stigma, shame, and violence. It includes: the ability to understand the benefits, risks, and responsibilities of sexual behavior; the prevention and care of disease and other adverse outcomes; and the possibility of fulfilling sexual relationships. (p. 41)

This chapter acknowledges the various social and cultural impacts on an individual's sexual health decision-making while in college. Additionally, we address some current trends in the field of sexual health and provide recommendations for college professionals. Strategies for student affairs professionals and other campus leaders are outlined, including how to create a campus environment that supports critical, honest dialogue surrounding sexual health.

Sexual Health Behaviors

Why should university and college professionals be concerned about students' sexual health behaviors? Isn't this personal behavior that can have little effect on college student life? The reality is that sexual health is a public health issue and individuals' sexual health decisions can affect those around them. For college students, sexually transmitted diseases (STDs), also referred to as sexually transmitted infections (STIs), and unplanned pregnancy can cause great amounts of stress or in some instances could cause a student to disengage with the institution. This may include withdrawal from the institution, as well as a negative impact on academic performance and personal relationships. One positive impact on a relationship could be that a concerned student who is pregnant may find a supportive and strong bond with her parent. A possible negative impact could be a student with an STI having trouble telling a parent that he or she needs support because of feelings of shame or guilt about contracting an STI.

Not all students are sexually active; many of them are not. It is important to acknowledge and provide supportive services to students who choose abstinence. Often, students not engaging in sexual activity feel silenced and invisible at their institutions. A quality campus effort on sexuality programming will provide a voice and visibility for these students. What a good program is will be discussed later in this chapter. Using the word "abstinence" may not be enough to engage students. It is important to talk with students about the many reasons for their sexual health choices and to inform others how they define being sexually abstinent. Some students may relate better to terminology such as "postponing sex" rather than abstinence, and some students prefer to create their own definition.

What are the sexual behavior trends of college students? According to the CDC's 2013 Youth Risk Behavior Surveillance System (YRBSS) (2013b), 46.8% of students in high school (grades 9–12) have reported having sexual intercourse. The *National College Health Assessment II* (NCHA) *Executive Summary*, by the American College Health Association (ACHA), is one of the largest data sets of college student health in the nation. Since its inception in spring 2000, over 1 million college students have participated in the survey, with over 550 institutions participating. The data that follows is from the spring 2013 sample, with 123,078 students participating from 153 campuses (ACHA, 2013b).

Of the students surveyed, 34.8% were in a relationship while not living together and 16.1% were in a relationship while living together (ACHA, 2013b, p. 17). It is important to keep in mind that some students are married, as 9.8% reported in the survey (ACHA, 2013b, p. 17). The majority of the students reported being in a relationship, while 39.7% did not report being in a relationship (ACHA, 2013b, p. 17). Students may not describe their relationships as monogamous (having a relationship with one partner or one partner at a time). Some students may be in non-monogamous relationships. People who are in non-monogamous relationships are transparent with their partners, which is different from cheating on a partner in a monogamous relationship, in which participants are not aware of the other partner's activity. Students may be in relationships that practice polygamy (practice of having more than one spouse at a time), swinging (when couples participate in sexual relationships with other people), or polyamory (non-monogamous behavior singles or partners in committed relationships engage in sexual activities with others recreationally or socially). This is but a short list of the many ways students may describe their relationships.

There may be misperceptions about college-age students and sexual activity. If only looking to the media, movies, and TV shows for validation of sexual behavior, we might think that many students are having sex and possibly with multiple partners. But the data paints another picture. In the last 12 months 29.6% reported no sexual partners, 44.5% stated that they had one sexual partner, and 10.2% stated that they had two (ACHA, 2013b, p. 10). For students reporting that they had been sexually active in the past 30 days, more reported engaging in vaginal sex and oral sex respectively (49.6% and 44.7%) than in anal sex (5.5%). For students engaging in sex, they reported using the following methods of contraception during their last sex act: the male condom (61.9%), the contraceptive pill (60.4%), and the withdrawal method or "pulling out" (27.6%) (ACHA, 2013b, pp. 10–11). If the occurrence of the withdrawal method is surprising, be assured that students are also surprised by this information. However, the withdrawal method may be used with other forms of contraception, such as the male condom and the contraceptive pill, therefore increasing the effectiveness of each. It may also be used on its own, which is not the most reliable method (particularly when it comes to STI transmission). Of the students surveyed, 11.1% stated that they or their partner reported using emergency contraception in the past 12 months (ACHA, 2013b, p. 11). Consent is an important part of healthy sexuality and acknowledges the needs, desires, and boundaries of everyone involved. It requires mutual understanding and active, assertive agreement between all partners and freedom from coercion, substances, and assumptions. Consent is a process and should always be addressed in the absence of, or while in, any type of relationship. Healthy, consensual, positive sexual experiences require having open, honest communication between and among all partners; acknowledging each person's needs, desires, and boundaries; and having the ability to articulate these to all partners. This can be difficult in situations where alcohol is involved. Research shows that 20% of students surveyed reported that they were drinking while having unprotected sex (ACHA, 2013b, p. 9). Consent is one of the reasons why sexuality educators try to educate students on the effects of alcohol on the body from a pleasure perspective, including discussions about how the body may be impacted, in addition its effect on the brain and decision-making. Many students are unaware that alcohol may actually decrease sensations of touch in addition to impacting blood flow in the body, which may then affect pleasure, erections, or orgasm.

Sexual Orientation and Gender Identity

Sexual orientation and gender identity can be complete book topics by themselves. With that said, we are going to give a brief description of both of these concepts.

Sexual orientation and gender identity are concepts that can confuse people. According to GLAAD (Gay and Lesbian Alliance Against Defamation) (n.d.), Sexual Orientation refers to an individual's enduring physical, romantic and/or emotional attraction to another person(s) including lesbian, gay, bisexual, pansexual and heterosexual orientations. Sexual orientation also refers to a person's sense of identity based on those attractions, related behaviors, and membership in a community of others who share those attractions.

The National Center for Transgender Equality (NCTE) (2014), refers to gender identity as a person's internal sense of being male, female, or something else. Because gender identity is internal, one's gender identity is not always visible to others. "Gender refers to the socially constructed roles, behaviors, activities, and attributes that a given society ascribes to boys and men or girls and women. These influence the ways that people act, interact, and feel about themselves. While aspects of biological sex are similar across different cultures, aspects of gender may differ. The term transgender is an umbrella term for persons whose gender identity, gender expression or behavior does not align with their sex assigned at birth" (NCTE, 2014). Some students identify as gender-nonconforming or gender variant, which means that how a person communicates their gender or gender expression does not correspond with society's expectations of gender (NCTE, 2014). Sexual orientation and gender identity are not the same constructs. People who are gender-nonconforming or identify as transgender may define their sexual orientation as gay, straight, pansexual, queer, or bisexual, the same as nontransgender or gender-confirming people. Both sexual orientation and gender identity are on a continuum, and people may not find a definition or "box" that they feel fits them. Some students are more comfortable using the term "queer" to describe sexual orientation or gender identity or both. What is most important for college professionals to know is to use the language that our students use to describe their sexual orientation or gender identity. For example, if a woman who is in a relationship with another woman uses the word "gay" to describe her orientation (rather than the term lesbian), the professional should mirror the language of the student and use the terminology of "gay." If a student identifies as gender-nonconforming or transgender, it is important to ask the student what pronoun or name they prefer rather than making an assumption. Most students would rather a professional ask this question than make assumptions about which pronouns they prefer, as it shows respect and kindness.

When professionals or students use the acronym LGBTQ, the LGBT (lesbian, gay, bisexual, and transgender) remain the same but the Q could mean "queer" or "questioning," or the Q could stand for both. Planned Parenthood Federation of America (n.d.) explains the terminology of "questioning": "It can take many years for people to understand their sexual orientation, and it can change over your lifetime—so a lot of people call themselves questioning, which means they aren't sure about their sexual orientation and/or gender identity." Talking with students, staff, and faculty on campus to find out the language that is used on your campus and in your region is important. Recognize that this language is evolving and changing.

Contraception

Another complex issue that requires investigation and knowledge is contraceptive methods. At times, a student may come to a faculty or professional staff member for advice or information about what methods are available to them, and it is important to know the basics. We often think of college students wanting to avoid pregnancy. However, for some this may not always be the case. Students vary in age, with some wanting to start a family. We also have to keep in mind that not all students are engaging in sexual acts or relationships that may put them at risk of pregnancy. For example, a male student who has sex with another male student does not need to be concerned about contraception related to pregnancy prevention but is at risk for STI transmission. Additionally, if a male student has sex with women, then the pregnancy concern can become very real. Teaching students about contraceptive methods, regardless of their sexual orientation or the type of sex (anal, oral, vaginal, or other forms of sex) they have, is beneficial when discussing risk reduction.

Currently, almost half of the 6.6 million pregnancies in the United States each year are unintended (Guttmacher Institute, 2013). High rates of sexual activity and inconsistent contraceptive use among college students place them at risk for an unintended pregnancy and STIs. The National College Health Assessment II, conducted in fall 2013, reported 70% of students are sexually active (defined as having oral, anal or vaginal sex in the last 12 months) (ACHA, 2013a). For those who reported having vaginal sex, only 46.5% reported using a condom during sex within the last 30 days (ACHA, 2013a, p. 10). This data is consistent with other studies on college students and sexual activity. The impact on student retention can be significant when dealing with an unplanned pregnancy, especially at community colleges. Nationally, unintended births account for nearly 1 in 10 dropouts among female students at community colleges, and 7% of dropouts among community college students overall (Prentice, Storin, & Robinson, 2012). Furthermore, 61% of community college students who have children after enrolling do not complete their postsecondary education (Bradburn, 2002).

While college students are at risk for an unintended pregnancy, it is important to emphasize that they are also at risk for a sexually transmitted infection. From a sexual health educator perspective, the prevention of STIs is just as important and can have life-threatening consequences if left untreated. When discussing the different types of contraceptive methods and attempting to understand a student's sexual health decision-making, a more comprehensive approach is recommended. For example, to validate and acknowledge all college students and sexual behaviors, a more inclusive approach to contraception should include contraceptive methods to prevent unintended pregnancy as well as STIs. For example, not everyone engages in vaginal intercourse or can get pregnant. By emphasizing only pregnancy prevention, the complete benefits of contraceptive methods are not being promoted, and some students may feel alienated.

For those students who want to prevent an unintended pregnancy and STIs, there are several very effective contraceptive methods available. Because there are so many choices, it is important to consider lifestyle, cost, and effectiveness in prevention of STIs and pregnancy, as well as discussing the various methods.

STIs

According to the CDC's fact sheet entitled Incidence, Prevalence, and Cost of Sexually Transmitted Infections in the United States (2013a, p. 1), in reference to STIs "America's youth shoulder a substantial burden of these infections." College-age students may be more susceptible for STIs because most STIs don't have symptoms, students lack resources (healthcare or safer sex options), students face dating violence and assault, and students' anatomy is still developing (CDC, 2011). However, a person at any age can contract an STI. The CDC estimates that "there are more than 19.7 million new STIs in the United States each year. While most of these STIs will not cause harm, some have the potential to cause serious health problems, especially if not diagnosed and treated early. Young people (ages 15–24) are particularly affected, accounting for half of all new STIs, although they represent just 25% of the sexually experienced population" (CDC, 2013a, p. 2).

Students today often misunderstand HIV/AIDS treatment to be a cure. This leads to students being less concerned about this STI, thinking that it is easily managed by taking a pill. Often this STI is talked about because of the epidemic and its impact from the 1980s and 1990s. Because of this, students are aware of this disease but are unclear about other STIs. While there are four STIs common among college students, other STIs may also be common, depending on the location of institution and the community both within and around the institution. While getting college-specific data is difficult, there is much information about STIs among 18–24 year olds. The common STIs in the college population are: (1) human papilloma virus (HPV); (2) chlamydia; (3) gonorrhea; and (4) herpes (see Table 6.1).

HPV is one of the most common STIs in the United States today (CDC, 2013a). Several strains of HPV have no signs or symptoms; nor do these strains cause concern, and they may go away on their own. However, there are strains that can cause genital warts and there are strains that cause cancer in the oropharynx (back of the throat, tongue, and tonsils), cervix, vulva, vagina, anus, and penis (CDC, n.d.c). These strains can also go undetected. There is no test for men, although women can be tested through a Pap test and/or HPV test (CDC, n.d.g).

TABLE 6.1 Information Adapted from the Centers for Disease Control and Prevention

Name	Type	Curable	Treatable	How common	Vaccine	Health impacts
HPV (human papilloma virus)	Virus	No	Yes	Very	Yes, up to nine strains	Some strains cause cancer; some genital warts
Chlamydia	Bacteria	Yes	Yes	Very	No	Untreated may cause infertility in men and women or pelvic inflammatory disease (PID) in women
Gonorrhea	Bacteria	Yes	Yes	Very	No	Untreated may cause infertility
Herpes	Virus	No	Yes	Very	No	Can cause sores

Students seem to be more familiar with chlamydia and gonorrhea, which are both bacterial infections. Both are curable, but reinfection can occur for untreated partners, so it important for all persons having sex to obtain treatment at the same time. The CDC (n.d.b) reports an increase in antibiotic-resistant gonorrhea, which makes treatment more challenging. Since the majority of STIs have no symptoms, it is important to encourage students to seek testing if they are starting a new relationship, have had sex with several partners, or engaged in other behaviors that may increase their risk of exposure to STIs.

Another STI that students are familiar with is herpes. While students are aware of it, they often confuse it with HPV. There are two strains of herpes: HSV1 and HSV2 (CDC, n.d.d). The reason for this distinction is because HSV1 is very common; many people know it as cold sores. It can be transmitted through kissing (a greeting kiss, parental kiss, or partner kiss), sharing water bottles, lip balm, drinking through same straw and touching a sore then rubbing one's eye. This strain is not necessarily transmitted through sex, but it can be transmitted through oral sex with someone who has the infection. Both of these types of herpes may express symptoms; but sometimes people don't have symptoms or might have mild symptoms that they don't recognize as herpes (CDC, n.d.d). Only a healthcare provider will be able to type test a sore from a person to determine which kind they have.

Safer Sex Strategies

Using the terminology "safer sex" instead of "safe sex" is important because we can make sex safer only by using different strategies, but engaging in sexual activity is not risk-free. Using the language "safe sex" can provide a false sense of security. It is important for students to know how to reduce their risk of contracting STIs if they are engaging in sexual contact. Some of these methods differ from the contraception methods mentioned earlier. Students can use either the male "external" condom or the female (internal) condom as both contraception and STI prevention. Other products for safer sex can include dental dams or sheaths of plastic or latex, nonlatex gloves, and lubrication. Often times, lubrication is not mentioned as a safer sex strategy. It is an important part of safer sex for two reasons: it helps keep the latex or nonlatex products from breaking due to friction, and it increases pleasure. Sometimes students are resistant to use these safer sex products because they think that they may reduce sensation or be restrictive. This is why it is important for lubrication to be a part of the conversation, as it helps increase sensation. To address students' concerns about fit, it is important to discuss that condoms come in all shapes and sizes. It is important for people to find their best fit.

Other safer sex strategies include getting vaccinations, reducing sexual partners, abstaining or postponing sex, and getting tested for STIs (CDC, n.d.e). Students may decrease their risk of contracting STIs by reducing the number of sexual partners they have. It is important for students, regardless of age, to know and share their STI status with all sexual partners. Some students get tested annually, while some may choose to get tested with every new partner. The CDC (n.d.f.) recommends the following screening guidelines:

- All adults and adolescents from ages 13 to 64 should be tested at least once for HIV.
- Annual chlamydia screening for all sexually active women younger than 25 years, as well as older women with risk factors such as new or multiple sex partners, or a sex partner who has a sexually transmitted infection.
- Yearly gonorrhea screening for all sexually active women younger than 25 years, as well as older women with risk factors such as new or multiple sex partners, or a sex partner who has a sexually transmitted infection.
- Syphilis, HIV, chlamydia, and hepatitis B screening for all pregnant women, and gonorrhea screening for at-risk pregnant women, starting early in pregnancy, with repeat testing as needed, to protect the health of mothers and their infants.
- Screening at least once a year for syphilis, chlamydia, and gonorrhea for all sexually active gay, bisexual, and other men who have sex with men (MSM). MSM who have multiple or anonymous partners should be screened more frequently for STIs (i.e., at three- to six-month intervals).
- Anyone who has unsafe sex or shares injection drug equipment should get tested for HIV at least once a year. Sexually active gay and bisexual men may benefit from more frequent testing (e.g., every three to six months).

There are a number of strategies that campuses can implement to assist students with STI awareness. A campus could host annual, monthly, or weekly STI screening days, free for students. Campuses could work with local health departments or waive the fee for the day for a certain number of students. Some campuses use MTV's (Viacom Media Networks, 2014) "GYT" or Get Yourself Talking, Get Yourself Tested campaign to raise awareness and destigmatize testing. Campuses can also offer safer sex supplies, such as condoms (male and female), lubrication, and dental dams.

Sexual Health Decision-Making for College Students

What goes into a student's decision-making with regard to sexual health? Individual factors certainly affect college student decision-making. More importantly, the social cultural contexts in which they make these decisions play a significant role. College offers students unique yet challenging opportunities to grow both personally and professionally.

From a very young age, we are taught that sex and sexuality are an integral part of being human—what to wear, how to act, who we should be attracted to, and whether or not and when to have sex. These influences originate from religion, the media, personal experiences, education, culture, peers, and parents, among others. Unfortunately, the messages we receive often contradict each other. For example, our educational system teaches us that our sexuality is so sacred that public school curricula rarely address the comprehensiveness of sexuality. Conversely, popular media glamorizes sex and frequently portrays sexuality inaccurately. In the media there is an unrealistic portrayal of beauty, sex is easy and doesn't require communication, and has little to no consequences. As one can imagine, it can be confusing for young adults to make decisions while being bombarded with conflicting messages; this presents hypocrisy. It is no wonder that sexual decision-making is an intricate yet complex process affected by personal experience and sociocultural influences.

Although there are some nontraditional students who are older than 24 years of age, the majority of college students are 18 to 24 years old. For those in this age group many things uniquely impact decision-making. This stage of development signifies a relatively immature brain, specifically the prefrontal cortex, a part of the brain linked to higher-order cognitive functioning and emotional regulation, both deemed instrumental in decision-making (Shad et al., 2011). In addition to developing physiologically, college students are forced to mature socially very quickly. For many, this is the first time away from home with relatively little supervision. There is increased access to substances such as alcohol and other drugs, and reduced knowledge in how to navigate the health care system.

Social Norms, Pressure, and Expectancies

During this stage of life, young adults are discovering who they are both personally and professionally, what they enjoy, and what risks they can take and are willing to take, while often looking to their peers for cues about the appropriateness of certain types of social behavior. The fear of not fitting in and/or being regarded as "different" during this developmental stage in life fuels this pressure to act according to sexual scripts. One example of this phenomenon is the decision to engage in sexual activity. The perception of peers' sexual behaviors, either overestimation or underestimation, has been found to impact sexual behavior (Brandhorst, Ferguson, Sebby, & Weeks, 2012; Lewis, Litt, Cronce, & Blayney, 2014). In a smaller study of 322 college students, participants' frequency of sexual activity was directly related to their perception of peer sexual activity. When peer sexual activity was perceived to be low, the frequency of sexual activity of the participants was low; a similar relationship was found for moderate to high levels of perceived peer sexual activity (Brandhorst, Ferguson, Sebby, & Weeks, 2012).

The overwhelming perception among most college students is that there is pressure to have sex, thus leading to a greater intention to have sex, earlier sexual debut, and a greater frequency of subsequent sexual behaviors (Buhi & Goodson, 2007). In addition to perceived peer norms, students with a greater frequency of sexual communication with their peers were significantly more likely to expect that sex would be pleasurable, but yet significantly less likely to endorse the social or health risks of engaging in sex. This data suggests that sexual communication among peers has a lasting effect. During young adulthood, peers may be particularly effective in influencing what students expect regarding sex. In addition, accurate representation and broad dissemination of information about sexual behavior can relieve some of the social pressures reported by college students (Ragsdale et al., 2014).

Although the influence of peers is significant, the role of parents and a young person's feeling of connectedness to their parents and school, particularly among young women, is an important factor influencing sexual health decision-making (Schalet, 2011). For example, the quality of relationship with parents and shared activities with the mother were strongly associated with delayed sexual debut for adolescent girls. These findings have been replicated in several smaller studies among college-aged women. One such study of 52 college women demonstrated that reminders of paternal disengagement increased women's activation of sexual thoughts, sexual permissiveness, and negativity toward condom use (DelPriore & Hill, 2013). This phenomenon has been replicated in a smaller study with college students using priming procedures. Conversely, greater parental monitoring and supervision predicted earlier sexual debut, increased frequency of sex, and number of partners, which in turn predicted greater sexual risk (Buhi & Goodson, 2007).

So why is this important to someone in student affairs or other leadership positions at a college or university? Students are more comfortable with adults than they have been in years past, and some report strong relationships with their family. With this in mind, students' family can have a positive impact on their decision-making when a parent or family discusses expectations and norms around sexuality (CDC, n.d.a).

College students may also have a skewed perception of their risk when it comes to sex. Although some college students may engage in sex with multiple partners, use condoms inconsistently, and report engaging in sexual activity while under the influence of alcohol and/or drugs, college students often claim they are in control of their sexual situation and believe they are at little risk (Roberts & Kennedy, 2006). Accurate and timely perception of risk is important for college students to be successful in their college career. Gardner and Steinberg (2005) found that in comparison to adults, the decisions individuals aged 18 to 22 make are riskier in the presence of the peers than made alone. Relative to adults, adolescents are more susceptible to the influence of their peers in risky situations. One of the reasons determined was that adolescents focus more on the benefits rather than the costs of risky behavior, and that compared with adults, adolescents have less ability to act independently of the influence of others (Gardner & Steinberg, 2005).

Cognitive Development

Oftentimes, when studying sexual health, people tend to focus their attention on the physical aspect of sex, disregarding the comprehensiveness of sexuality. Studies have proven that high-risk decision-making necessitates greater cognitive challenges, and thus requires more brain activity, particularly in the prefrontal activation area of the brain, compared to purely reward-related behavior. The prefrontal cortex (PFC) of the brain is responsible for conflict monitoring and response inhibition pivotal in decision-making in adults. Differences in the PFC during adolescence are thought to contribute to frequent underestimation of risks and risk-taking behaviors (Shad et al., 2011). It is important to keep this in mind when offering programming or trying to discern how college students are making decisions surrounding sexual health. Being cognizant of our limitations and the preexisting experiences students come to college with is important in developing effective sexual health programming. We must come to terms with what we can do to support our students and realize that behavior change is difficult and complex. Sometimes we see behavior change during their time in college, or sometimes we are moving them into a contemplation stage of behavior change for the process to happen after the college years. Being realistic about our expectations and working with the knowledge that while in college, students are young adults still growing and maturing are vitally important.

In addition to the cognitive development of students, attending college represents a dramatic shift in their social cultural environment. Much of the literature suggests there is a specific "culture of sex on college campuses." In one study, the majority of students agreed that having sex is a part of the college experience, with "hookup" sex being the most prevalent, and considered an inevitable form of romantic relationships while in college (Garcia, Reiber, Massey, & Merriweather, 2012). What traditionally was considered the gold standard for relationships among youth (long term exclusivity that encourages trust, intimacy, and support) has now shifted to more casual dating patterns. Within these types of relationships, being intimate comes first, with the determination of a longer-term relationship coming later, if at all.

Hookup sex, according to the literature, is defined as any sexual interactions that occur outside of a committed, romantic relationship (Claxton & van Dulmen, 2013). Some believe that hookup sex provides emerging adults with opportunities for sexual exploration (Owen, Quirk, & Fincham, 2013; Stinson, 2010). Others suggest that hookup sex is associated with negative emotional states and reactions related to attitudes about relationships and sexual behavior (Burnett et al., 2014). No matter the outcome, positive or negative, sexual behavior rates among college students are the same, and it is just their relationship patterns that are different than in the past.

Although there are quite a few studies about sexual health decision-making among this age group, much of the research lacks methodological rigor. For example, there is an absence of theoretical underpinnings when research studies on sexual health have been conducted. Working within a theoretical framework strengthens the results and allows for study replication. Additionally, much of the research relies on a convenience sample and therefore prevents the investigator from drawing any casual relationships, does not control for selection biases, and limits the investigator's ability to generalize the findings. More specifically, the gaps in the literature related to sexual health include examinations of refusal or negotiation skills and subsequent sexual behavior and intention. With the large amount of relationship research, there is little investigation on the contributing factors of hooking up and the prevalence of STIs among the college population, specifically among men.

Professional Spotlight: Sexuality Educators

Some institutions have sexuality educators on their campuses, while others rely on health educators, health promotion staff, or a nurse to provide sexual health information on their campuses. For those staff members who are health educators, health promotion staff, or nurses, they often have varied responsibilities. Providing sex education is one of the many tasks that are required. Because of this, it can be difficult for the person to know the most current research or have time to develop evidence-informed strategies for his or her campus. A way for people to remain current is to review the websites for the Centers for Disease Control and Prevention Sexual Health, Guttmacher Institute, Advocates for Youth, and Rutgers University Sex Etc. and review different journals, such as the *American Journal of Sexuality Education, Sexuality & Culture, Sex Education: Society and Learning,* and *Sexual Health*. Given the varied sizes of institutions and budgets, not all institutions can afford to have a person dedicated to this topic for any length of time.

Sexuality educators or health educator/promotion staff who provide sexual health education to their campus can be found providing a range of educational/ prevention strategies. Sexuality educators on campus may use the social ecological model in their work. This model helps to address several needs, including interpersonal, intrapersonal, organizational, community, and public policy. For example, a sexuality educator may conduct a survey of the campus, and may talk with key stakeholders to assess the needs of students. In addition to these strategies, a sexuality educator may also host focus groups or discussions with students or may also review national trends of the population through surveys and national data on the population. Professionals can review the aggregated data to address subpopulations, such as nontraditional students, married students, students with disabilities, students who identify with religions or ethnicities, and racial minorities. Once a sexuality educator understands the needs of the campus, they can implement different strategies, such as STI testing, supporting improved access to safer sex options and contraception, and teaching students skills such as assertiveness or negotiation of safer sex or how to use safer sex methods correctly. A sexuality educator may also use social media and other media platforms to destigmatize common myths and perceptions held in our culture. Sexuality educators may work directly on policies and procedures on campus. Some sexuality educators are working on Title IX policies on their campus (United States Department of Education, n.d.). Other strategies may include a sexuality educator assisting with implementing gender-neutral spaces on campus, including bathrooms, or working with the campus health center to provide free STI testing.

Another viable option for campuses involves using peer education. Peer education involves using trained students to deliver messaging, resources, education, and/or skills to other students. Students can also impact their peers informally by providing resources and information to peers when professionals may not be available. Often, peer educators are asked questions outside of the "office hours" of the institution. Even as professionals adjust their schedules to make themselves available, there typically is not enough staff to answer students' questions. This is where effective peer education can be helpful. Furthermore, peers may feel more comfortable speaking with another student than a person in authority.

Campus Applications

Many of these examples are about the professional person providing sexual health information on campus. How can other professionals, including faculty, student affairs, and other staff, be proactive or supportive? A current or future leader at institutions of higher education can be supportive of sexual health work by addressing the following points:

- Assessment: Support staff in collecting campus data on sexual health in addition to supporting their comparing national and regional data to inform campus efforts.
- Consultation: Encourage staff to provide one-on-one educational appointments to directly address students' needs.
- Education and outreach: Provide peer education and integrate sexual health education into other academic subject areas, such as psychology, English, and sciences, in addition to offering sexual health courses to students. Also, support outreach activities across campus, including free STI testing and access to safer sex products. Sexual health is only one component of a person's overall health and can intersect with alcohol and or other drugs, mental health, relationship stress, and affect academics.
- Training: Provide training for different constituents of campus leaders, including student workers, residence assistants (RAs), peer educators, and Greek life and professional staff.
- Policies: Work with the health center to provide free testing and treatment. Work with residential life department to mandate sexual health programming offered by the appropriate office. Mandate that healthcare providers be trained in special populations such as lesbian, gay, bisexual, transgender, or queer (LGBTQ), and that healthcare providers address students' sexual health as a part of overall preventative health care.
- Professional development and leadership: Encourage the sexual health educator to be actively involved in presenting at conferences or in other leadership capacities (regionally or nationally). Full-time collegiate sexual health professionals are in a unique position to be leaders in the field of sexuality, being in an academically challenging environment that may require them to remain more current in the field than part-time sexual health professionals or generalists on college campuses.

Summary and Conclusions

It is imperative that college professionals consider the complexity of sexuality and its impact on college students' lives. This chapter explores the multiple factors contributing to sexual health decision-making among college students. Prevention, early detection, and effective interventions are critical to reducing sexual health risks and promoting positive sexuality. Students may consult student affairs professionals, advisors, deans, or other university officials for advice on these types of issues. Examining the impact of different constructs, including culture and students' morals and family values, is important when assisting students with their decision-making processes. Contextually, college is a time of self-exploration, learning, and navigating a new environment. We can assist students during this time by being open and guiding them to the best resources both on and off campus.

References

American College Health Association (ACHA). (2013a). *National College Health Assessment II: Reference group data report, fall 2013.* Retrieved from http://www.acha-ncha.org/docs/ACHA-NCHA-II_ReferenceGroup_DataReport_Fall2013.pdf

American College Health Association (ACHA). (2013b). *National College Health Assessment II: Reference group executive summary, spring 2013.* Retrieved from http://www.acha-ncha.org/docs/ACHA-NCHA-II_ReferenceGroup_ExecutiveSummary_Spring2013.pdf

Bradburn, E.M. (2002). *Short-term enrollment in postsecondary education: Students background and institutional differences in reasons for early departure.* Washington, DC: National Center for Education Statistics, US Department of Education.

Brandhorst, S.R., Ferguson, B., Sebby, R.A., & Weeks, R. (2012). The influence of peer sexual activity upon college students' sexual behavior. *North American Journal of Psychology, 14*(1), 111–122.

Buhi, E. R., & Goodson P. (2007). Predictors of adolescent sexual behavior and intention: A theory-guided systematic review. *Journal of Adolescent Health, 40,* 4–21.

Burnett, A. J., Sabato, T. M., Ott Walter, K., Kerr, D.L., Wagner, L., & Smith, A. (2014). The influence of attributional style on substance use and risky sexual behavior among college students. *College Student Journal, 48*(2), 325–336.

Centers for Disease Control and Prevention. (2011). 2011 sexually transmitted diseases surveillance. Retrieved from http://www.cdc.gov/std/stats11/adol.htm

Centers for Disease Control and Prevention. (2013a). *CDC fact sheet: Incidence, prevalence, and cost of sexually transmitted infections in the United States.* Retrieved from http://www.cdc.gov/std/stats/sti-estimates-fact-sheet-feb-2013.pdf

Centers for Disease Control and Prevention. (2013b). *Youth risk behavior survey.* Retrieved from http://www.cdc.gov/mmwr/pdf/ss/ss6304.pdf

Centers for Disease Control and Prevention. (n.d.a). Adolescent and school health. Retrieved from http://www.cdc.gov/healthyyouth/protective/index.htm

Centers for Disease Control and Prevention. (n.d.b). Antibiotic-resistant gonorrhea. Retrieved from http://www.cdc.gov/std/gonorrhea/arg/default.htm

Centers for Disease Control and Prevention. (n.d.c). Basic information about HPV-associated cancers. Retrieved from http://www.cdc.gov/cancer/hpv/basic_info/index.htm

Centers for Disease Control and Prevention. (n.d.d). Genital herpes—CDC fact sheet. Retrieved from http://www.cdc.gov/std/herpes/stdfact-herpes-detailed.htm

Centers for Disease Control and Prevention. (n.d.e). Sexually transmitted diseases (STDs). Retrieved from http://www.cdc.gov/std/prevention/

Centers for Disease Control and Prevention. (n.d.f). STD & HIV screening recommendations. Retrieved from http://www.cdc.gov/std/prevention/screeningReccs.htm

Centers for Disease Control and Prevention. (n.d.g). What should I know about screening? Retrieved from http://www.cdc.gov/cancer/cervical/basic_info/screening.htm

Centers for Disease Control and Prevention, Health Resources and Services Administration Advisory Committee on HIV, Viral Hepatitis, and STD Prevention and Treatment. (2012). *Record of the proceedings.* Retrieved from http://www.cdc.gov/maso/facm/pdfs/CHACHSPT/20120508_CHAC.pdf

Claxton, S. E., & van Dulmen, M.H.M. (2013). Casual sexual relationships and experiences in emerging adulthood. *Emerging Adulthood, 1*(2), 138–150. doi:10.1177/2167696813487181

DelPriore, D.J., & Hill, S.E. (2013). The effects of paternal disengagement on women's sexual decision making: An experimental approach. *Journal of Personality and Social Psychology, 105*(2), 234–246.

Garcia, J.R., Reiber, C., Massey, S.G., & Merriweather, A. M. (2012). Sexual hookup culture: A review. *Review of General Psychology, 16,* 161–176. doi:10.1037/a0027911

Gardner, M., & Steinberg, L. (2005). Peer influence on risk taking, risk preference and risky decision making in adolescence and adulthood: An experimental study. *Developmental Psychology, 41*(4), 625–635.

GLAAD. (n.d.). GLAAD media reference guide: Lesbian/gay/bisexual glossary of terms. Retrieved from http://www.glaad.org/reference/lgb

Guttmacher Institute. (2013, December). Unintended pregnancy in the United States. Retrieved from http://www.guttmacher.org/pubs/FB-Unintended-Pregnancy-US.html

Lewis, M. A., Litt, D. M., Cronce, J. M., & Blayney, J. A. (2014). Underestimating protection and overestimating risk: Examining descriptive normative perceptions and their association with drinking and sexual behaviors. *Journal of Sex Research, 51*(1), 86–96.

National Center for Transgender Equality. (2014). *Transgender terminology*. Retrieved from http://transequality.org/sites/default/files/docs/resources/TransTerminology_2014.pdf

Owen, J., Quirk, K., & Fincham, F. D. (2013). Toward a more complete understanding of reactions to hooking up among college women. *Journal of Sex and Marital Therapy,40*(5), 396–409. doi:10.1080/0092623X.2012.751074

Planned Parenthood Federation of America. (n.d.). All about LGBTQ at a glance. Retrieved from http://www.plannedparenthood.org/teens/lgbtq/all-about-lgbtq

Prentice, M., Storin, C., & Robinson, G. (2012). *Make it personal: How pregnancy planning and prevention help students complete college.* Washington, DC: Author.

Ragsdale, K., Bersamin, M. M., Schwartz, S. J., Zamboanga, B. L., Kerrick, M. R., & Grube, J. W. (2014). Development of sexual expectancies among adolescents: Contributions by parents, peers and the media. *Journal of Sex Research, 51*(5), 551–560.

Roberts, S. T., & Kennedy, B. L. (2006). Why are young college women not using condoms? Their perceived risk, drug use, and developmental vulnerability may provide important clues to sexual risk. *Archives of Psychiatric Nursing, 20*(1), 32–40.

Schalet, A. T. (2011). Beyond abstinence and risk: A new paradigm for adolescent sexual health. *Women's Health Issues, 21*(3), S5–S7. doi:10.1016/j.whi.2011.01.007

Shad, M. U., Bidesi, A. S., Chen, L., Thomas, B. P., Ernst, M., & Rao, U. (2011). Neurobiology of decision-making in adolescents. *Behavioural Brain Research, 217*, 67–76.

Stinson, R. D. (2010). Hooking up in young adulthood: A review of factors influencing the sexual behavior of college students. *Journal of College Student Psychotherapy, 24*(2), 98–115. doi:10.1080/87568.220903558596

Viacom Media Networks. (2014). MTV's "It's your (sex) life." Retrieved from http://www.itsyoursexlife.com/about

United States Department of Education. (n.d.). *Questions and answers to Title IX and sexual violence.* Retrieved from http://www2.ed.gov/about/offices/list/ocr/docs/qa-201404-title-ix.pdf

7

Alcohol
Reaching Students Through Education and Intervention

SHANNON K. BAILIE, JASON R. KILMER, AND M. DOLORES CIMINI

The evolution of approaches to college student drinking prevention and intervention has advanced significantly within the last 50 years. What we once addressed as an issue focusing on morals and values has evolved into an evidence-based, scientifically rigorous field of study, utilizing brief interventions and strategic ecological approaches. We may still be battling media exaggerations portrayed in films like *Animal House* and *Old School* and unfortunately even films targeting younger audiences, like *Monsters University*. But the good news is while Hollywood may continue to produce movies based on misinformed norms that serve only to reinforce dangerous social standards, we as a field of researchers and practitioners know the landscape of college alcohol is more complex and varied than Hollywood would have us believe. In addition, we have reached a significant moment in this journey, and we are now equipped, better than ever, with the tools and knowledge of what works with this population (e.g., Brief Alcohol Screening and Intervention with College Students) and what doesn't ("Just Say No," scare tactics, wrecked car displays, and goggles that simulate being intoxicated). The progress we have made in this field is dramatic, even by Hollywood standards. In this chapter we will focus on what currently represents best practices for prevention of alcohol-related harms, by breaking down the science and providing accessible examples of how prevention efforts can fit into a larger ecological model of education, outreach, and intervention appropriate for our college campuses.

College Student Alcohol Use

Over three-quarters (75.6%) of college students report that they have consumed alcohol at least once in the past year, and over half (57.9%) report that they have been drunk at least once in the same time frame (Johnston, O'Malley, Bachman, Schulenberg, & Miech, 2014). When considering past month drinking, the numbers reflect smaller prevalence rates, with 63.1% who report any use and 40.2% who report having been drunk (Johnston et al., 2014). Thus, in a given month on a college campus, most students (almost 60%) either do not drink at all or, if they make the choice to drink, do so in a way that does not involve getting drunk. Although campuses tend to focus on the at-risk or high-risk students who drink excessively, students who abstain can also be an important target of prevention efforts to extend and prolong their abstinence, as can those who drink in a light to moderate way.

There is well-documented variability in patterns of alcohol consumption, such that school breaks (e.g., spring break), many holidays or weekends surrounding holidays (e.g., Halloween, New Year's Eve, St. Patrick's Day), and personally relevant events (e.g., twenty-first birthdays) reflect elevated alcohol use and even a greater number of unwanted consequences (Del Boca, Darkes, Greenbaum, & Goldman, 2004; Neighbors et al., 2011; Tremblay et al., 2010). At colleges or universities with a strong football culture, high-profile game days (both home and away) are among the heaviest drinking days from September to December (Neal & Fromme, 2007). There are also groups of students for whom rates of drinking could be higher than the general student body, and for whom there may also be considerable variability in patterns, including students in fraternities and sororities (Kilmer & Larimer, 2008) and intercollegiate athletes (Martens, Dams-O'Connor, & Beck, 2006). Among student-athletes, rates of abstinence increase during the season in which they are competing, suggesting the potential for increased risks during the off-season (Martens, Dams-O'Connor, & Duffy-Paiement, 2006; Yusko, Buckman, White, & Pandina, 2008). Thus, when campuses screen or collect data from their students, it is important to be aware of these atypical days and high-risk events, and to ask the questions about alcohol use that paint the most accurate picture of what a student's drinking looks like. Additionally, as campuses consider ways to best meet the needs of their students, event-specific prevention offered around high-risk times of year is an emerging possibility (e.g., Lee et al., 2014).

College student alcohol use, and the possible risks associated with it, is not a new phenomenon. In 1945, Dr. Clements Collard Fry at Yale University wrote the first peer-reviewed journal article addressing college student alcohol use. Impressively, he had already recognized the importance of considering the context of (and reasons behind) excessive alcohol use. His article opens with, "Drinking is a common index of a college student's emotional reactions to the complex variety of situations and problems in his [or her] life" (Fry, 1945, p. 243). While motives for drinking can (and do) vary, it is incredible to see this emphasis on the potential role of alcohol use, and the suggestion that alcohol could be used for coping, well before college campuses increased the attention being paid to student health and mental health needs, and well before a literature on college student substance use had been established. In his concluding paragraph, Dr. Fry states, "It is the obligation of the university, which should be concerned with the health of its students, to view alcoholism as a possible symptom of emotional disturbance, in need of psychiatric attention, rather than as a form of behavior calling for customary disciplinary action" (Fry, 1945, p. 248). Although now, 70 years later, alcoholism tends to be associated with references to an alcohol use disorder (and can be a loaded term for many), his plea for colleges to focus on their students' health needs and approach these issues beyond a purely judicial or punitive way is exceptional.

Nationally, campus chief student affairs officers report that alcohol is involved with 57% of residence hall damage, 58% of violent behavior, 32% of suicide risk,

65% of acquaintance rape, 26% of attrition, and 38% of physical injury (Anderson & Gadaleto, 2012). NIAAA (2002) data reports 1,825 students dying every year due to alcohol-related causes.

Education and Prevention

Fortunately, several successes in reducing the harms associated with college student alcohol use have been achieved over several decades (Kilmer, Cronce, & Larimer, 2014). Many of the most significant advances in college student drinking prevention were developed by Dr. G. Alan Marlatt (Kilmer, Palmer, Cronce, & Logan, 2012), who very boldly suggested harm reduction approaches in place of the "Just Say No," abstinence-only programs prevalent at the time. If there is a misconception surrounding harm reduction, it is often the belief that it is anti-abstinence and necessarily equals moderation; yet, nothing could be further from the truth. The optimal outcome from a harm reduction intervention is, in fact, abstinence, since this is the most harm- and risk-free goal. Harm reduction approaches acknowledge, however, that any steps toward reduced risk are steps in the right direction.

Prior to the development of Marlatt's programs, education-only and, typically, abstinence-only approaches were utilized. Unfortunately, these did not result in changes in behavior, and, at best, increased participants' knowledge (Hanson, 1982). Something was missing, and the Alcohol Skills Training Program (ASTP) seemed to be a major piece filling that prevention gap (Kivlahan, Marlatt, Fromme, Coppel, & Williams, 1990; Miller, Kilmer, Kim, Weingardt, & Marlatt, 2001). ASTP differed from other programs at the time by acknowledging that participants, even those under 21, might make the choice to drink. The group-based program did not encourage alcohol use, but instead examined ways that those who make the choice to drink could do so in a less dangerous or less risky way if they so choose. The skills training component of ASTP focused on setting a limit based on blood alcohol concentration (BAC) and utilizing various protective behavioral strategies and harm reduction techniques to adhere to this limit and reduce unwanted effects throughout the drinking occasion. Compared to an abstinence-only intervention and a control group, participants in ASTP achieved significant reductions in alcohol use and related consequences.

The Alcohol Skills Training Program set the foundation for the development of the Brief Alcohol Screening and Intervention for College Students (BASICS) program (Dimeff, Baer, Kivlahan, & Marlatt, 1999). Other advances in understanding and facilitating behavior change also were hugely influential at the same time. Providers and researchers were conceptualizing different levels of readiness to change behavior, and acknowledged that some individuals may not be considering change at all (i.e., precontemplation), some may be ambivalent about or weighing the pros and cons of change (i.e., contemplation), while others are making changes (i.e., action) (Prochaska & DiClemente, 1991). For those in the precontemplation or contemplation stage, an action stage request (like "just say no") reflects a potential disconnect between what is being asked and where the individual might be in terms of his or her readiness to change. The development of motivational interviewing (Miller & Rollnick, 1991) provided a clinical approach that emphasized meeting people where they are in terms of their readiness to change, and helped to address this disconnect. Motivational interviewing is a nonjudgmental, nonconfrontational clinical approach utilized to elicit personally relevant reasons to change and to explore and resolve ambivalence (when applicable). Baer et al. (1992) compared the group-based Alcohol Skills Training Program to an individually delivered, motivational interviewing–based feedback session, and found that both groups significantly impacted alcohol use compared to a control group (with no differences between the intervention conditions). The intervention involving a one-on-one review of personalized feedback led to the development of BASICS.

BASICS is an individually focused intervention that involves an alcohol screening, followed by a feedback session. During the feedback session, data from the alcohol screening are summarized on a personalized feedback sheet, and a facilitator trained in motivational interviewing reviews the feedback with the student. When the student identifies unwanted effects related to alcohol use that he or she would like to see eliminated or reduced, the facilitator elicits and explores strategies for making changes. Compared to a high-risk control group and a general college student control group, students who participate in BASICS had significant reductions in their alcohol use and related consequences a full four years after the intervention (Baer, Kivlahan, Blume, McKnight, & Marlatt, 2001; Marlatt et al., 1998). Subsequent research has highlighted the importance and value of combining skills training strategies with motivational enhancement techniques in achieving reductions in drinking and related consequences (Cronce & Larimer, 2011; Larimer & Cronce, 2002, 2007). As technology has advanced and alternative delivery options have evolved, efforts have been made to implement interventions via computer, the web/Internet, and even cell phone and text messages (Cronce, Bittinger, Liu, & Kilmer, in press). Any one program, prevention effort, or intervention—regardless of delivery method—will be most impactful when part of a comprehensive strategy that includes work with the campus as a whole as well as the surrounding community (National Institute on Alcohol Abuse and Alcoholism [NIAAA], 2002).

A component of environmental strategies includes policies, and, importantly, consistent enforcement of policies. Campuses are encouraged to immediately educate students about policy guidelines and penalties (including the suggestion to send policies to students and their parents before they even begin their college career) so that students know what is and is not acceptable. The key, then, is consistent enforcement of those policies, since inconsistent enforcement creates mixed messages and could suggest that "rules are made to be broken" (NIAAA, 2002, p. 22). Student support for policies and enforcement of policy is generally much higher than many administrators would predict, and Saltz (2007) has demonstrated that students consistently underestimate the support that their peers have for policies.

Common Myths Surrounding Alcohol Use

There are several myths or misunderstandings surrounding alcohol and its effects that could contribute to students' initiation of alcohol use or the maintenance of high-risk drinking practices. While no means an exhaustive list, the following are some domains in which there may be opportunities for student life and student affairs professionals, as well as faculty members, to correct information in the context of formal prevention programs or even informal conversations.

"Alcohol makes me funnier, more social, and more flirty . . ."

One need look no further than essentially any commercial for alcohol to see the portrayal of a magical elixir that will enhance most social situations. Students can identify several interpersonal positive outcomes anticipated from the consumption of alcohol—yet, does alcohol really make these things happen? The answer to this question has a solid foundation in research using the balanced placebo design (George, Gilmore, & Stappenbeck, 2012; Kilmer et al., 2012). In a simulated bar setting (e.g., the University of Washington's Behavioral Alcohol Research Laboratory, or "BARLAB"), students over 21 who drink alcohol (and who have signed consent forms acknowledging that they may be served alcohol over the course of the experiment) are told they are being offered drinks that contain alcohol (which either contain alcohol or are placebos) or drinks that are alcohol-free (which either are, in fact, alcohol-free or contain alcohol). Students who believe they have been drinking, even when they receive an alcohol-free drink, nevertheless act more social, outgoing, talkative, flirtatious, and confident. Students who believe they are drinking alcohol-free beverages yet actually receive alcohol do not demonstrate interpersonal changes; although they may feel the effects of alcohol, they attribute what they are feeling to factors other than alcohol (e.g., being tired, being clumsy, or being warm). Research clearly shows that the social or interpersonal effects of alcohol are due more to expectations than to the alcohol itself. For students considering a change in their drinking, a barrier to making a change could be the concern that they will miss out on the social effects of alcohol if they drink less or stop drinking; yet, the science suggests these effects were never coming from the alcohol to start with.

"I need to sober up quickly—coffee, a cold shower, or exercise will make that happen."

The oxidation of alcohol is driven by a liver enzyme, alcohol dehydrogenase. The action of this liver enzyme results in the steady decrease of blood alcohol concentration (BAC, which describes the percentage of alcohol in the bloodstream) over time. While different sources report slightly different oxidation rates (e.g., .015% per hour to .017% per hour, or even as low as .012% per hour), the rate of oxidation is commonly estimated as the reduction of .016% from one's BAC per hour (Dimeff et al., 1999). This becomes simple math in the context of the legal limit. A student at .080% at midnight will not reach .000% until 5:00 a.m. A student at .160% at midnight will not reach .000% until 10:00 a.m. A student at .240% at midnight will not reach .000% until 3:00 p.m. the next day! This has significant implications for students who may be attending class or practice the next morning still under the influence of alcohol, as well as students who attempt to "sleep off" their buzz with the intent of driving the next day. Despite attempted remedies like coffee, a cold shower, or exercise, these do not speed up the rate of oxidation (at best, these strategies could make a person temporarily feel more alert, yet, because their BAC and associated effects remain unchanged, could have a false sense of security or safety). Students who try to eat (bread seems to be a popular choice) to "soak up" the alcohol are likely (1) misunderstanding that while eating prior to or while drinking can slow down the rate of absorption, eating after drinking does not help one sober up more rapidly, and (2) forgetting that the alcohol to be oxidized is in the blood stream.

"I can 'hold my liquor'—that means I handle alcohol better than other people."

Students may view tolerance, the phenomenon by which it takes more of a substance for someone to feel the expected effect, as a sign of status separating those who can "hold their liquor" from the "lightweights." Often, they misunderstand the difference between tolerance and blood alcohol concentration (BAC)—a person with tolerance will have the same BAC as a person without, meaning that the person with tolerance is not getting the cues or signs that suggest how impaired he or she may actually be. From the standpoint of risk for addiction, tolerance is one of the criteria for an alcohol use disorder, so it is clearly undesirable from a public health standpoint. However, studies examining the development of tolerance suggest significant overdose risks for students who feel they can "hold their liquor."

Siegel and Ramos (2002) remind readers of the principles of classical conditioning, such that a stimulus unrelated to another stimulus can, after repeated pairings, elicit a conditioned response (e.g., a dog salivating when a bell rings after the bell was repeatedly paired with the presentation of food). There is strong evidence that if someone drinks around the same set of cues (e.g., the same fraternity basement, the same room in a residence hall, the same bar), those cues become paired with the presentation of alcohol to the body. Why does this matter? Because alcohol slows down the central nervous system, and because the body tries to maintain homeostasis, these cues that signal that alcohol is coming can, over time, result in the body making an anticipatory response in the direction opposite of the substance's effect. For example, they explain that in response to receiving a central nervous system depressant (like alcohol) that slows down central nervous system functions, cues associated with the introduction of alcohol to the body (e.g., a particular room or bar) could, over time, signal to the body that alcohol is about to be consumed, resulting in the compensatory response of essentially trying to counteract the drug (Siegel, 2005). Then, if an individual drinks the same amount at the time this compensatory response is made, the subjective feelings of intoxication will not be as pronounced (i.e., the depressant effects of alcohol are masked, to some degree, by the compensatory effects elicited by the stimuli). Consequently, the person drinks more and will, over time, likely develop tolerance. This situational specificity of tolerance (Siegel, 2005) means that if someone with tolerance goes to a completely new environment away from cues that would typically prompt the conditioned compensatory response, this compensatory response will fail to occur. If the person drinks the same amount he or she typically drinks in the absence of this compensatory response, the full depressant effects will be experienced and the results could be devastating. This has significant implications for incoming students, since our campuses represent new sets of friends, new living environments, and new cues—tolerance can literally fail to follow them to the new environment. This also suggests that students on road trips to sporting events, trips for spring break, and, certainly, students studying abroad must be aware that the same amount they typically consume could affect them much more significantly in this new environment.

Peer Influence and Peer-Delivered Interventions

The powerful influence of peers on college student behavior is well documented in the literature. National surveys suggest that college students regard their peers as a credible and trusted source of information. Within the broad scope of the public health model, there are many arenas in which trained peer educators can serve as allies to assist in our prevention efforts, from the delivery of broad-based, universal interventions to individual-focused, early interventions. For example, these students, when trained and supervised, can help us develop, implement, and evaluate campus-wide social norms media campaigns that reduce alcohol and other drug use and related risk behaviors, carry out educational, informational, screening, and brief interventions, and operate referral services, such as hotlines, under professional supervision.

Across the broad scope of peer-based interventions, the theoretical and research literature on models of social influence offers support for focusing on peer influences as a key element of interventions designed to reduce excessive alcohol consumption. This includes research on perceived norms for drinking, social motives or expected social benefits of drinking, and modeling of heavy drinking as risk factors (Carey, 1993; Larimer, Irvine, Kilmer, & Marlatt, 1997; Paschall, Ringwalt, & Flewelling, 2002; Wood, Read, Palfai, & Stevenson, 2001). Theoretical models of social influence (Bandura, 1977) have stressed peer influences on a range of behaviors, and empirical evidence suggests the social context is of particular relevance for college student drinking (Carey, 1993, 1995). In particular, drinking attitudes and behaviors of peers are among the strongest correlates of adolescent alcohol use/abuse (Hawkins, Catalano, & Miller, 1992; Perkins, 2002). Within the college campus setting, peer and social influences are highly salient and frequently involve alcohol (Borsari & Carey, 2001; Collins, Parks, & Marlatt, 1985; Costa, Jessor, & Turbin, 1999). Specific peer influences related to college drinking include alcohol offers, social modeling, and perceived descriptive and injunctive norms (Graham, Marks, & Hansen, 1991; Larimer et al., 1997; Wood et al., 2001). Perceived descriptive norms include perceptions or misperceptions about what constitutes typical drinking behavior among peers (Reno, Cialdini, & Kallgren, 1993). College-age drinkers typically overestimate the amount of alcohol use and problems among peers (Baer & Carney, 1993; Baer, Stacy, & Larimer, 1991; Borsari & Carey, 2001). Consistent with the concept of "injunctive norms" (judgments of what is appropriate behavior; see Reno et al., 1993), students also misjudge the prevailing attitudes of others toward alcohol use and intoxication (Berkowitz &

Perkins, 1986; Prentice & Miller, 1993; O'Leary Tevyaw, Borsari, Colby, & Monti, 2007). Inaccurate perceptions of norms and attitudes regarding alcohol may result in the reinforcement and perpetuation of abusive drinking patterns.

The foregoing findings suggest that both broad-based and individually tailored peer education interventions for college drinking aimed at individual risk factors should incorporate normative correction, challenge expectations of social benefits of drinking, and provide models of responsible attitudes toward drinking. Recent research offers support that group-specific live and interactive interventions that deliver normative feedback designed to correct misperceptions of alcohol-related group norms have been effective in reducing drinking behavior at up to a six-month follow-up and that changes in perceived norms mediated the reductions in drinking (Cimini et al., 2009; LaBrie, Hummer, Neighbors, & Pedersen, 2008). Based on work in the area of peer influence as well as brief interventions for alcohol use among college students, the implementation of novel, technologically advanced, group-based, brief alcohol interventions delivered by trained and closely supervised peer educators that address the correction of norm misperceptions warrants further exploration, both with regard to their effectiveness in reducing alcohol use and in their practical efficiency and cost-effectiveness when delivered within college and university settings (Cimini et al., 2009).

Screening & Outreach Services

Broad-based screening of students who present at counseling centers and health centers is one important strategy for reaching students who may be struggling with alcohol use or who are experiencing negative consequences as a result of drinking (Larimer, Cronce, Lee, & Kilmer, 2005). As noted earlier in this chapter, a large portion of students who do choose to drink are doing so in a moderate way, but for those students who are struggling with dependence or who are experiencing and identifying negative consequences associated with drinking, the challenge remains in identifying and connecting to those students. Almost all (96%) of students with an alcohol use disorder (i.e., at the time of the study, either alcohol abuse or alcohol dependence based on *DSM-IV* criteria) receive no alcohol services of any kind (Wu, Pilowsky, Schlenger, & Hasin, 2007).

Universal screening can be an effective tool in reaching students who are exhibiting signs of an alcohol use disorder (AUD). Martens et al. (2007) screened students who came in for their regularly scheduled appointments in health and counseling centers. The students were screened for alcohol use disorders using the Alcohol Use Disorder Identification Test (AUDIT). Screening not only identified students who were at risk but also connected those students to a brief intervention, BASICS (Brief Alcohol Screening and Intervention for College Students). As a result of screening, students who were identified as being at risk ended up receiving an evidence-based intervention that resulted in reports of decreases in alcohol use, better understanding of drinking norms, and increases in protective strategies for students. Screening combined with an effective intervention like BASICS can be an important part of a comprehensive approach to addressing alcohol-related concerns on college campuses.

In addition to screening, another strategy for reaching students who may be struggling with alcohol use as well as other co-occurring mental health issues is strategic outreach. We know that not all students access health and mental health centers on campus, and therefore a challenge remains: How do campuses connect with students who are not accessing current services? At the University of Washington, Health & Wellness, a department in Student Life, actively seeks out students who have "hit the radar" as students of concern; the department utilizes a proactive intervention strategy to reach students rather than waiting for them to access services on campus. Health & Wellness often reaches students who are at the highest risk of falling through the cracks, students who are not connected in one way or another to support services on campus. Through a network of partnerships and collaborations, Health & Wellness gathers police reports, faculty concerns, and incident reports from the residential and Greek life offices to identify the students who may be in need of intervention, referrals, and support. The department also works collaboratively to consult with and advise faculty and staff to address concerns early on in an attempt to prevent a situation of stress from escalating into a student in distress.

Connections within student life offices and beyond are crucial for creating a holistic response for students who are in need of support. Students who are struggling with substance use may have co-occurring mental health concerns. For example, we know that a diagnosis of depression carries increased risk for co-occurring substance abuse or anxiety disorder (Weissman et al., 1996). Also a co-occurrence of depression and alcohol or other drug use increases the risk of suicide (Ross, 2004). Multidisciplinary departments like Health & Wellness are able to address complex and co-occurring concerns. In addition to the outreach services, a department versed in a variety of evidence-based interventions is able to assess and address a wide range of issues by having programs like Alcohol and Other Drugs Education, Sexual Assault, Stalking, Harassment, and Relationship Violence Information Service, and Suicide Intervention all housed in one department. The flexibility to address multiple issues in one department allows that department to meet the student's needs without having to juggle numerous referrals or trips across campus. Programs like Health & Wellness at the University of Washington are designed to create and manage a holistic response for students.

Changing Campus Culture

We have discussed several strategies in this chapter for holistic prevention, education, and intervention. So the question remains: How do we as faculty, staff, and administrators pull this all together? Is it simply enough to have a month dedicated to alcohol awareness as well as resources provided for AUD at orientation? Promising practices would tell us otherwise. We have a variety of ways and means of connecting to our students on campus. Programs based on a holistic and ecological model that incorporate a multifaceted approach to responding to alcohol and other health concerns, practices similar to a public health approach, seem to be making promising impacts on student health and mental health issues (Hunt & Eisenberg, 2009). This may sound daunting for administrators charged with education and intervention programs on campus. But what we can hope to accomplish is that by making advances in education around alcohol and other drugs we can also impact on other co-occurring campus health and safety concerns. When we help students to better understand their limits with alcohol we can help them recognize risky situations around sexual encounters and obtaining consent. When we discuss the impacts that a depressant like alcohol can have on someone in a depressive state, we can also address the risk factors of suicidal ideation and alcohol use. When we turn to bystander education and peer education to supplement our alcohol education, we can empower our students with the skills to be able to speak up and intervene when they are concerned about a friend's mental health. We as campus administrators, faculty, and staff have an opportunity to revolutionize the way we address health on our campus by breaking down the old barriers and silos that have traditionally separated programs like alcohol education, sexual assault prevention, and suicide prevention. We can create strategic prevention programs designed to address the impacts alcohol can have on students navigating sex and consent. We can talk about the risk factors involved in alcohol use and help our students connect the dots between alcohol abuse and co-occurring mental health concerns. If we utilize evidence-based education and interventions that have proven to be effective, we can begin to build a holistic health map that reaches beyond the once-a-month awareness campaign or health center brochure.

Implications and Future Directions for Student Life

The office of student life is uniquely situated to work collaboratively across campus, bridging the world of research and academics with service providers on campus. We are not constrained by academic specialties and can use our centralized positions on campus to bring together the best of what academia has to offer. Student life professionals can take the lead in planning comprehensive programs to reach students who may be having difficulty not only with alcohol use but also with other issues related to health or mental health by incorporating multiple strategies, from education and screening to intervention and support, using the framework of a comprehensive approach.

Student life professionals are naturally inclined and often already well placed to collaborate on social norming campaigns with student leaders and peer-education groups. These partnerships can address the dangerous and often misinformed perceptions of existing drinking cultures on campus. As identified earlier, peer education can play a crucial role in preventive education, especially around risky occasions like spring breaks and other holidays, by campaigning with relevant social norms and highlighting preventative measures to reduce unintended negative consequences of drinking for students who choose to drink. National networks, like BACCHUS, are leading initiatives across campuses in peer education programs by supporting students' academic and personal success and building skills in student leaders to address campus health and safety issues (NASPA, 2014). Student life professionals can be the change agents by reaching across academia, bridging disciplines, and bringing together evidence-based interventions. With the skills and the support of both administration and students, we can create strong programs that have real impacts on student health. Student life offices can reach the next level of impacting health by including strategic outreach mechanisms to connect with students who might not seek help on their own. A cohesive, campus-wide plan for education around alcohol can help us create blueprints for addressing other co-occurring health and mental health concerns, allowing us to build a foundation of prevention and intervention on a variety of topics. Dramatic and powerful changes, worthy of a Hollywood ending, can be a reality on each campus.

References

Anderson, D., & Gadaleto, A. (2012). The College Alcohol Survey: The national longitudinal survey on alcohol, tobacco, other drug and violence issues at institutions of higher education. 1979–2012. Unpublished results. George Mason University and West Chester University. Retrieved from www.caph.gmu.edu

Baer, J.S., & Carney, M.M. (1993). Biases in the perceptions of the consequences of alcohol use among college students. *Journal of Studies on Alcohol, 54*, 54–60.

Baer, J.S., Kivlahan, D.R., Blume, A.W., McKnight, P., & Marlatt, G.A. (2001). Brief intervention for heavy drinking college students: 4-year follow-up and natural history. *American Journal of Public Health, 91*, 1310–1316.

Baer, J.S., Marlatt, G.A., Kivlahan, D.R., Fromme, K., Larimer, M., & Williams, E. (1992). An experimental test of three methods of alcohol risk reduction with young adults. *Journal of Consulting and Clinical Psychology, 60*, 974–979.

Baer, J.S., Stacy, A., & Larimer, M. (1991). Biases in the perception of drinking norms among college students. *Journal of Studies on Alcohol, 52*, 580–586.

Bandura, A. (1977). *Social learning theory*. Englewood Cliff, NJ: Prentice- Hall.

Berkowitz, A.D., & Perkins, H.W. (1986). Problem drinking among college students: A review of recent research. *Journal of American College Health, 35*, 21–28.

Borsari, B., & Carey, K.B. (2001). Peer influences on college drinking: A review of the research. *Journal of Substance Abuse, 13*, 391–424.

Carey, K.B. (1993). Situational determinants of heavy drinking among college students. *Journal of Counseling Psychology, 40*, 217–220.

Carey, K.B. (1995). Alcohol-related expectancies predict quantity and frequency of heavy drinking among college students. *Psychology of Addictive Behaviors, 9*, 236–241.

Cimini, M.D., Martens, M.P., Larimer, M.E., Kilmer, J.R., Neighbors, C., & Monserrat, J.M. (2009). Assessing the effectiveness of peer-facilitated interventions addressing high-risk drinking among judicially mandated college students. *Journal of Studies on Alcohol and Drugs, 16*, 57.

Collins, R. L., Parks, G. A., & Marlatt, G. A. (1985). Social determinants of alcohol consumption: The effects of social interaction and model status on the self-administration of alcohol. *Journal of Consulting & Clinical Psychology, 53*, 189–200.

Costa, F.M., Jessor, R., & Turbin, M.S. (1999). Transition into adolescent problem drinking: The role of psychosocial risk and protective factors. *Journal of Studies on Alcohol, 60*, 480–490.

Cronce, J.M., Bittinger, J.N., Liu, J., & Kilmer, J.R. (in press). Electronic feedback in college student drinking prevention and intervention. *Alcohol Research: Current Reviews*.

Cronce, J.M., & Larimer, M.E. (2011). Individual-focused approaches to prevention of college student drinking. *Alcohol Research & Health, 34*, 210–221.

Del Boca, F.K., Darkes, J., Greenbaum, P.E., & Goldman, M.S. (2004). Up close and personal: Temporal variability in the drinking of individual college students during their first year. *Journal of Consulting and Clinical Psychology, 72*(2), 155–164.

Dimeff, L.A., Baer, J.S., Kivlahan, D.R., & Marlatt, G.A. (1999). *Brief alcohol screening and intervention for college students (BASICS).* New York, NY: Guilford Press.

Fry, C. C. (1945). A note on drinking in the college community. *Quarterly Journal of Studies on Alcohol, 6,* 243–248.

George, W. H., Gilmore, A. K., & Stappenbeck, C. A. (2012). Balanced placebo design: Revolutionary impact on addictions research and theory. *Addiction Research and Theory, 20,* 186–203.

Graham, J.W., Marks, G., & Hansen, W.B. (1991). Social influence processes affecting adolescent substance use. *Journal of Applied Science, 76,* 291–298 .

Hanson, D. J. (1982). The effectiveness of alcohol and drug education. *Journal of Alcohol and Drug Education, 27,* 1–13.

Hawkins, J.D., Catalano, R.F., & Miller, J.Y. (1992). Risk and protective factors for alcohol and other drug problems in adolescence and early adulthood: Implications for substance abuse prevention. *Psychological Bulletin, 112,* 64–105.

Hunt, J., & Eisenberg, D, (2009). Mental health problems and help-seeking behavior among college students. *Journal of Adolescent Health, 46,* 3–10.

Johnston, L.D., O'Malley, P. M., Bachman, J.G., Schulenberg, J.E., & Miech, R.A. (2014). *Monitoring the Future national survey results on drug use, 1975–2013: Vol. 1. Secondary school students.* Ann Arbor: Institute for Social Research, University of Michigan.

Kilmer, J.R., Cronce, J.M., & Larimer, M.E. (2014). College student drinking research from the 1940s to the future: Where we have been and where we are going [Supplemental material]. *Journal of Studies on Alcohol and Drugs, 75*(17), 26–35.

Kilmer, J.R., & Larimer, M.E. (2008). Case study: Drinking among sorority and fraternity students in the United States. In M. Martinic & F. Measham (Eds.), *Swimming with crocodiles: The culture of extreme drinking* (pp. 228–232). New York, NY: Routledge.

Kilmer, J.R., Palmer, R.S., Cronce, J.M., & Logan, D.E. (2012). Reducing the harms of college student drinking: How Alan Marlatt changed approaches, outcomes, and the field. *Addiction Research and Theory, 20,* 227–235.

Kivlahan, D.R., Marlatt, G.A., Fromme, K., Coppel, D.B., & Williams, E. (1990). Secondary prevention with college drinkers: Evaluation of an alcohol skills training program. *Journal of Consulting and Clinical Psychology, 58,* 805–810.

LaBrie, J. W., Hummer, J. F., Neighbors, C., & Pedersen, E. R. (2008). Live interactive group-specific normative feedback reduces misperceptions and drinking in college students: A randomized cluster trial. *Psychology of Addictive Behaviors, 22,* 141–148.

Larimer, M.E., & Cronce, J.M. (2002). Identification, prevention, and treatment: A review of individual-focused strategies to reduce problematic alcohol consumption by college students [Supplemental material]. *Journal of Studies on Alcohol, 63*(14), 148–163.

Larimer, M.E., & Cronce, J.M. (2007). Identification, prevention, and treatment revisited: Individual-focused college drinking prevention strategies 1999–2006. *Addictive Behaviors, 32,* 2439–2468.

Larimer, M.E., Cronce, J.M., Lee, C.M., & Kilmer, J.R. (2005). Brief intervention in college settings. *Alcohol Research & Health, 28*(2), 94–104.

Larimer, M.E., Irvine, D.L., Kilmer, J.R., & Marlatt, G.A. (1997). College drinking and the Greek system: Examining the role of perceived norms for high-risk behavior. *Journal of College Student Development, 38,* 587–598.

Lee, C. M., Neighbors, C., Lewis, M. A., Kaysen, D., Mittmann, A., Geisner, I. M., . . . Larimer, M. E. (2014). Randomized controlled trial of a spring break intervention to reduce high-risk drinking. *Journal of Consulting and Clinical Psychology, 82*(2), 189–201.

Marlatt, G.A., Baer, J.S., Kivlahan, D.R., Dimeff, L.A., Larimer, M.E., Quigley, L.A., . . . Williams, E. (1998). Screening and brief intervention for high-risk college student drinkers: Results from a two-year follow-up assessment. *Journal of Consulting and Clinical Psychology, 66*(4), 604–615.

Martens, M.P., Cimini, M.D., Barr, A.R., Rivero, E.M., Vellis, P.A., & Desemone, G.A. (2007). Implementing a screening and brief intervention for high-risk drinking in university-based health and mental health care settings: Reductions in alcohol use and correlates of success. *Addictive Behaviors, 32*, 2563–2572.

Martens, M. P., Dams-O'Connor, K., & Beck, N. C. (2006). A systematic review of college student-athlete drinking: Prevalence rates, sport-related factors, and interventions. *Journal of Substance Abuse Treatment, 31*, 305–316.

Martens, M. P., Dams-O'Connor, K., & Duffy-Paiement, C. (2006). Comparing off-season with in-season alcohol consumption among intercollegiate athletes. *Journal of Sport & Exercise Psychology, 28*, 502–510.

Miller, E., Kilmer, J. R., Kim, E. L., Weingardt, K. R., & Marlatt, G. A. (2001). Alcohol skills training for college students. In P. M. Monti, S. M. Colby, & T. A. O'Leary (Eds.), *Adolescents, alcohol and substance abuse: Reaching teens through brief intervention* (pp. 183–215). New York, NY: Guilford Press.

Miller, W. R., & Rollnick, S. (1991). *Motivational interviewing: Preparing people for change.* New York, NY: Guilford Press.

NASPA. (2014). BACCHUS initiatives. Retrieved from http://www.naspa.org/constituent-groups/groups/bacchus-initiatives

National Institute on Alcohol Abuse and Alcoholism. (2002). *A call to action: Changing the culture of drinking at U.S. colleges.* Bethesda, MD: National Institutes of Health, DHHS (NIH Publication No. 02–5010).

Neal, D. J., & Fromme, K. (2007). Hook 'em Horns and heavy drinking: Alcohol use and collegiate sports. *Addictive Behaviors, 32*(11), 2681–2693.

Neighbors, C., Atkins, D. C., Lewis, M. A., Lee, C. M., Kaysen, D., Mittmann, A., . . . Rodriguez, L. M. (2011). Event-specific drinking among college students. *Psychology of Addictive Behaviors, 25*, 702–707.

O'Leary, T. A., Brown, S. A., Colby, S. M., Cronce, J. M., D'Amico, E. J., Fader, J. S., . . . Monti, P. M. (2002). Treating adolescents together or individually? Issues in adolescent substance abuse interventions. *Alcoholism: Clinical and Experimental Research, 26*, 890–899.

O'Leary Tevyaw, T., Borsari, B., Colby, S. M., & Monti, P. M. (2007). Peer enhancement of a brief motivational interview with mandated college students. *Psychology of Addictive Behaviors, 21*, 114–119.

Paschall, M. J., Ringwalt, C. L., & Flewelling, R. L. (2002). Explaining higher levels of alcohol use among working adolescents: An analysis of potential explanatory variables. *Journal of Studies on Alcohol, 63*, 169–178.

Perkins, H. W. (2002). Surveying the damage: A review of research on consequences of alcohol misuse in college populations. *Journal of Studies on Alcohol Supplement, 14*, 91–100.

Prentice, D. A., & Miller, D. T. (1993). Pluralistic ignorance and alcohol use on campus: Some consequences of misperceiving the social norm. *Journal of Personality & Social Psychology, 64*, 243–256.

Prochaska, J. O., & DiClemente, C. C. (1991). The transtheoretical approach. In J. C. Norcross & M. R. Goldfried (Eds.), *Handbook of psychotherapy integration* (pp. 300–334). New York, NY: Basic.

Reno, R. R., Cialdini, R. B., & Kallgren, C. A. (1993). The transsituational influence of social norms. *Journal of Personality and Social Psychology, 64*, 104–112.

Ross, V. (2004). Depression, anxiety, and alcohol or other drug use among college students. Higher Education Center, US Department of Education. Retrieved from www.higheredcenter.org

Saltz, R. F. (2007). How do college students view alcohol prevention policies? *Journal of Substance Use, 12*, 447–460.

Siegel, S. (2005). Drug tolerance, drug addiction, and drug anticipation. *Current Directions in Psychological Science, 14*, 296–300.

Siegel, S., & Ramos, B.M.C. (2002). Applying laboratory research: Drug anticipation and the treatment of drug addiction. *Experimental and Clinical Psychopharmacology, 10*, 162–183.

Tremblay, P. F., Graham, K., Wells, S., Harris, R., Pulford, R., & Roberts, S. E. (2010). When do first-year college students drink most during the academic year? An Internet-based study of daily and weekly drinking. *Journal of American College Health, 58*(5), 401–411.

Weissman, M. M., Bland, R. C., Canino, G. J., Faravelli, C., Greenwald, S., Hwu, H. G., . . . Yeh, E. K. (1996). Cross-national epidemiology of major depression and bipolar disorder. *Journal of the American Medical Association, 276*(4), 293–299.

Wood, M. D., Read, J. P., Palfai, T. P., & Stevenson, J. F. (2001). Social influence processes and college student drinking: The mediational role of alcohol outcome expectancies. *Journal of Studies on Alcohol, 62*, 32–43.

Wu, L., Pilowsky, D. J., Schlenger, W. E., & Hasin, D. (2007). Alcohol use disorders and the use of treatment services among college-age young adults. *Psychiatric Services, 58*, 192–200.

Yusko, D. A., Buckman, J. F., White, H. R., & Pandina, R. J. (2008). Alcohol, tobacco, illicit drugs, and performance enhancers: A comparison of use by college student athletes and nonathletes. *Journal of American College Health, 57*, 281–289.

8

Prescription and Illicit Drug Abuse
Changing the Narrative
DAVID S. ANDERSON AND TOM HALL

Overview

Drugs have been a part of world cultures for centuries. Whether it is the opium culti-vated in lower Mesopotamia 5,400 years ago and the use of cannabis as medicine 4,000 years ago (Guerra-Doce, 2014), the invention of heroin by the Bayer Corpo-ration (Kahn, 2006), or the use of LSD to understand mental illness (Sandison & Whitelaw, 1957), substances have been around us, for various reasons, for a very long time. For many people, their purpose was medicinal treatment; for others, they were used as a way to relax. There were those who used substances to experiment for effects, and those who just wanted to experience a "different world," an "altered state," or a "high." Some people were curious and living on the edge, and some used drugs only because it seemed to be the thing to do, or because others were doing it (Goode, 1989).

If drugs have been around for what seems like forever, why bother with it now? What makes any of us think that we can make a difference? In short, while pre-scription drug abuse among college students is a growing concern (McCabe, 2008), other illicit drug abuse has long been a concern. Traditional drugs of abuse include hallucinogens, stimulants, opiates, and tranquilizers. Drug abuse is cyclical from one generation to another. The changing legal landscape surrounding marijuana has many concerned (Cerdá, Wall, Keyes, Galea, & Hasin, 2012).

This chapter provides an understanding of prescription and illicit drugs and focuses on a broad perspective of these substances and some frameworks and strategies that can extend beyond our current concerns. Some specific informa-tion is also provided about several current drugs of concern. Attention is provided to ways in which campus personnel at all levels can better address substance abuse, and to how they might alter their conversations with students and colleagues about drugs. A brief understanding and new insights about misconceptions of sub-stance use may provide direction to college personnel who interact with students. Through this understanding, both broad and specific, we can better educate and prepare our students about substance use, misuse, and abuse, ultimately leading them to make healthy, safe, and appropriate decisions.

Some Contextual Considerations

The focus of this chapter is on the illicit use of substances. Illicit is defined here as generally not accepted by society, and largely illegal. While there may be general agreement that heroin is illicit, where does marijuana stand? Moreover, how does this change as laws about marijuana are reconsidered? Similarly, how about the use of Adderall during exam periods; is that illicit?

Second, it is fair to say that virtually everyone has some experience with substance use. Some people have used drugs prescribed by a physician, and some have experimented with drugs. Some have used someone else's drugs, and others know friends, family members, or acquaintances who have used drugs. The point is that drugs are around all of us, and everyone has some knowledge or experience with drugs at some level. Therefore, it is reasonable to expect that everyone has some opinions or perspectives, and, while these may be valid from his or her personal perspective, they may not be globally true. This chapter seeks to provide some factual knowledge and offers some fresh perspectives.

Third, this chapter does not focus on drugs prescribed by a physician for a medical purpose. Rather, the chapter is about illegal or illicit use. As such, the chapter focuses on those who use both illegal and off-label prescription drugs for self-medication or cognitive enhancement.

Fourth, why are prescription and illicit drugs in the same chapter? Illicit drug use includes recreational use of prescription drug as well as illegal use of controlled substances.

Finally, as part of the contextual underpinnings of this chapter, it is helpful to have a different perspective about prescription and illicit drug misuse. This builds upon two items already noted: the long-term presence of substances throughout the history of the world, and the experience that virtually everyone has, at some level, with substance use. This assessment builds upon the often-cited "War on Drugs" widely touted in this country over recent decades, institutionalized by the naming of a "drug czar." The premise of such a "war" is that prescription and illicit drug misuse must be eradicated or eliminated. Rather than taking a "win or lose" position on drugs, the approach offered in this chapter is based on the view that substance misuse must be better managed. By redefining the framework, we can be more deliberate and practical when handling campus problems associated with substances abuse.

The Nature of the Problem

Some of the best, long-term national data comes from the Monitoring the Future study (MTF). Johnston, O'Malley, Bachman, Schulenberg, and Miech (2014) reported annual rates of marijuana use by full-time college students to be 35% (40% of men and 33% of women). Illicit drug use other than marijuana was reported by full-time college students to be 19% (23% of men and 16% of women). Full-time college students' yearly prevalence of nonmedical use of Adderall was 11% (13% of men and 9% of women). Annual usage rates of other substances include the following: cocaine (3%), hallucinogens (4%), narcotics other than heroin (5%), amphetamines (11%), sedatives (3%), tranquilizers (4%), and heroin (0.3%).

Johnston et al. (2014) report full-time college student 30-day marijuana use was 21% (28% of men and 16% of women). Illicit drug use other than marijuana was reported by full-time college students to be 8% (10% of men and 7% of women). Thirty-day use of other substances includes the following: cocaine (0.9%), hallucinogens (1%), narcotics other than heroin (1.5%), amphetamines (5.3%), sedatives (0.9%), tranquilizers (1.2%), and heroin (0.2%).

Between 1980 and 1991, the annual rate of illicit drug use dropped from 56% to 29% and between 1992 and 2001 peak annual use of any illicit substance did not exceed 38% (Johnston et al., 2014). After a decrease in 2006 (34%) an increase was observed in 2013 (39%) (Johnston et al., 2014). Data indicate illicit drug use appears to be trending upward. In addition to increases in all illicit substance use, the annual rate of illicit substance use other than marijuana increased between 2008 and 2013 from 15% to 19%. The availability of street-level prescription medication is believed to account for this increase.

Marijuana use has exhibited similar patterns, with 51% reporting annual use in 1980, and then declining to 27% in 1991. However, the current annual marijuana rate of 36% is the highest since 2006 (Johnson et al., 2014). In 2013 daily use of marijuana reported by college students was 5% (Johnston et al., 2014). This is the highest daily rate of use since 1981. We can expect continued growth in marijuana use as more states legalize medicinal and/or recreational use.

Further, 10% of people age 18–25 reported nonmedical uses of pain relievers in the last year (SAMHSA, 2013). According to the 2013 American College Health Association (ACHA) National College Health Assessment, 15% of college students reported using prescription drugs that were not prescribed to them within the last year, including:

- 8% who reported using stimulants (e.g., Ritalin, Adderall);
- 8% who reported using painkillers (e.g., OxyContin, Vicodin, Codeine);
- 4% who reported using sedatives (e.g., Xanax, Valium); and
- 3% who reported using antidepressants (e.g., Celexa, Lexapro, Prozac, Wellbutrin, Zoloft).

These rates demonstrate the current and continuing need to address substance abuse among students. While the majority of students are not abusing substances (as was the case over 30 years ago), the concern is with those students who are abusing these substances. The concern is with their overall health (including potential substance dependence issues), academic performance, personal development, and potential for negative consequences.

Beyond substance use rates, it is important to also acknowledge the consequences associated with the use of various substances. While these vary based on the individual, the substance, and various other factors, physical consequences may include impaired vision, poor judgment, risky behavior (driving under the influence), injury, sleep disturbances, violent behavior, loss of balance, overdose, sexually transmitted diseases, loss of coordination, and drug tolerance leading to substance use disorders. Emotional consequences can include irritability, anxiety, paranoia, mood swings, loss of confidence, depression, argumentativeness, and insecurity. From a cognitive perspective, consequences can include forgetfulness, decreased concentration, loss of short-term and long-term memory, poor work performance, irrational comments, slurred speech, lack of coherent thoughts, lowered attention, and bad judgment. Socially, consequences can include undeveloped social skills, disheveled appearance, relationship difficulties, family troubles, regretful behavior, isolation, embarrassing statements, and stressed friendships. Legal consequences can include charges for use of a controlled substance, driving while under the influence, reckless driving, endangering behavior, and other behaviors in violation of state or federal law, local ordinance, or campus policy. This listing provides a sense of the wide range of negative consequences that can occur.

Why People Use Substances

An understanding of why people use substances provides an opportunity to redirect potentially harmful and dangerous behavior. The reality is that college students, as well as people in general, use prescription and illicit drugs for a variety of reasons. Students' use of substances is organized around four broad clusters: physical, emotional, social, and cognitive. Physical reasons may be to relax, to sleep, to be more alert, to reduce withdrawal effects, to get a buzz or high, to front-load, to unwind, or to forget. Emotional reasons include numbing pain, to drown sorrows, to escape, to boost self-esteem, to gain confidence, and to feel good. Social goals involve using substances because others do, to share the experience with others, to change the mood, to experiment, to loosen up, to be friendly, to celebrate, and to enjoy life. Cognitive reasons are to focus attention, to stay alert, to improve memory, to be more creative, to organize thoughts, to better appreciate the scene, and to participate in a rite of passage.

The focus here is to attend to the causes of someone's illicit substance use. More specifically, what is the individual trying to achieve with his or her use of the substance? With the desired effect, are there other ways of achieving that effect? With this knowledge, we can propose other approaches that would address or answer these issues, without the health, safety, legal, and other problematic factors associated with the use of substances.

Educational approaches can include workshops and discussion groups about the facts related to illicit drugs and the illegal use of prescription drugs; they may include fact sheets and campaigns, lectures and educational programs, and peer education. They may also include in-service training so that staff members are communicating appropriate messages about substances, not reinforcing myths and misinformation, and directing students to various resources as needed.

Environmental strategies can include policy development, consistent enforcement, tiered sanctions based on repetition or severity of offense, substantive and student-developed alternative activities, and a positive campus environment that would obviate students' needs based on the range of causal factors underlying substance use. That is, listen to students' reporting of reasons for use, and design strategies that seek to address those same needs and issues. This is all part of the campus environment and campus culture that student affairs professionals foster.

Interpersonal approaches include one-on-one or small group discussions with students who have been involved with some of these substances. This may include assessments, psychoeducational approaches, and substance abuse intervention or treatment. The purpose of these strategies is to halt the harmful use of substances, to avoid acute negative consequences, and to address potential or actualized substance dependence.

With any of these approaches, and particularly those involving interaction with students, it might be appropriate and helpful to ask a student who has used (or is contemplating using) illicit or prescription drugs a question about their use—specifically, "What was it you were or are trying to achieve?" A deeper query may be, "If the use of illicit or prescription drugs was your solution to a problem or answer to a question, what was the question or problem that triggered your drug use?"

The goal is to reduce the risk of potential harm to our students, by striving to have them choose healthier and substance-free ways of coping with college life. Campus personnel have an opportunity to guide and help these students achieve their goals, without the personal, physical, emotional, and legal or campus conduct complications.

An Overall Understanding of Substances and the Human Body

Drugs are classified into different categories. A range of various classifications exists, depending on the purpose of the organizational schema. There are classifications based on factors such as the law (drug schedules), disease or condition, overall effects, or dependence potential. For this chapter, the legal framework and the general effects are examined.

Legally, there are five drug schedules. Schedule I includes drugs that have no currently accepted medical use, and which are viewed as having a high potential for abuse; examples within this schedule include heroin, LSD, ecstasy, peyote, and marijuana. While Schedule II also has a high risk of abuse, medical use is accepted with severe restrictions; examples include codeine, morphine, oxycodone, opium, amphetamine, fentanyl, and methadone. Schedule III, with abuse potential, has current medical treatment use and includes pentobarbital, dronabinol, anabolic steroids, and various narcotic drugs. Schedule IV drugs have a currently accepted medical benefit and have a lower potential for abuse than the drugs in previous categories; examples include Xanax, Valium, and Klonopin. Schedule IV drugs may lead to limited physical or psychological dependence relative to drugs in Schedule III. Schedule V drugs have currently accepted medical use and have a lower threshold for dependence relative to Schedule IV. Schedule V drugs include but are not limited to Robitussin, Lomotil, and Lyrica.

For general effects, consider three very broad conceptual groups: uppers, downers, and hallucinogens. Uppers include stimulant drugs, such as cocaine and crack, amphetamines, and nicotine. Downers include sedative-hypnotics, narcotics, and alcohol. Hallucinogens include LSD, peyote, and mescaline. Some drugs may cross over into different categories: Ecstasy is both an upper and a hallucinogen, and marijuana is generally viewed as a downer, but with some hallucinogenic properties. As a related note, some classifications take this three-group framework and further separate out the opiates from the depressants. They may also separate alcohol from other depressants; further, nicotine and caffeine may be separated from other stimulants. A helpful summary chart from the National Institute on Drug Abuse, with general classifications, substances, trade names, and effects, is shown in Table 8.1.

These general classifications—whether broad (uppers, downers, hallucinogens) or more focused groupings—help in understanding the general effects of substances on the body. Within each of these drug groupings are specific substances. For example, within the sedative-hypnotic category of benzodiazepines, many medically approved substances are used to address anxiety and sleep, including Xanax, Valium, Halcion, Centrax, and Rohypnol. Pharmaceutical companies are continuously refining and testing the substances available for medical use, to obtain the desired results for an individual, with no or minimal side effects. Physicians understand that "one size does not fit all" and that patients respond differently to various medications.

Notable is that this brief discussion focuses on authorized medical use; this does not address the unauthorized or clandestine production of substances not part of the medical system. There are individuals who use controlled substances manufactured for medical purposes, but diverted for nonprescribed medical or "off-label" (nonmedical) recreational use. An additional concern is the use of substances prepared in an unauthorized or clandestine setting. Questions should be raised about the quality and purity of these substances, and what is actually included in them. Not only are these types of substances illegal, but also they pose significant health risks and safety concerns important to recognize and share with our students.

Perhaps the most helpful framework is that which describes the physical effects of substance use. Seven principles help us understand the biological properties of substances.

Properties of the Substance. The primary factor is based on the substance ingested. If a person consumes a stimulant, the effects will be dramatically different from those of a sedative-hypnotic. With illicit drugs, such as cocaine, heroin, ecstasy, and others, the question is what is really in the substance. These substances are often altered or "cut" with unknown ingredients.

Characteristics of the Individual. This factor explains different effects of the same substance on different individuals. This includes gender, weight, body fat, age, prior experience, expectations, and the presence of food or other substances (including alcohol). It also includes factors such as body metabolism or other genetic aspects, affecting the speed and nature of substances being processed by the body. There are predisposing factors involving the brain's neurotransmitters, including neurological deficiencies.

Setting. The circumstances under which a substance is taken influence the effects of a drug. Whether this is alone or with others, in a place that is viewed as safe versus vulnerable to risky circumstances, makes a difference with how a person experiences the drug. With hallucinogens, for example, users often report having had a "good trip" or a "bad trip," with a significant factor being the person(s) with

TABLE 8.1 Selected Substances of Abuse and Their Effects

Drug classification	Trade name or other names	Duration (hours)	Usual method	Primary effects	Overdose effects
Narcotics					
Heroin	Diamorphine, horse, smack, black tar, *chiva, negra* (*black tar*)	3–4	Injected, snorted, smoked	Euphoria, drowsiness, respiratory depression, contracted pupils, nausea	Slow and shallow breathing, clammy skin, convulsions, coma, possible death
Morphine	MS Contin, Roxanol, Oramorph SR, MSIR	3–12	Oral, injected		
Hydrocodone	Hydrocodone w/ acetaminophen, Vicodin, Vicoprofen, Tussionex, Lortab	3–6	Oral		
Hydromorphone	Dilaudid	3–4	Oral, injected		
Oxycodone	Roxicet, oxycodone w/ acetaminophen, OxyContin, Endocet, Percocet, Percodan	3–12	Oral, injected		
Codeine	Acetaminophen, guaifenesin or promethazine w/codeine, Fiorinal, Fioricet, or Tylenol w/codeine	3–4	Oral, injected		
Other narcotics	Fentanyl, Demerol, methadone, Darvon, Stadol, Talwin, Paregoric, Buprenex	Variable	Oral, injected, snorted, smoked		

(*Continued*)

TABLE 8.1 (Continued)

Drug classification	Trade name or other names	Duration (hours)	Usual method		Primary effects	Overdose effects
Depressants						
Gamma-hydroxybutyric acid	GHB, liquid ecstasy, liquid X, sodium oxybate, Xyrem	3–6	Oral		Slurred speech, disorientation, drunken behavior without odor of alcohol, impaired memory of events, interacts with alcohol	Shallow respiration, clammy skin, dilated pupils, weak and rapid pulse, coma, possible death
Benzodiazepines	Valium, Xanax, Halcion, Ativan, Restoril, Rohypnol (Roofies, R-2), Klonopin	1–8	Oral, injected			
Other depressants	Ambien, Sonata, meprobamate, chloral hydrate, barbiturates, methaqualone (Quaalude)	2–6		Oral		
Stimulants						
Cocaine	Coke, flake, snow, crack, *coca*, *blanca, perico, nieve*, soda	1–2	Snorted, smoked, injected		Increased alertness, excitation, euphoria, increased pulse rate and blood pressure, insomnia, loss of appetite	Agitation, increased body temperature, hallucinations, convulsions, possible death
Amphetamine/methamphetamine	Crank, ice, cristal, krystal meth, speed, Adderall, Dexedrine, Desoxyn	2–4		Oral, injected, smoked		
Methylphenidate	Ritalin (Illy's), Concerta, Focalin, Metadate	2–4	Oral, injected, snorted, smoked			

(Continued)

TABLE 8.1 (Continued)

Drug classification	Trade name or other names	Duration (hours)	Usual method	Primary effects	Overdose effects
Other stimulants	Adipex-P, Ionamin, Prelu-2, Didrex, Provigil	2–4	Oral		
Hallucinogens					
MDMA and analogs	(Ecstasy, XTC, Adam), MDA (love drug), MDEA (Eve), MBDB	4–6	Oral, snorted, smoked	Heightened senses, teeth grinding and dehydration	Increased body temperature, electrolyte imbalance, cardiac arrest
LSD	Acid, microdot, sunshine, boomers	8–12	Oral		
Phencyclidine and analogs	PCP, angel dust, hog, love boat, Ketamine (Special K), PCE, PCPy, TCP	1–12	Smoked, oral, injected, snorted		
Other hallucinogens	Psilocybe mushrooms, mescaline, peyote cactus, ayahausca, DMT, dextromethorphan (DXM)	4–8	Oral		
Cannabis					
Marijuana	Pot, grass, sinsemilla, blunts, mota, yerba, grifa	2–4	Smoked, oral	Euphoria, relaxed inhibitions, increased appetite, disorientation	Fatigue, paranoia, possible psychosis
Tetrahydrocannabinol	THC, Marinol	2–4	Smoked, oral		
Hashish and hashish oil	Hash, hash oil	2–4	Smoked, oral		

whom they used the substance. Another important factor is homeostasis or system equilibrium; for example, with continued opiate use, an individual's brain responds to environmental cuing. Frequent drug use leads to predictable routines prior to use. The human brain is capable of responding to physical cues associated with drug use and may react to an expected effect before the drug is ingested. This process alters the dosage effect.

Dosage. The intensity of a psychoactive substance is influenced by dosage or volume and concentration or purity of the active ingredient in the substance. For example, marijuana with a THC concentration of 15% will have greater effects than marijuana with a THC concentration of 8%, assuming similar rates of consumption.

Means of Preparation. This principle is coupled with the method of use and distance from the plant. This refers to the way in which the substance is prepared. A substance in pill form is designed to be swallowed whole, just as a chewable tablet is designed to be chewed and a time-release capsule is designed to be swallowed. Leafy substances can be smoked or cooked or chewed, and liquids can be drunk or injected.

Method of Use. Based on how the substance is prepared, it can be used as designed (e.g., drink liquids, swallow the pills, and smoke leafy substances). However, substances might be used in unintended ways, such as crushing pills and snorting or vaporizing or injecting. Consider a time-release capsule that is crushed and ingested all at once, resulting in immediate as opposed to gradual effects.

Distance from the Plant. This principle emphasizes that substances in nature are generally less potent and less addictive. As a natural plant becomes processed, the active ingredient typically gets more concentrated and may also have synthetic materials added. Consider the opium plant; the plant's primary active ingredient, morphine, is used for pain management and has its strength enhanced with various combinations of other additives; one highly addictive adaptation is heroin, a Schedule I drug.

Here are some additional considerations, important in understanding how substances affect the body.

- Physically, a drug that works as designed for one person may have different or problematic effects for another person. A physician who prescribes a drug for a patient takes into consideration his or her personal health, other prescriptions, and individualized factors. Further, sometimes prescribed drugs have side effects, so the aim is to prescribe a drug that maximizes the desired therapeutic effects while minimizing adverse side effects. If a substance causes negative consequences for a patient, the physician will likely try to find a different medication that does not have the same side effects, while maintaining the overall effectiveness.
- Most college students are between the ages of 18 and 25. Because of the plasticity of the brain during these years substances such as marijuana may lead to persistent cognitive deficits (Feinstein, Richter, & Foster, 2012). The developing brain is thus more vulnerable to the effects of various substances (Squeglia, Jacobus, & Tapert, 2009).

- Overall, the body does not know anything about the substance(s) being put into it; it just responds. It doesn't know why a person is using the substance, where it was prepared, whether it is pure, or whether additives are included. It doesn't know what other substances are in the body (prescription, over-the-counter, herbal, or illicit), with potential interaction effects. It just responds to what is ingested.
- Many drugs have the potential for dependence; this is true regardless of whether the substance is an illicit drug or a prescription drug. Some individuals become dependent on a substance, and others do not, even though their usage patterns may be identical. The reason dependence happens isn't precisely clear, but it's based on lots of factors, primarily predisposing genetic as well as constitutional factors, such as lifestyle behaviors, diet, exercise, and stress management (Swendsen & Le Moal, 2011). Couple these personal factors with frequency and dosage of the use of the substance, and some individuals become harmfully involved and dependent while others do not. Physical dependence progresses along a continuum of use, misuse, abuse, dependence, and addiction. Dependence and addiction are manifest in the inability to stop using a drug despite its physical and emotional harms.
- With all substances—legal and illegal, licit and illicit—there is much that is known and much that remains unknown. Just as new knowledge continues to evolve over time, new substances continually appear on the street (both prescribed and illicit). Labs associated with pharmaceutical companies continue to develop and test new drugs to meet various diseases and ailments; similarly, clandestine labs also create new substances to meet the continual demand.

Marijuana: A Brief Overview

Specific attention to marijuana (cannabis) is provided here because of the changing climate nationally surrounding this substance. Daily or almost daily marijuana use has reached a 30-year high among college students (Johnston et al., 2014). It is worth noting that death directly caused by marijuana use is minimal to nonexistent; that is, an individual does not overdose from marijuana consumption. This does not, however, mean that marijuana is not implicated in deaths; consider marijuana-impaired driving or other impaired judgments. Second, marijuana has adverse effects; research indicates marijuana can affect critical thinking skills and memory (Ilan, Smith, & Gevins, 2004). Third, addiction does occur with marijuana; while milder than dependence on many other substances, an individual can be diagnosed with a marijuana dependence disorder (Dennis, Babor, Roebuck, & Donaldson, 2002).

The current potency of marijuana raises new concerns about the prevalence of cannabis use disorders. A comparison of samples seized by the Drug Enforcement Administration between 1995 and 2008 revealed the percentage of the primary active ingredient tetrahydrocannabinol (THC) in marijuana increased from 3% to 9% (Mehmedic et al., 2010). The increased potency of marijuana raises concerns about adolescent brain development and the risk of dependence. Educators are concerned about research findings that link diminished academic achievement and marijuana use (Brook, Stimmel, Zhang, & Brook, 2008). In addition to learning deficits, the onset of mental health disorders may be associated with chronic marijuana use. Volkow, Baler, Compton, and Weiss (2014) report that chronic marijuana use, especially when initiated during adolescence, negatively impacts lifetime achievement. Marijuana use is also associated with addiction to other substances, which exacerbates concerns about potential deficits in academic achievement and psychosocial development among adolescent marijuana users.

Despite concerns raised by the medical and public health community, the stigma attached to marijuana use is diminishing. Favorable attitudes about marijuana have led to marijuana being viewed as a safer alternative to prescription drugs for treating a myriad of medical conditions, including but not limited to chronic pain, epilepsy, nausea, wasting syndrome, and glaucoma. The status of marijuana as medicine has bolstered assertions that recreational marijuana use is less harmful than alcohol.

The evolving legal scene related to marijuana has led to new challenges. Impaired driving is one of the challenges. Whitehill, Rivera, and Moreno (2014) found that 44% of male students drove after smoking marijuana and 51% rode with a driver who was under the influence of marijuana. O'Malley and Johnston (2013) caution "despite considerable progress in reducing driving under the influence of alcohol or riding with a driver who has been drinking, driving or riding after marijuana use is on the rise" (p. 2034). While the effects of alcohol impairment on driving are better understood than the effects of marijuana impairment on driving, accident and injury trends are emerging that highlight the risks of buzzed driving. Marijuana-impaired driving is similar to alcohol-impaired driving; both substances impede one's ability to safely operate a motor vehicle (Li et al., 2012). Specific concerns about marijuana-impaired driving include disturbances in one's depth perception, reaction times, and vehicle rate of speed. Initiatives that legalize medical or recreational marijuana that do not prescribe legal limits for marijuana-impaired driving are concerning for traffic safety organizations. Common definitions for marijuana-impaired drivers are inconsistent; THC levels that define marijuana intoxication range between 2 and 5 nanograms per milliliter. The lack of availability of roadside testing kits to determine THC levels is also problematic. When consistent THC levels for legal impairment are established, it will remain difficult for a marijuana user to know how many hits it takes to cross the legal threshold.

College and community policy makers are faced with several unanswered questions related to the unintended consequences of marijuana legalization. How will campuses adapt policy to allow for medical use of marijuana on campus? Will students who use medical marijuana have the option of living on campus? Health marketing campaigns could highlight protective factors associated with moderate marijuana use. Will health promotion efforts include risk reduction strategies similar to those for alcohol? Will resident assistants hold floor meetings to discuss how to smoke or consume marijuana responsibly? Will social marketing campaigns highlight the number of students who have only one or two tokes per week? How juxtaposed are these responsible use messages with decades of rhetoric for prohibition and punishment? How will faculty and staff discuss these issues, including their own experiences? These are just a few questions with which college personnel may be confronted in the foreseeable future.

Prescription Drugs as "Study Aids"

The incidence of misuse of prescription stimulants, such as Adderall or Ritalin, is second only to marijuana for college students (McCabe, Teter, & Boyd, 2006). Noteworthy among college students is the use of prescription stimulants as a way of enhancing study skills during the exam period at the end of an academic term. Many college students view Adderall as part of college life (DeSantis & Hane, 2010). Adderall and other stimulants prescribed to treat attention-deficit/hyperactivity disorder (ADHD) appear to increase mental acuity for some; however, it is unclear if these effects improve the ability to process complex information and increase recall among normal, healthy adults (Farah, Haimm, Sankoorikal, & Chatterjee, 2009; Franke, Bagusat, Rust, Engel, & Lieb, 2014). Placebo or expectancy effects may explain the perceived benefit of intermittent Adderall use as a study drug (Looby & Earleywine, 2011). Students may use study drugs to cope with pressure to perform academically or to "cram" prior to a final exam or important project. The perception among students of increased pressure to perform academically may be a partial explanation for the use of study drugs.

Adderall has physical, legal, and disciplinary consequences. Obtaining prescription stimulants without a physician's order bypasses a physical exam and a review of medical history. Contraindications related to off-label use (use in a way not specified by the FDA with its approved uses) include the risk of serious side effects. The most common side effects include sleep and appetite disruption, as well as personality changes. Less common side effects include seizures and disturbance of cardiac function. In addition to legal consequences, there is risk of dependency from using any controlled substance, including off-label use of prescription stimulants.

The perception that off-label prescription stimulant use is inconsequential is concerning for health professionals and educators. Permissive attitudes toward off-label stimulant abuse may lead to serious harm for the user. Until more is known about the long-term effects of using stimulants for academic doping, it is prudent to err on the side of caution. Many students believe off-label prescription stimulants are readily accessible and pose little harm to the user. The notion that prescription stimulants are safer than nonprescribed stimulants is generally true in relation to potency. The effect of any controlled substance (prescription or illegal) is variable, and requires the care and expertise of medical personnel. It is important for higher education professionals to challenge myths and misperceptions that the dosage and effects of controlled substances (especially prescription) are well known and therefore safe.

An Emerging Concern: Heroin

Heroin use is not typically associated with college students. However, the use of heroin among college students deserves our attention. According to the National Survey on Drug Use and Health (NSDUH), the number of past-year heroin users in the United States nearly doubled between 2005 and 2012, from 380,000 to 670,000, and heroin overdose deaths increased by almost 50% (Centers for Disease

Control and Prevention, 2012). Heroin use is not only an urban problem but also an emerging problem in rural and suburban areas. Healthcare providers and counselors are now more likely to see students who are abusing heroin (Lambie & Davis, 2007).

Several factors may explain heroin use among youth; the street cost of heroin is often less than illicit prescription pain medication, and heroin use is seen as a substitute for illicit use of prescription pain medication. Powerful prescription pain medication was introduced in the 1990s to treat chronic severe pain. However, in the past decade pain medication became easily available as a street drug. Recreational users' illicit use of prescription pain medication, misperceived as a "safe" alternative to heroin, coupled with easy access, fueled the popularity of prescription opiates in recent years. The increased purity of heroin is also a factor in its growing acceptance. Previous generations of heroin users injected heroin to get the effect; because of increased potency, today's heroin users have the option of snorting or smoking heroin. Some students believe heroin can be managed as long as the route of administration excludes intravenous injection. This, of course, is untrue.

The cost of illicit pain medication has increased due to new regulatory systems that track patient access to prescribed controlled substances. Unfortunately a great number of young people who abused prescription medications are turning to illicit street drugs because of the difficulty of obtaining prescription painkillers. Regular opiate abuse leads to tolerance and ultimately increased dosing. Eventually the opiates have no euphoric effect and are needed to avoid physical illness resulting from withdrawal. Sadly, for the addict, nausea, diarrhea, muscle soreness, fever, and chills replace the euphoria heroin previously induced. Campuses can better prepare for managing the challenges of re-emerging heroin use with early intervention. Screening in campus health centers and counseling centers is a first step; a second step is helping students who have a substance use disorder locate treatment resources. Heroin use is highly stigmatized, and users typically feel intense guilt and shame. Parents also experience similar feelings after their student is treated for heroin use. Historically, young people do not present for their first treatment episode with an opiate addiction; alcohol or stimulant abuse is more common. However, access to prescription opiates has changed the landscape and many more young adults are presenting to treatment for the first time with an opiate addiction.

Addiction, Dependence, and Substance Use Disorder

According to the American Society of Addiction Medicine (ASAM), addiction is a primary, chronic disease of brain reward, motivation, memory, and related circuitry. The consensus among medical providers is that addiction has a physical beginning, stemming from an individual's physiological or genetic characteristics. Addicts are thought to have a predisposition to chemical dependence because of a genetic or pathophysiological vulnerability that causes chemical dependence (Le Moal & Koob, 2007). The American Psychiatric Association publishes the *Diagnostic and Statistical Manual of Mental Disorders (DSM)*, the fifth edition (2013) being the most recent version. The *DSM-V* is a classification of mental disorders, and provides healthcare providers uniform descriptions of mental disorders and standard criteria for the evaluation and diagnosis (American Psychiatric Association, 2013).

The *DSM-V* combines previous categories of substance abuse and substance dependence into a single disorder, substance use disorder, measured on a continuum from mild to severe. Each particular substance is addressed as a separate use disorder (e.g., alcohol use disorder, stimulant use disorder), but nearly all substances are diagnosed based on the same overarching criteria. The criteria for substance use disorder include the following: larger amounts of a drug taken over a longer period of time than intended; a persistent desire to or unsuccessful effort to cut down use; a great deal of time spent in activities necessary to obtain and use the drug and recover from its effects; a craving or strong desire to use a substance; social role impairment; social or interpersonal problems caused or exacerbated by drug use; important social, occupational, or recreational activities given up or reduced; and hazardous use, withdrawal, and tolerance. Having two or more of these criteria within a 12-month period serves as the basis for a clinical diagnosis.

Terminology on this issue is important. Thus, it is important that faculty and staff on campus are aligned with the most current and clinically appropriate language, even though this same audience of professionals is not made up of clinicians. Physicians and behavioral health professionals recognize the addicted person does not choose to become an alcoholic or addict, nor does the illness stem from a lack of willpower, which was a commonly held view in our society for years. Sadly, the perception that addiction is a moral or character issue still resonates with many on college campuses and in surrounding communities.

Campus Prevention Strategies

Campus personnel need to determine the overall framework within which the use of illicit and prescription drugs will be handled. A legalistic or policy approach, while necessary, does not constitute the entire approach. Negative consequences and problematic behavior must be addressed. They must also be viewed as opportunities to become involved in the lives of students, to address, and, ideally, halt problematic behavior. Since substance use disorders are understood on a continuum, it is better (yet often more difficult) to address the behavior at earlier stages. Early intervention is critical from two broad perspectives. First, it can help reduce the harm to an individual or others, regarding the behavior itself and the immediate consequences. Second, it is helpful for impeding the development of substance use disorder. The strategies identified here can be helpful for each of these, as they can help redirect or minimize immediate harm (e.g., impaired driving) as well as make a difference with the progression along the continuum of the substance use.

In recent years, many campuses have implemented harm reduction strategies as part of their health promotion efforts. Harm reduction strategies are grounded on cognitive behavioral theory (CBT). Education is an important part of harm reduction. Personalized feedback is an important part of teaching individuals how their thoughts, beliefs, and attitudes activate emotions that influence their decision to use illicit substances. Motivational enhancement theory (MET) is a complementary strategic intervention to limit substance use harm to the individual and society. Cognitive behavioral and motivational enhancement strategies are useful tools, including imparting nonbiased information essential to motivating self-awareness and change. An important assumption related to motivational enhancement is that people change when they are ready to do so. Lastly, harm reduction strategies address social integration and community.

Typically, students experience negative consequences before being referred for an assessment by a mental health professional. Early intervention is within the scope of responsibilities for student affairs professionals, peer educators, and faculty members. Academic advisors, resident assistants, parents, and friends are often the first to recognize the onset of poor academic performance, interpersonal conflict, and dysthymia. It is important for nonclinicians to recognize signs of both negative consequences associated with substance abuse and indicators of a potential substance use disorder; further, it is important for these individuals to have the confidence to intervene. Providing personalized normative feedback about alcohol consumption is an effective intervention strategy that may be provided by nonmedical or mental health professionals. In addition, the Alcohol Use Disorder Identification Test (AUDIT) and the Cannabis Use Disorder Identification Test (CUDIT) are each 10-question assessment instruments that are easy to administer and score by nonclinical staff. Online programs designed to assess risk related to marijuana use and provide normative feedback are also readily available. The establishment of a broad array of integrated intervention approaches is necessary for finding, engaging, and enabling students to seek help.

The philosophy of harm reduction incorporates nonjudgmental and noncoercive approaches based on positive regard and the belief that all individuals can engage in self-directed change. Critics of harm reduction are apprehensive that students may interpret these approaches as implicit approval of risky or illegal behavior. However, it is important to point out that harm reduction does not ignore health threats associated with dangerous behavior. Effective intervention moves clients toward action, and any movement in the direction of change toward less danger and harm, and greater health and safety, is desirable. With the changing legal climate and public opinion on marijuana use, discussions are warranted on campus regarding the appropriate adaptation of harm reduction strategies for marijuana use, as well as for all illicit substances.

Campus Intervention and Treatment Strategies for Substance Use Disorder

Campus health centers, counseling centers, and dean of students offices often interact with students in need of substance abuse care. Three different but related strategies are examined in this section: substance use intervention, treatment, and recovery or aftercare. A brief, nonjudgmental assessment of adverse consequences related to a student's substance use, displaying concern for their academic and personal success, provides a platform to make referrals to campus healthcare providers who can provide a biopsychosocial assessment. A clinical assessment determines the nature and extent of substance use; it may be determined that the individual does not have a substance use disorder, but needs counseling or intervention to address problematic behavior. Should there be a clinical diagnosis, a determination is made about what treatment may be most appropriate, and an intervention or treatment plan is created and implemented. If a student reports a history of a substance use disorder, a referral to recovery support resources is advised. Collegiate recovery programs (CRC) are expressly designed for this student population. Campus CRC programs often incorporate an array of support services, including but not limited to academic advising, alternative housing options, academic scholarships, support groups, and substance-free social activities. How campuses respond to students in recovery or with untreated substance use disorders differs; some campuses do not have campus-based intervention, treatment, or CRC services. Students may be referred to noncampus-based providers for substance abuse intervention or treatment. An alternative approach is for campuses to offer substance abuse clinical intervention, treatment services, and CRC programs.

Typical campus-based intervention includes an agreement between the therapist and the student to monitor his or her substance use and report all use in counseling sessions. Intervention strategies include teaching students how to identify protective behaviors designed to reduce unintended consequences related to substance use. Applying protective behaviors taught by campus interventionists leads to personalized plans for reducing a student's substance use. When students make a plan to reduce their substance use, therapists assist them in developing strategies to cope with high-risk situations that are coupled with substance abuse.

Substance abuse treatment differs from substance use intervention. A standard treatment plan includes specific goals, objectives, and tasks linked to abstinence or risk reduction. Treatment may lead to a referral to a residential or hospital program or an intensive outpatient program. Inpatient hospitalization is recommended for students who need detoxification, followed by intensive treatment within a residential setting. Inpatient hospitalization varies from several days to a few weeks. Residential care usually lasts 28 days or more. Sometimes patients move to aftercare residences for several months before returning to college. Intensive outpatient treatment programs provide 9 or more hours of counseling per week and typically run for 12 weeks. Patients who attend intensive outpatient treatment are frequently required to also attend self-help groups. Students referred to inpatient or intensive outpatient treatment may be granted a medical withdrawal from classes. Typically students who require this level of substance abuse treatment need to take a break from their studies and focus on recovery. An advantage of providing on-campus treatment services for students is better coordination of care between healthcare providers and better access to academic advising, legal services, and other services offered by the university. Campus-based treatment providers collaborate with medical and behavioral health professionals. Outpatient treatment provided by campus-based providers is typically more affordable for students and is likely to reduce disruption to students' academic studies.

The disadvantage of providing on-campus treatment includes the costs of providing access to substance abuse treatment care. Some campuses may not have the infrastructure to provide campus-based substance abuse treatment services, including staffing and appropriate expertise. Philosophical concerns may limit the scope of mental health and behavioral health services provided on campus. Some university administrators do not want their campus to be perceived as having, or perceived as catering to, substance-dependent students. Another downside to providing on campus treatment services is the real or perceived concerns about the confidentiality of campus-based substance use intervention or treatment. Well-meaning faculty and nonmedical staff may not understand the need to maintain student confidentially and discuss referrals with peers or colleagues. On-campus treatment may increase the possibility of stigma attached to those individuals referred to these campus services or known to be receiving services.

Lastly, recovery from substance addiction is different from substance use treatment or intervention. It is important to recognize characteristics of both students in recovery and students in treatment. Student in recovery recognize their addiction and understand how to avoid people, places, and thinking that lead to relapse. Students returning to campus after treatment often need additional academic advising and support. However, students in recovery have developed a commitment to sobriety and are resolute to maintain their sobriety. Because of their determination and resolve, students in recovery often perform academically as well or better than other student cohorts (Botzet, Winters, & Fahnhorst, 2008). These students look for opportunities to experience a "normal" college experience without the worn-out "rite of passage" narratives. They lead by example and show it is possible to enjoy football tailgating, attend parties, and experience campus traditions without the influence of alcohol and other drugs. Students in recovery create new campus traditions that engage students who are looking for an alternative to the "party" scene.

Self-Help Groups

Peer-led support or self-help groups are an important part of self-change and reflection regardless of whether one chooses an abstinence-only or harm reduction substance abuse treatment strategy. Within peer-facilitated support groups, recovery becomes a lived experience apart from prescribed therapeutic activities of professionally led treatment programs. Three different support groups are highlighted in this chapter. First, 12-step programs are the most widely recognized support groups, with an ongoing history of success dating back to the 1940s. Alcoholics Anonymous is the largest of all the 12-step programs; Narcotics Anonymous is the second largest and accommodates members who are recovering from addiction to alcohol and other drugs. The focus of this abstinence-based approach is recovery from the physical, mental, and emotional consequences of the loss of control and a commitment of oneself to a higher power in order to facilitate recovery. The process of working through universal "steps" is intended to substitute self-centered beliefs and actions with a greater awareness of how their addictive behaviors result in dysfunctional relationships.

Second, SMART Recovery is a nonfaith-based, peer-facilitated support group centered on cognitive behavioral theory. It is also based on abstinence from substances. SMART Recovery supports (a) individual progression toward motivation to remain sober, (b) strategies to cope with urges to abuse substances, (c) dealing with attitudes, beliefs, and behaviors that lead to substance abuse, and (d) mindfulness.

Lastly, Harm Reduction, Alcohol Abstinence and Management Support (HAMS), informed by harm reduction, does not require or encourage abstinence. This non-judgmental approach to support provides individuals help to make desired changes in their behavior. Individuals who use alcohol and other drugs are welcomed and supported regardless of whether they choose safer use, reductions in use, or quitting altogether.

Conclusions

The chapter has been designed to provide an overview, and an imperative, regarding the importance of addressing prescription and illicit drug abuse among college students. Grounded in the concept of helping students seek healthier, safer, and more effective ways of meeting their needs, the focus of this chapter has been upon identifying some of the more current issues surrounding illicit drug abuse. Further, since the landscape regarding these substances continues to evolve with the presence of new substances and new interest in older or existing substances, it is important that campus personnel remain vigilant about students' behavior, perceptions, and attitudes.

No quick fixes for this subject matter exist. What is important is to have a healthy perspective that seeks to reshape the campus culture, and the role of illicit and prescription drug abuse within that setting. Part of this reshaping is a changed conversation among professionals and between professionals and students. It is vital to harness the numerous resources that do exist regarding substances, intervention, treatment, and recovery. Finally, this can be viewed as an opportunity to reshape our campuses and provide students with skills and attitudes helpful for better addressing the various challenges and opportunities they will face during their own lifetimes.

References

American College Health Association. (2013). American College Health Association-National College Health Assessment II: Reference Group Executive Summary, Spring 2013. Hanover, MD: Author.

American Psychiatric Association. (2013). *Diagnostic and statistical manual of mental disorders* (5th ed.). Washington, DC: Author.

Botzet, A. M., Winters, K., & Fahnhorst, T. (2008). An exploratory assessment of a college substance abuse recovery program: Augsburg College's StepUP Program. *Journal of Groups in Addiction & Recovery, 2*(2–4), 257–270.

Brook, J.S., Stimmel, M.A., Zhang, C., & Brook, D.W. (2008). The association between earlier marijuana use and subsequent academic achievement and health problems: A longitudinal study. *American Journal on Addictions, 17*(2), 155–160.

Centers for Disease Control and Prevention, National Center for Health Statistics. (2012). Multiple Cause of Death 1999–2010. http://wonder.cdc.gov/

Cerdá, M., Wall, M., Keyes, K.M., Galea, S., & Hasin, D. (2012). Medical marijuana laws in 50 states: Investigating the relationship between state legalization of medical marijuana and marijuana use, abuse and dependence. *Drug and Alcohol Dependence, 120*(1), 22–27.

Dennis, M., Babor, T.F., Roebuck, M.C., & Donaldson, J. (2002). Changing the focus: The case for recognizing and treating cannabis use disorders. *Addiction, 97*(s1), 4–15.

DeSantis, A.D., & Hane, A.C. (2010). "Adderall is definitely not a drug": Justifications for the illegal use of ADHD stimulants. *Substance Use & Misuse, 45*(1–2), 31–46.

Farah, M.J., Haimm, C., Sankoorikal, G., & Chatterjee, A. (2009). When we enhance cognition with Adderall, do we sacrifice creativity? A preliminary study. *Psychopharmacology, 202*(1–3), 541–547.

Feinstein, E.C., Richter, L., & Foster, S.E. (2012). Addressing the critical health problem of adolescent substance use through health care, research, and public policy. *Journal of Adolescent Health, 50*(5), 431–436.

Franke, A.G., Bagusat, C., Rust, S., Engel, A., & Lieb, K. (2014). Substances used and prevalence rates of pharmacological cognitive enhancement among healthy subjects. *European Archives of Psychiatry and Clinical Neuroscience, 264*(1), 83–90.

Goode, E. (1989). *Drugs in American society.* New York, NY: Knopf.

Guerra-Doce, E. (2014). The origins of inebriation: Archaeological evidence of the consumption of fermented beverages and drugs in prehistoric Eurasia. *Journal of Archaeological Method and Theory,* 1–32. doi:10.1007/s10816-014-9205-z

Ilan, A.B., Smith, M.E., & Gevins, A. (2004). Effects of marijuana on neurophysiological signals of working and episodic memory. *Psychopharmacology, 176*(2), 214–222.

Johnston, L.D., O'Malley, P.M., Bachman, J.G., Schulenberg, J.E., & Miech, R.A. (2014). *Monitoring the Future national survey results on drug use, 1975–2013: Vol. 2. College students and adults age 19–55.* Ann Arbor: Institute for Social Research, University of Michigan.

Kahn, R.B. (2006). Myth, misunderstanding & stigma. In M. Stanford & D. Avoy (Eds.), *Professional perspectives on addiction medicine* (pp. 99–104). Santa Clara, CA: Santa Clara Valley Health & Hospital System, Department of Alcohol & Drug Services, Addiction Medicine and Therapy Division.

Lambie, G.W., & Davis, K.M. (2007). Adolescent heroin abuse: Implications for the consulting professional school counselor. *Journal of Professional Counseling: Practice, Theory & Research, 35*(1), 1–17.

Le Moal, M., & Koob, G.F. (2007). Drug addiction: Pathways to the disease and pathophysiological perspectives. *European Neuropsychopharmacology, 17*(6), 377–393.

Li, M.C., Brady, J.E., DiMaggio, C.J., Lusardi, A.R., Tzong, K.Y., & Li, G. (2012). Marijuana use and motor vehicle crashes. *Epidemiologic Reviews, 34*(1), 65–72.

Looby, A., & Earleywine, M. (2011). Expectation to receive methylphenidate enhances subjective arousal but not cognitive performance. *Experimental and Clinical Psychopharmacology, 19*(6), 433.

McCabe, S.E. (2008). Screening for drug abuse among medical and nonmedical users of prescription drugs in a probability sample of college students. *Archives of Pediatrics & Adolescent Medicine, 162*(3), 225–231.

McCabe, S.E., Teter, C.J., & Boyd, C.J. (2006). Medical use, illicit use and diversion of prescription stimulant medication. *Journal of Psychoactive Drugs, 38*(1), 43–56.

Mehmedic, Z., Chandra, S., Slade, D., Denham, H., Foster, S., Patel, A.S., Ross, S.A., Khan, I.A., & ElSohly, M.A. (2010). Potency Trends of 9-THC and Other Cannabinoids in Confiscated Cannabis Preparations from 1993 to 2008. *Journal of Forensic Sciences, 55*(5), 1209–1217.

O'Malley, P.M., & Johnston, L.D. (2013). Driving after drug or alcohol use by U.S. high school seniors, 2001–2011. *American Journal of Public Health, 103*(11), 2027–2034.

Sandison, R.A., & Whitelaw, J.D.A. (1957). Further studies in the therapeutic value of lysergic acid diethylamide in mental illness. *British Journal of Psychiatry, 103*(431), 332–343.

Squeglia, L. M., Jacobus, J., & Tapert, S. F. (2009). The influence of substance use on adolescent brain development. *Clinical EEG and Neuroscience, 40*(1), 31–38.

Substance Abuse and Mental Health Services Administration (SAMHSA). (2013). *Results from the 2012 National Survey on Drug Use and Health: Summary of national findings.* Rockville, MD: U.S. Department of Health and Human Services.

Substance Abuse and Mental Health Services Administration (SAMHSA). (2014). *Results from the 2013 National Survey on Drug Use and Health: Summary of national findings.* Rockville, MD: U.S. Department of Health and Human Services. Retrieved from http://www.samhsa.gov/data/sites/default/files/NSDUHresultsPDFWHTML2013/Web/NSDUHresults2013.pdf

Swendsen, J., & Le Moal, M. (2011). Individual vulnerability to addiction. *Annals of the New York Academy of Sciences, 1216*(1), 73–85.

Whitehill, J. M., Rivara, F. P., & Moreno, M. A. (2014). Marijuana-using drivers, alcohol-using drivers, and their passengers: Prevalence and risk factors among underage college students. *JAMA Pediatrics, 168*(7), 618–624.

Volkow, N. D., Baler, R. D., Compton, W. M., & Weiss, S. R. (2014). Adverse health effects of marijuana use. *New England Journal of Medicine, 370*(23), 2219–2227.

Section 3
Intellectual Wellness

9

Study and Writing Skills
Fostering Students' Academic Development and Engagement

DANIELLA OLIBRICE

Introduction

Institutions of higher education have an obligation to support students—be they traditional high school students, first-generation college students, or adult students returning to college after a long hiatus from higher education—in achieving economic independence. The way colleges can do this is by providing opportunities, inside and outside the classroom, for students to develop the habits, attitude, and skills necessary for becoming successful students, workers, and citizens. Current research and reports from the workforce speak of a "skills gap," while employers cite a lack of "career readiness" among college graduates.

A discussion of the value of postsecondary education in terms of the greater economic, social, and democratic well-being of American society as a whole is provided in this chapter. The pivotal role that higher education personnel can play in reinvigorating student engagement and skills development in order to better prepare students for the world of postgraduation is presented. Examples of workshops, activities, and lessons that can be offered on campus are outlined. Great emphasis is placed on students' development of specific skills, such as critical thinking, time management, organization, and academic writing, as these are competencies most valued in college and that are easily transferrable to the workplace. These recommendations are intended to be part of a campus plan for addressing the levels of academic and career readiness among all student populations that are typically found in under-resourced, underfunded, and heavily enrolled academic institutions. Finally, the recommended strategies are worthy of consideration when thinking about approaches to improving student retention, graduation, and postgraduation employment.

The Need for a Better Educated and Skilled Workforce

Academic institutions are best equipped to support students' development of strong academic, writing, and critical thinking skills. Some studies have found a significant link between being academically prepared—meaning that one has developed and mastered the skills and habits necessary for academic success—and having those skills necessary for making a successful transition from college life to the workforce (Arum & Roksa, 2014; Association for Career and Technical

Education, n.d.; Constantine, Kindaichi, & Miville, 2007). As workplaces have become increasingly technological and complex, so have employer demands and expectations of workers in the United States.

The types of study skills, strategies, and habits that individuals acquire as they move from middle school to high school often carry over into college. Too often it takes receiving poor grades during the first year or semester of college, and being put on academic probation, for a student to realize that the strategies used in high school might not be as effective in college. While individuals might be motivated to develop compensatory skills in order to perform well on the job because the rewards are more immediate or tangible, such as a salary or promotion, performing well in college can have an impact on the quality of individuals' experience as students and can affect their future beyond college, including their employability. Regardless of whether the emphasis is on the traditionally aged student, the nontraditional adult student, or the first-generation college student, higher education plays a pivotal role in helping students build the study, writing, and critical thinking skills that can positively affect the quality of their learning, employability, and overall quality of life postgraduation.

Academic and Career Readiness

Educational institutions at all levels, K–16, are under pressure to better prepare students for the job market. At the same time, American students are constantly being measured and judged based on their performance on various statewide, national, and international tests designed to determine what they know, how well the school system is working, teacher effectiveness, and their ability to participate and compete in our increasingly technology-driven, global societies and economies. Depending on whom you speak to, the terms "college ready" and "career ready" may be used interchangeably to describe the shift in our thinking about the level and type of skills and knowledge needed to enter the workforce. Growing employer expectations of job applicants' qualifications and the decreasing number of well-paying jobs with lower education requirements, such as a high school diploma, have pushed adults to enroll in certificate and degree programs so as to remain competitive in the labor market. According to the Association for Career and Technical Education (n.d.), career readiness means having the type of skills needed to enter a "career with family-sustaining wages and opportunities for advancement," and it involves three major skill areas:

1. *Core academic skills* and the ability to apply those skills to a concrete situation in order to function in the workplace and in routine daily activities;
2. *Employability skills* (such as critical thinking and responsibility) that are essential in any career area;
3. *Technical, job-specific skills* related to a specific career pathway.

A review of policy briefs produced by different organizations regarding academic and job readiness has identified a range of academic skills that an individual can learn while in college that are applicable to the workplace; they are the ability to:

- Read different genres and types of materials, especially informational texts;
- Adhere to conventions of English grammar and spelling;
- Interpret tables, graphs, charts, and pictures related to content in a text;
- Write in a persuasive, expository, or descriptive manner;
- Analyze, interpret, and display data and statistics;
- Work in teams and present work orally;
- Apply quantitative reasoning for problem-solving;
- Speak another language or have an awareness that languages reflect cultures;
- Understand the scientific method and possess insight into the big ideas and organization of knowledge in the sciences. (Conley, 2012; Olson, 2007)

The National Association of Manufacturers and the New York City–based Conference Board, a global independent business membership and research association, surveyed employers about college graduates and their overall preparedness: they reported that graduates lack both academic and basic employability skills. Among those identified were everyday social skills, verbal and nonverbal communication, attendance, punctuality, and the ability to read and follow instructions, interview appropriately, and manage time, projects, and workload, including being able to apply knowledge to the real world (Olson, 2007). A review of the types of competencies mentioned reveals some overlap between those associated with college readiness and those associated with career readiness. In fact, one would argue that exposure to college-level courses increases one's career readiness, and colleges are essential for reducing the skills gap. Therefore, institutions of higher education, especially community colleges, should receive more funding rather than less in order to give all students, especially those with the greatest need and most at risk, with the tools for academic and postgraduation success. This success would include making a smooth transition to a 4-year college, with clear goals about choice of major and occupation.

The College's Role in Increasing Employability Skills

Attending college also provides individuals with opportunities to develop and sharpen skills valued by employers. Among the skills that have been reported are: critical thinking and analysis, teamwork, sound judgment, problem-solving, public speaking, writing, professional appearance, punctuality, reliability, initiative, flexibility, and honesty. All divisions within an academic institution, on both the academic and student affairs sides, must design opportunities for students to develop and exercise these values, attitudes, and skills through the school's curriculum and by virtue of the college student experience.

Among the ways of doing this are: (1) requiring students take courses that involve group work, oral presentations, and the production of visual or multimedia products for course assignments; (2) connecting students to internships, work-study, research projects, and cooperative programs with local business and industry for at least two semesters to increase and deepen experiential learning; (3) urging them to participate in clubs and student government as a way of improving services and building teamwork and collaborative learning; and (4) providing opportunities for students to develop a strong network beyond college.

While many already do, academic institutions—both community and 4-year colleges—must articulate early to their students what those highly valued skills and experiences are that employers want, and guide them toward acquiring these. Furthermore, the office of career services and student development must be well attuned to the college's offerings because of their link to the world of work, and be adept at helping students translate their coursework and credentials for future employers. Their role is central in terms of conveying information about in-demand occupations, educational requirements for entry-level occupations, labor market data, social media and research tools for finding work, and experiential learning opportunities to students during their time in college. This information is very useful for students in choosing academic majors and securing their future postgraduation.

Furthermore, career advising staff should be more integrated in academic departments, academic program planning, and other campus services, to ensure that conversations about college majors, disciplinary requirements, and occupational outlook are not postponed to the senior year. Instead, these conversations should be happening during freshman orientation and throughout the student's time in college. Also, they need not be conversations that only career services staff should initiate; faculty should also be involved by staying informed and abreast of opportunities within their field. Given their greater access to students, they can play a key role in exposing students to occupations that students on their own would not have known existed. In addition, faculty should incorporate in their courses expectations, assignments, and activities that build and extend students' skills so that they are better able to function in the workplace postgraduation. This is where having faculty who are "in the field" or practitioners with a foot in academia *and* industry can be very valuable because they can serve as mentors, introduce students to others in the field, and help expand students' networks. While these are not new practices, these are the types of linkages to the world of work that can better support students' transitions from college to work.

Postsecondary Education for Traditional and Nontraditional Students

Once enrolled in college, the unprepared and unsupported student can face many barriers that, if not dealt with properly and early, can quickly become insurmountable. Among the challenges may be being away from home for the first time, making decisions about how to manage academic and social pressures, keeping ties with family and friends back home who may still rely on the student for emotional support from a distance, and lacking sufficient financial aid in order to carry the cost of tuition and other expenses over the four years or more of study. For some, this can be an energizing and exciting period because it is about learning, questioning, and exploring. For others, not grasping new ideas or concepts quickly can deepen insecurity, and a lack of confidence carried over from high school or previous academic experience grows. Feelings of inadequacy or shame may become overwhelming because they are associated with past failures, such as low grades, academic probation, dropped classes, early withdrawals, and things left undone and incomplete.

On the other hand, the return to college can represent a new opportunity or second chance for an adult student. Going to college helps them develop expertise and learn new academic and nonacademic skills: the broadening of a social and professional network, the accomplishment of a goal, and acquisition of a recognized and valuable credential. Consider adults who left school in their early twenties in order to enter the workforce and who had great successes there as they climbed the career ladder. Nonetheless, the lack of a terminal degree continued to gnaw at them. Sometimes, it takes a life-changing event, such as a layoff or being passed over for a promotion, to decide that getting a college degree should be their next goal.

For the traditional student the goal may be less personal or more abstract. The decision to go to college may come from parental or peer pressure, and may not always be clearly directed at gaining skills for a specific job. However, it is expected that the experience of college should have a greater impact on young adults intellectually and developmentally as they move from late adolescence to early adulthood. For adults, it is expected that they have gone through the maturation stage, and thus the issues they face as students are somewhat different. They are more concerned with how their learning applies to their lives and careers. Often, adult learners have greater motivation because they see the link between their education and their sense of purpose and direction. Usually, they do not want to waste time on assignments that seem vague or purposeless. To a certain extent, younger students may feel the same way, but may express their resistance differently.

For the military veteran, going to college is related to concerns about returning to civilian life and immersing themselves in an environment with a different set of rules. Given the hierarchical, highly structured, and regimented nature of military life, veterans are expected to have comparable levels of readiness as working adults. Yet, they face other challenges. As they make the transition from military to civilian life, they may suffer from psychological and physical injuries, as well as other stressors associated with adult life. Some professionals who have taught veterans report that these students may adapt well to most of the demands of college life; they are punctual to class, disciplined about assignment deadlines, demonstrate natural leadership, have respect for authority, and follow instructions, but they are less adept at being autonomous and have trouble with ambiguity.

For higher education personnel, whether administrators, faculty, or student services staff, particularly at underfunded and under-resourced institutions, communicating effectively is vital with students who are the most at risk, ensuring that they are availing themselves of all the resources that exist on campus. The ultimate goal of the programs devised by academic affairs and student services is to transform ill-prepared, anxious, and unconfident students into knowledgeable, self-assured, and focused individuals who will be ready to undertake any challenge that life brings, them after completing their degree. In other words, a solid college education should provide individuals with the skills for leading a healthful, purposeful, and satisfactory life.

Habits of Mind: The Skills, Behaviors, and Attitudes of the Successful

In order to do well in college, students need to exhibit the attitude and observe habits that will allow them to be effective learners. These have been referred to as the "habits of mind," an idea that was first developed by professor of education Art Costa and his coauthor, Bena Kallick. Costa and Kallick surveyed the works of various authors who had done research on effective thinking, successful people, and intelligent behavior, and they discovered that successful people from a variety of backgrounds and occupations have identifiably common characteristics. These characteristics can be best described as *intellectual* behavior that leads to *effective* actions. Their book, *Learning and Leading With the Habits of Mind: 16 Essential Characteristics for Success* (2008), written as a guide for schoolteachers and administrators who seek to teach their students higher-level thinking skills, describes the habits as a "composite of many skills, attitudes, cues, past experiences and proclivities" (Costa and Kallick, 2008, as cited in Association for Supervision and Curriculum Development, 2015, pp. 1–2). They constitute intelligent behavior because it is what intelligent people do when they encounter a challenge for which the resolution is not readily obvious. The 16 habits are described ahead.

Habits of Mind

1. **Persistence**: Staying with a task, staying focused, and not giving up.
2. **Managing impulsivity**: Remaining calm and taking time to think before acting.
3. **Listening with empathy and understanding**: Taking the time to understand and listen to someone else's perspective and emotions.
4. **Thinking flexibly**: Looking at something another way and being able to change perspectives, generate alternatives, and consider options.
5. **Metacognition (thinking about your thinking)**: Being aware of one's thoughts, strategies, feelings, and actions and their effects on others.
6. **Striving for accuracy**: Checking work again, always doing one's best, setting high standards, and finding ways to improve.
7. **Applying past knowledge**: Using what one learns, accessing prior knowledge, and applying it to new situations.
8. **Questioning and posing problems**: Having a questioning attitude, knowing what data are needed, developing questioning strategies to produce those data, and finding problems to solve.
9. **Thinking and communicating with clarity and precision**: Being clear and striving for accurate communication in both writing and speaking, such as avoiding generalizations, distortions, deletions, and exaggerations.

---

10. **Gathering data through all senses:** Paying attention to the world around you and gathering data through all senses: taste, touch, smell, hearing, and sight.
11. **Creating, imagining, and innovating:** Trying a different way, generating new and novel ideas, fluency, and originality.
12. **Responding with wonderment and awe:** Enjoying the process of figuring something out, finding the world awesome and mysterious, being intrigued with phenomena and beauty, and being passionate.
13. **Taking responsible risks:** Being adventurous, living on the edge of one's competence, and trying new things constantly.
14. **Finding humor:** Finding the whimsical, incongruous, and unexpected, and being able to laugh at oneself.
15. **Thinking interdependently:** Being able to work and learn from others in reciprocal situations, and working in a team.
16. **Remaining open to continuous learning:** Learning from experiences, having humility when admitting one doesn't know something, and resisting complacency.

> Adapted from Association of Supervision and
> Curriculum Development (2015), Chapter 2:
> "Describing Habits of Mind" by Arthur L. Costa.

Costa and his supporters argue that these characteristics or dispositions can be taught, cultivated, observed, and assessed. Individuals can develop these habits through formal learning experiences as well as through informal means—through their everyday experiences and interactions. Nevertheless, the college environment should provide the structure to further develop these habits among its students, as part of its curriculum.

Core Academic Skills: Access, Support, and Strategies for Success

In the context of this chapter, academic skills constitute the ability to prepare, be organized and clear about one's purpose and goals, to manage one's time, communicate appropriately, and seek support in order to perform well in college. The development of these skills should be reinforced in students through continuous interaction with advisers, faculty, mentors, college staff, classmates on campus, and off campus with family, work colleagues, church members, and other affiliations that the student may have. Academic administrators and faculty can design interventions or services that will better prepare students for managing all aspects of student life. Examples of practices already in place at certain institutions will be described in the sections that follow. These include practices that can occur before students enroll and afterwards.

At the pre-enrollment stage, communication between admissions, the registrar, academic departments, and student advisement staff is essential. Student affairs and advisement staff can harness information about an incoming class to develop services that will address some of the challenges a student may encounter. One strategy is to have entering students develop a profile by completing a questionnaire or survey that will give administrators a full picture of the student's situation. This includes, for instance, identifying whether the student will need accommodations due to a disability or support for accessing affordable housing, child care, technology, books, and other supplies or materials, transportation, additional income beyond financial aid in order to support themselves and dependents while in school, or other services. The point is to get to know the students beforehand in order to be responsive to their needs, and devise strategies to address them. In the event that institutional priorities and resources are such that some of these cannot be addressed within the institution, local resources or other alternatives can be identified to assist the student, such as the office for disability or accessibility services or a nonprofit that provides social services.

Communication: Staying Connected

During orientation, staff from student affairs, academic advisement, and instructional technology or technological support should convey to their students the message of: (1) "being and staying connected" to the school by logging into the college portal regularly, and (2) making sure to secure their login information. The loss of login information results in the loss of time and opportunity, especially where it concerns announcements about important deadlines, grants, scholarships, and services available on the campus throughout the academic year. In order to ensure compliance, a reward system could be put into place whereby administrators from academic affairs, with the support of the technology support division, reward compliance with prizes in the form of gift cards to the bookstore, cash credits for meals at the cafeteria, partial membership to the campus gym, or other incentives.

Using light-hearted and attention-getting approaches to draw student engagement is often well appreciated and creates greater connection between the student body and the institution in the long run. For fully online programs, assigning IT staff to deliver information at orientation as part of the welcome that virtual students receive would be ideal. Besides making accessible a student handbook with procedures, policies, and rules for online conduct, a series of activities could be designed to encourage community and affiliation. In her book *Discussion-Based Online Teaching to Enhance Student Learning: Theory, Practice and Assessment* (2004), Tisha Bender offers insight and techniques for facilitating student learning in the context of fully online and hybrid courses. She advises instructors to be as explicit as possible about their expectations for students with regard to their interaction with the course content. The ambiguity and unease that may arise from lack of physical proximity can be assuaged by: (1) stating at the outset of an online or hybrid course how frequently students should log in and participate and how often they can expect their teacher to be available online, and being very clear about what 24/7 availability really means; (2) informing students how participation is graded quantitatively in terms of percentage of the overall class grade, and describing what quality participation should look like, especially when students are required to contribute to discussion topics; and (3) posting in the syllabus and reinforcing rules for civility with clear expectations about how to be "positive, sensitive, consideration, polite and tolerant" (Blankespoor, 1996, as cited in Bender, 2004, p. 59).

In addition to offering an online orientation for students on how to navigate the class's online environment, consider incorporating a "virtual lounge" into the design of an online course. A virtual lounge can be created simply by putting up the first discussion forum to which students are invited to post personal introductions that can be read by their fellow classmates. It should be a low-stakes "warm-up" discussion thread that should take place before the course begins. The course instructor should start by posting a biographical statement and the syllabus. Throughout the semester, in order to maintain the feeling of camaraderie, students should be invited to go to the virtual lounge and partake in community-building exercises. Other tips Bender offers include designing an informal first discussion topic that is "so enticing, so intriguing and so marvelous that they really do not want to miss out on it" (p. 47); having students interview each other; asking students to write short descriptive stories about themselves to be shared online; and even having a telephone conversation with each student at the beginning of the semester. These methods and others recommended by Bender and others acknowledge how overwhelming and anxiety-provoking online learning can be for those new to the experience. It is also a response to the low completion rates typically seen among exclusively online learners.

Supporting students toward becoming smart consumers of technology and achieving information literacy should be an additional priority of academic institutions with high enrollments of students from disadvantaged backgrounds. Technological access and knowledge level the playing field and break down barriers between those who have been historically disadvantaged and those with greater privilege and access to technology, resulting in a society with greater distribution of resources and raising human capital overall.

Technology and Information Literacy

In addition to providing access to technology, instructional technology departments as well as academic advisement should be able to gauge each student's technological accessibility as it relates to his or her course load and requirements. Making workshops available throughout the semester to students on learning management systems—that is, Blackboard—and basic Microsoft suite software—that is, Word, Excel, and PowerPoint—is key in ensuring that these tools enable student learning rather than hinder it. In some cases, attendance at these workshops should be mandatory, especially in contexts where it is recognized that students may not possess adequate technological skills. During the weeks before classes begin, students should have access to support with setting up an email account and logging into the school's online portal from school and home. As is the current practice in many schools, students should have access through a login and password combination to a portion of the school's website, where all content that pertains to their life as a student (e.g., academic calendar, course schedules, deadlines, services, announcements) can be read, retrieved, and interacted with.

Information literacy is a bundle of skills that individuals living in our increasingly technological society need to master in order to attend to the myriad forms of information that they encounter daily through email, Facebook, Twitter, and other media. It is also very closely tied to critical thinking. The ability to discern, critique, and judge the quality of the information encountered is key to not being easily manipulated by media, interest groups, politicians, and other parties that might want to do us harm.

As a prerequisite to the traditional term paper, students are usually asked to research books, articles, and publications from credible, peer-reviewed, or reputable sources. Those with limited information literacy may not always understand from the outset what is behind this requirement. The point is to raise students' awareness and urge them to ask themselves with regularity: What is credible? What is peer-reviewed? What is considered reputable? They may ask: Why does this matter? Isn't everything published in print or on the Internet true or real? There is a tendency to believe everything, including photographs, seen on television, in magazines, and on the Internet as real. However, the growing sophistication of our technology has rendered all forms of media questionable.

At many schools, a librarian or an instructional technology staff member could offer a series of noncredit workshops or a semester-long credited course in information literacy, held at the school's library or in a computer lab. If it is held at the library, it can include a tour of the facilities as way to acquaint students with its resources and staff. Along with learning how to evaluate media, students learn how to use electronic databases, search for peer-reviewed materials, become acquainted with reference materials, get trained on how to integrate and cite sources properly in order to avoid plagiarism, and gain awareness of the different types of information media—all worthy skills that will serve students beyond their time on campus. The course should also equip students with the awareness and ability to discern credible and reliable sources. Sessions should be dedicated to plagiarism and strategies to avoid it.

Time Management

Time management is not only about how much time to allot to activities but also an approach to better distribute one's energy and efforts over a period of time, and avoid unnecessary stress. Human beings living in the Western world tend to think of time as measured by minutes, hours, days, weeks, months, years, or more, but depending on the task and how much energy is needed to fulfill it, one's perception of time can be unreliable. We tend to underestimate how much time it takes to accomplish something, especially when it concerns school assignments or projects, because we are by nature optimistic about our abilities, situation, and resources. It is a blind spot we all share. Psychologists who study this phenomenon have attributed it to having an overinflated sense of competence, intelligence, or ability. Social psychologists observe that, as human beings, we do not easily see our own flaws and we rarely receive accurate feedback from others. It is only during those times where one's performance is being evaluated for a job, for a school grade, or in a formal competition that we receive an objective assessment of our abilities or lack thereof.

Dunning states, "In a subjective area like intelligence, for example, people tend to perceive their competence in self-serving ways. A student talented in math, for instance, may emphasize math and analytical skills in her definition of intelligence, while a student gifted in other areas might highlight verbal ability or creativity. Another problem is that in many areas of life, accurate feedback is rare. People don't like giving negative feedback . . . so it's likely we will fail to hear criticism that would help us improve our performance" (DeAngelis, 2003, p. 60).

The main takeaway is to recognize that in order to make progress and learn, we must practice self-reflection and seek constructive feedback from those who have our best interest in mind, such as our advisers, counselors, classmates, colleagues, and supervisors. A discussion of this perspective could help incentivize students to push themselves more academically and in all their pursuits, with a strong reminder that they should be competing with themselves rather than against others.

Once students are enrolled and taking classes, faculty members and advising staff should work closely with student life staff to design activities to better immerse students in the college community. This can be in the form of a workshop that incorporates a lot of discussion, small group activities, hands-on exercises, and practical tips for students. The workshop's aim is to instill in students skills involving time management, study activities, communication, and community. Students are given planners and guided through a series of exercises that will push them to think about their time and commitments: what are their daily, weekly, and monthly personal and work obligations and academic commitments for the semester? How much time can be allocated to each activity, such as chores at home (e.g., laundry, going to the gym, food shopping, cooking, commuting or transportation, child/elder care, studying)? How much time can be devoted to study tasks and what time of the day can these be done? Can tasks be broken down into sizeable, manageable chunks (e.g., during lunch breaks, while commuting)?

The activities of mapping out weekly commitments, assignments, and deadlines for each class with dates for papers, quizzes, and exams and creating a timeline and "to do" or "goal and outcome" lists with dates as to when tasks will be completed are the types of organizational aids that can help alleviate anxiety and provide structure. Ultimately, the point is to help students develop a mechanism or tool for managing demands so they are achievable. Consequently, it is less about "things happening to me" and more about "things I can make happen."

Students should be asked to consider how much time, according to what kind of schedule, they would be able to devote to studying. Can certain organizational tasks like putting notes and class handouts into a binder be done during a lunch break, early in the morning, or before bed? Can reviewing class notes be done during a commute or while doing other household chores that may not require full attention (e.g., sitting in a laundromat or waiting room)? Can time be taken early in the day before the bustle of the day begins? In addition, keeping a "to do" list can aid one's memory and help one focus on goals and deadlines. It should also be stressed to students that dedicating some time for recharging and reconnecting with family, friends, and one's community is also important. While there may be times during the semester at midterm and during finals where it may seem particularly difficult to set time aside for this, staying connected to others and seeking some form of diversion can maintain and restore one's spirit and health.

Academic advisors, faculty, and tutors should be explicit with students about the different types of activities that can be called "studying." While many students may think they know this, studying comprises a *series* of activities that can be best described as a process. The following list, while not fully exhaustive, can be compiled into a handout distributed to students to ignite their thinking about what studying means. A companion exercise is to have students devise their own list of study strategies they have found personally helpful.

The Activities and Habits Associated With Studying

- Read the assignment carefully, making sure that one is clear about what the assignment is and how it is expected to be done. This should be done while in class or shortly after the class, to give ample time to ask questions and get clarification.
- Read assigned texts and notes taken during class in distributed chunks of time between class meetings.
- Review and rewrite notes taken during class, including notes, lectures, and slides created by the instructor.
- Write up summaries and outlines of class lectures and concepts from assigned readings.
- Review summaries and outlines of class lectures and assigned readings.
- Compile lists of definitions for new concepts or theories learned in class or from assigned texts by paraphrasing and using one's own words.
- Map out key ideas, concepts, or theories by using concept mapping, diagramming, or other visual language; using presentation-style software can be helpful.
- Prepare discussion points of main ideas or concepts on index cards that are portable and can be reviewed anywhere—such as during a lunch break or while commuting.
- Annotate assigned readings by writing directly on the page of the book or article as a way of having an imaginary dialogue with the author of the text. Attaching notes next to a passage of interest is another way of doing this, using Post-it notes for loaned books. Ask questions like, how much am I understanding of this? What is the main idea or takeaway from this section, text, or book? Does this represent my experience? How does this connect to what I have read before?

- Flip through the textbook to understand its structure and preview the topics covered. Scan the table of contents, the chapter headings, subheadings, review questions, definitions, and how the topics flow together. How are the topics and concepts sequenced and scaffolded, whether from simplest to more complex, or from the very general to the specific?
- Organize a study group. Discuss how to choose study partners, divide up reading assignments, and share the study load. Identify how to share notes on readings and test comprehension of concepts or theories. The best way to learn is to teach; being able to dialogue and explain a theory to a study partner can support better retention and fluency.
- Know what study and learning styles work best. Is one's preference to hear a lecture or is there a need to see ideas mapped out visually? Is information retained better after doing a hands-on exercise?
- Develop multiple drafts of a written paper and get feedback from peers and course instructors throughout the semester.
- Get acquainted with the college library and available resources, as well as accessing various electronic databases for articles, books, publications, and reports relevant to the area of interest or academic discipline.
- Find credible sources and be aware of the difference between peer-reviewed publications and opinion or editorial pieces; understand the importance of seeking reliable sources in academia and any public discourse.
- Understand authorial responsibility to the audience and avoid plagiarism. If ideas, words, images, or other media are being borrowed or referred to in one's work, be careful about giving credit, and always acknowledge correctly the source of the content.

Technologically Supported Student Monitoring

It is customary that, throughout a semester, student affairs personnel, faculty, and academic departments communicate with students through a student portal that can be accessed through the school's website. This allows students to receive necessary support, feedback, and insight about their performance. It is also keeps students focused on minigoals they may have set with the aid of their academic advisers, course instructors, mentors, or tutors. The portal allows key student services staff and the student to monitor progress reports entered by advisers, faculty, and others involved with the student throughout the course of a semester. At City University of New York's Lehman College in Bronx, New York, administrators from academic advisement, departments, faculty, the registrar, and other divisions have access to a system called Degree Works, in which all data about enrolled students can be inputted, searched, and viewed by the student, and the college's administrative and academic staff, with the right level of privilege and access, can view the student's full record. Ideally, by or before midterms, communications between the various academic and student services departments should be so well coordinated that students who are at risk and low-performing can be identified early and specific interventions can be devised by a committee comprised of an academic adviser, faculty, and academic support staff assigned to the student's case. Questions that may be addressed include:

- Is the student keeping up with assignments?
- Is the student showing up to all of his or her advisement and tutoring sessions?
- Is the student's class attendance steady?
- How well connected to the campus and involved in activities is the student?
- Is the student seeking help for any crises and does the student know where to go to seek support?
- If the student is struggling, what can be put in place to ensure that the semester is not a loss for the student?

Faculty should play an active role in reporting through an academic alert system students who are at risk. This academic alert system is used for communication between faculty and academic support services so that appropriate campus interventions are put into place to meet students' needs, whether they be purely academic or personal. The point is to remove any barriers that may arise for the student, and create a holistic on- and off-campus support system that identifies and addresses any factors that may escalate into a crisis.

Critical Thinking and the Writing Process

In his book *Engaging Ideas: The Professor's Guide to Integrating Writing, Critical Thinking, and Active Learning in the Classroom*, Bean (2011) sees a link between writing, learning, and critical thinking. Referring to John Dewey, he defines critical thinking as the "engagement with a problem" because problems evoke "students' natural curiosity and stimulate both learning and critical thought" (pp. 2–3). "Only by wrestling with the conditions of the problem at first hand, seeking and finding his own way out, does [the student] think" (cited in Bean, 2011, p. 3). By engaging in problem-solving one develops critical thinking.

Bean refers to a 15-year study of college professors conducted by Bain (2004), who found that the most effective teachers were the ones who presented their students with "intriguing, beautiful, or important problems, authentic tasks that will challenge them to grapple with ideas, rethink their assumptions, and examine their mental models of reality" (cited in Bean, 2011, p. 3). It is when students are given a problem at "an appropriate level of difficulty" that "a natural critical thinking environment" occurs (Bain, 2004, as cited in Bean, 2011, p. 3).

The symbiotic relationship between writing and critical thinking seems obvious because "writing is both a process of doing critical thinking and [a] product that communicates the results of critical thinking. Instead of thinking of writing as merely a communication skill, it should be thought of as a critical thinking task because it requires that a writer asks different questions, such as 'Is the writing interesting? Does it show a mind actively engaged with a problem? Does it make an argument?'" (Bean, 2011, p. 4). The writing of multiple drafts is in itself an act of problem-solving. During this act, the writer is trying to refine the core of what she wants to convey to her reader; she begins to imagine who this reader is and anticipates the kinds of questions the reader might have upon reading her text. Ultimately, the goal of academic writing isn't merely to communicate or be clear; it should be to address a "subject matter problem" and present this to an audience (Bean, 2011). One could add that the point of writing is to contribute one's thoughts to a greater conversation and to select within the boundaries of one's discipline a topic or subject about which one feels particularly energized to write. Therefore, having students begin by exploring current events and their own personal experience in juxtaposition with seminal theories and texts, accompanied by weekly journaling exercises, can be effective for motivating students to delve into seemingly difficult topics.

Discussion, Research, and Topic Development

One strategy used by skillful college teachers is to create opportunities during class where each student consults with his or her peers and instructor on the selection of a topic for a final paper. The classroom-wide dialogue between the student and the entire class is very effective at helping a student move from picking a generalized, often very broad topic to a more specific topic that is appropriate and feasible for a 15- to 20-page paper. Bean recommends "exploration tasks" that are intended to motivate students toward building arguments as a way of addressing a topical issue. A selection is listed here.

A Sample of Bean's Exploration Tasks for an Argument Addressing an Issue

1. Write out the issue your argument will address. Then write out your tentative answer to your issue-question. This will be your beginning thesis statement or claim.
2. What personal interest do you have in this issue? What personal experiences do you have with it? How does the issue affect you?
3. Who is the audience you need to persuade? What values, beliefs, and assumptions cause them to take positions different from yours? What evidence do they use to support their positions?
4. Through idea-mapping or freewriting, begin planning your own argument. What are the main reasons and evidence you will use to support your position?

Excerpted from Bean (2011, p. 140).

Throughout the academic year students should seek the support of a writing center or academic support center that helps students approach written assignments. This could be done through group workshops, individual tutoring sessions, online resources, and/or handouts about the college's expectations of student writing. Academic writing is a skill that has to be fostered both within and outside the classroom. Although Shaughnessy (1977) described learning to write academically as being akin to learning a new language, Elbow (1998) feels that it is more like "learning to speak to a new person or in a new situation" (p. 8). He sees good writing as the ability to write "with power, with eloquence on paper." Yet, he acknowledges the difficulty of the task because it involves two skills: being both creative *and* critical. The *critical* aspect comes into play when one must revise and pare down; the *creative* aspect has to do with being able to let one's ideas run freely. These are skills that come only from continual practice.

Espousing a perspective on the writing process that is very much in keeping with the idea of writing as a method for learning, Elbow (1998) strongly believes in the virtue of freewriting and doing it early on in a project because it is the "best all-around practice in writing" for getting as much as possible down on a page quickly without stopping. The product isn't the goal—the goal is to think without being too self-conscious about thinking. It's a form of brainstorming that gets pushed out from the head to hand and down to the paper. Elbow has many useful recommendations that both faculty and academic support staff can impart to students in order to allay their fear of producing those first sentences.

Key Lessons From Elbow's Writing With Power for Novice Writers

1. Do an outline only when you know well the ideas, incidents, or images that you want to use in your writing, and when you want to clarify and organize them;
2. Have a discussion or conversation about a topic before sitting down to write, or better yet, have an argument about it because it supports the trying out of "various ideas, approaches, and formulations" and analytic thinking;
3. Imagine that you are having a dialogue or debate with another author and you must make assertions, support reasons, and produce evidence;
4. Write a story about your thinking in order to clear any confusion you may have about your topic—this method allows the writer to "untangle bad snarls in your mind" and get you to see an issue from a less complicated lens;
5. Concentrate *less* on writing things correctly, slowly, and carefully the first time;
6. Understand that ideas need time to blossom or cook, or risk producing "dull" writing;
7. Realize that you can't always know what you think before you start writing because this emerges from the process.

Establishing Student Expectations About Writing

Rather than giving students rules about what good writing should look like, greater focus should be placed on developing their awareness of the different ways the process could look. This message should then be reiterated in class, writing workshops, and tutorials.

Setting Student Expectations About the Writing Process

1. Good writing doesn't just happen.
2. It takes thought and time. Start early.
3. Often you have to produce many drafts to achieve flow.
4. The more you write, the better you get.
5. Read often and as many different genres as possible.
6. Find good role models and inspiration wherever you can.
7. Get good support and help.
8. Find out what works for you. Do you write better in the morning or evening?
9. Keep a journal of ideas.
10. Be open to feedback.

Exposure to good models of writing and a variety of genres, such as the newspaper article, the editorial, the critique, the textbook, the memoir, autobiography, poetry, fiction, policy brief, and white paper, is crucial. Where it makes sense, faculty should incorporate different forms of texts and sources of data in order to enable their students to develop the skills needed to decode and interpret them. These discussions do not necessarily have to occur in only writing, composition, or literature courses. Encouraging students' appreciation for good writing by talking about favorite authors and what makes a good reader is an integral part of writing instruction, whether in the context of dedicated writing workshops or tutoring sessions, or across the college curriculum.

The ability to give and receive different forms of constructive feedback and feel comfortable with making mistakes because they are tied to learning and growth should also be recognized. For instance, the idea of the editor in terms of his or her role in all published works should be discussed vis-à-vis strategies for developing one's own "inner nice editor," as Elbow (1998) calls it. This editor should encourage you to think about and question what it is you are trying to express without judging or paralyzing your process. Finally, talking through a topic with a professor, classmates, or a tutor is a useful step in the process of building critical thinking and communication skills. It can help clarify ideas and narrow them down to specifics.

Being inarticulate about what one wants to express will make it difficult to pin it down in writing. This is why faculty should consider structuring lessons along the lines of the seminar, in which students are held as responsible for the tenor and tone of the class as is the professor. Within a seminar, each student is expected to come ready to actively discuss assigned texts with his peers and instructors, to lead the group in a debate in which smaller groups are asked to present a specific perspective, and present their analysis of issues or recent controversy in a coherent and thoughtful manner. Given that these kinds of learning situations may be demanding of and intimidating for students who are used to the more passive, lecture-based class structure, faculty who opt to use this method once in a while must develop the classroom management strategies and skills needed to effectively facilitate this more active and sometimes uncomfortable type of learning. It can support novice writers' ability to formulate a topic. The back-and-forth between the student, his or her peers, and the instructor can be crucial in laying bare the foundations of the topic of a paper.

Academic Preparation and Life Skills

With the exception of those that are directly occupational, employability skills can be developed by completing courses and engaging in experiences that a higher education institution offers its students through its curriculum. Mastery of a foreign language, statistical and quantitative knowledge, cultural competence and sensitivity to other perspectives, interaction with individuals from diverse backgrounds, basic understanding of scientific concepts and phenomena, verbal and written communication across contexts and media platforms, and willingness to experiment and be curious are at the core of most liberal arts–focused colleges. These are essentially life skills. This is why having different types of opportunities for students to exercise leadership and practice those highly valued skills is so powerful and enriching. These may be on campus through clubs, student-led newspaper/blogs, salons, speaker series, fundraisers, volunteer activities, and participation in peer mentoring and tutoring networks. These opportunities are what make the college environment a microcosm of society at large. It is in this way that attending college truly prepares an individual to participate in our fully interconnected and global society.

Conclusion

Given how important it is for all adults to achieve a postsecondary degree to enter and remain in the workforce, higher education institutions in the United States have a great imperative to offer the kinds of services and environments that will address the needs of their increasingly diverse student populations. Colleges must be well equipped to ease students' transition to college, encourage their resilience when faced with various challenges (both academic and nonacademic) as they progress through their studies, and nurture the determination and motivation necessary to help them achieve their academic, personal, and professional goals.

Many of the habits, attitude, and skills that employers report as lacking among college graduates are many of the ones that academic institutions seek to instill within their current and graduating students. The message to students about the value of a postsecondary degree, along with the kinds of meaningful experiential learning opportunities that could be achieved while pursuing it, should be communicated more loudly, clearly and earlier. Students should also be coached about the different ways to articulate and present what they have learned to employers and its potential value to the workplace.

Academic institutions must devise approaches to better prepare students who come with different levels of academic preparedness, dispositions to learning, and knowledge about the availability of occupations and their educational requirements. By designing innovative curricula and activities, integrating services and functions, and increasing collaboration among departments that are more responsive to student needs, colleges increase their ability to retain those students. Designing approaches to better support students' transition to college and from college to work demonstrates to students their institution's commitment to their short-term and long-term success. Once students feel that their institution cares about them and does a superlative job of preparing them for work or graduate study, the allegiance the students feel toward that institution will be invaluable. By creating environments and opportunities on campus that teach and reinforce the skills, values, and standards that are upheld in the workplace and our society, colleges are doing their students a great service by preparing them to become contributing members of our increasingly technological and global society. This, in turn, ensures that our system of higher education remains pivotal in positively transforming the aspirations and livelihood of the greatest number of individuals who dream of a degree as the ticket to economic independence.

References

Arum, R., & Roksa, J. (2014). *Aspiring adults adrift: Tentative transitions of college graduates.* Chicago, IL: University of Chicago Press.

Association for Career and Technical Education. (n.d.). What is "career ready"? Retrieved from http://www.acteonline.org

Association for Supervision and Curriculum Development. (2015). "Chapter 2: Describing the habits of mind by Arthur L. Costa." Retrieved from http://www.ascd.org/publications/books/108008/chapters/Describing-the-Habits-of-Mind.aspx

Bain, K. (2004). *What the best college teachers do.* Cambridge, MA: Harvard University Press.

Bean, J.C. (2011). *Engaging ideas: The professor's guide to integrating writing, critical thinking, and active learning in the classroom* (2nd ed.). San Francisco, CA: Jossey-Bass.

Bender, T. (2004). *Discussion-based online teaching to enhance student learning: Theory, practice and assessment.* Sterling, VA: Stylus.

Blankespoor, H.D. (1997). Classroom atmosphere: A personal inventory. In J. K. Roth (Ed.), *Inspiring teaching: Carnegie professors of the year speak* (pp. 24–33). Bolton, MA: Anker.

Conley, D.T. (2012, May 2). *A complete definition of college and career readiness.* Educational Policy Improvement Center. Retrieved from www.epiconline.org

Constantine, M.G., Kindaichi, M.M., & Miville, M.L. (2007). Factors influencing the educational and vocational transitions of Black and Latino high school students. *Professional School Counseling, 10,* 261–265.

Costa, A.L., & Kallick, B. (2008). *Learning and leading with habits of mind: 16 essential characteristics for success.* Alexandria, VA: Association for Supervision and Curriculum Development.

DeAngelis, T. (2003, February). Why we overestimate our competence: Social psychologists are examining people's patterning of overlooking their own weaknesses. *Monitor on Psychology, 34*(2), 60. Retrieved from http://www.apa.org/monitor/feb03/overestimate.aspx

Elbow, P. (1998). *Writing with power: Techniques for mastering the writing process* (2nd ed.). New York, NY: Oxford University Press.

Olson, L. (2007, June 12). What does "ready" mean? There is plenty of confusion about what it means to fully prepare students for life after high school. *Education Week, 26*(40), 7–8, 10–12. Retrieved from http://www.edweek.org/ew/articles/2007/06/12/40overview.h26.html

Shaughnessy, M. P. (1977). *Errors and expectations: A guide for the teacher of basic writing.* New York, NY: Oxford University Press.

Section 4
Physical Wellness

10
Sleep
Enhancing Bedtime Performance
MICHAEL McNEIL

Introduction

Sleep is a necessity, not a luxury.
—Dr. Safwan Badr, President, American Academy of Sleep Medicine

Not sleeping may just be the unofficial sport of college students. Societal acceptance of nonsleeping, along with social glorification of ideas like "all-nighters," is contributing to the sleep deficit that today's college students are experiencing. One in five college students reports staying up for 24 consecutive hours at least once in the past month (Lund, Reider, Whiting, & Prichard, 2010), contributing to erratic patterns of sleep among students. Sleep contributes to individual well-being through the connections to attention, focus, energy, and coping. Sleep is also directly linked to physical and psychological health. For students, faculty, and administrators it is wise to question ways in which college and university campuses are helping or hindering sleep quantity and quality.

To establish a framework for this chapter, consider the following:

- Sleep quantity is defined as the amount of sleep needed to feel rested, generally identified as 7–9 hours per night.
- Sleep quality is defined as restful, disruption-free sleep.
- Sleep regularity is defined as having a sleep pattern consistent with a schedule or routine and remaining consistent across days.
- REM sleep is defined as a period of deeper sleep characterized by rapid eye movement (REM), increased pulse and respiration, body movements, and dreaming.

While abundant scientific literature exists on the benefits of sleep, notably less is available on why college students tend to sacrifice sleep. It has become socially acceptable for college students to sacrifice sleep. Various theories have attempted to explain sleep avoidance tendencies, centering primarily in developmental stage–based explanations. Leading theories are tied to two key concepts: time management and the idea known as "fear of missing out." College students may choose a lifestyle that is expectant of less sleep despite having greater freedoms to schedule activity and sleep times. It has also been suggested that academic and social demands may produce irregular sleep schedules (Tsai & Lee, 2004). Clement, Janowski, Bouchard, Perreault, and Lepage (2002) may have said it best: "The time demands of academic life may have induced students to reduce time-consuming health behaviors, such as getting enough sleep" (p. 257). Examples include working students trying to find time to focus on academics and sacrificing sleep or students in highly competitive environments feeling pressure to shoulder a higher-volume course load, resulting in less time available for sleep.

According to the World Health Organization (1996), the links between health and the ability to learn cannot be separated. Researchers have discussed how schools will be able to reach their educational goals only when the students are healthy (Smith, 1996). It is important for postsecondary institutions to investigate the role of health in the academic performance of enrolled students. With greater accountability expected in higher education, schools should consider how sleep-related issues are linked to retention, dropout rates, and time to degree completion.

Students tend to be highly unaware of the impact that sleep can have on their abilities, going so far as to notably overestimate performance if lacking sleep. Despite perceptions of ability to perform, sleep deprivation reduces college student performance compared to rested individuals (Pilcher & Walters, 1997). When given a choice of problems on an assignment, sleep-deprived college students tend to select less challenging tasks, while not perceiving a reduction in effort. Sleep-deprived students may choose less difficult problem options to help ensure quality, and this problem selection decision implies that in coursework, students may opt for less difficult effort in an attempt to preserve higher achievement. "Adolescents, who often use sleep time as discretionary time and subsequently get insufficient sleep, may reduce their educational goals both inside and outside of the classroom" (Engle-Friedman et al., 2003, p. 123).

With the recognition that sleep plays a significant part in health (physical and mental), productivity, and safety, the U.S. Department of Health and Human Services (USDHHS) (2010) has included student sleeping in the Healthy People 2020 plan for the nation. An objective was included that calls for students getting an average of 8 hours of sleep per night. According to the USDHHS (2010), there is a need to "increase public knowledge of how adequate sleep and treatment of sleep disorders improve health, productivity, wellness, quality of life, and safety on roads and in the workplace" (p. 1).

State of Affairs

The problems with sleep appear to begin before students enroll in postsecondary education. Data from the Youth Risk Behavior Surveillance System (YRBSS) in 2013 showed that more than 68% of students in grades 9–12 got less than 8 hours of sleep per night on average (CDC, 2014).

Nearly three-quarters (73%) of college students report some level of sleep problems, including quantity and quality (Buboltz, Brown, & Soper, 2001). In 2013, data published by the American College Health Association (ACHA) showed that:

- More than 19% of students reported sleep difficulties that resulted in negative academic performance.

- More than a quarter of students (26.9%) reported sleep difficulties as being traumatic or difficult to handle.
- More than 88% of students reported getting enough sleep to feel rested on 5 or fewer days in the past week.
- Nearly 90% of students reported as least some problem with sleepiness during daytime activities.
- Nearly 60% of students reported feeling tired, dragged out, or sleepy during 3 or more days in the past week (ACHA, 2013b).

Despite all of the negative sleep experiences reported by students in the ACHA data, the overwhelming majority (98%) had not been treated by a professional for sleep. The ACHA data also highlights an information gap; more than half of students (52%) reported wanting to receive information on sleep from their institution, yet only half that number (25%) reported actually receiving sleep information (ACHA, 2013a). Sleep is one of the most desired health topics.

Researchers have noted that the negative experience of college students with sleep is higher than the average nonstudent adult population (Buboltz et al., 2001), suggesting that enrollment in postsecondary education may be a covariate to consider. There are likely unique elements of the college experience that may contribute to negative sleep experiences. In fact, sleep may be one issue that is consistently different compared to the general population (Clement et al., 2002).

While secondary school data notes that sleeping is better among males, the numbers tend to change once students enroll in college. Men in college sleep less and women sleep more, regardless of the weekday or weekend consideration, and age, gender, and race are all considerations when thinking about daytime sleepiness and how sleep is viewed and experienced by college students (Jean-Louis, von Gizycki, Zizi, & Nunes, 1998).

The sleep-wake cycle of a college student is generally characterized by insufficient sleep duration, lower quality of sleep, delayed onset of sleep, and daytime napping (Brown et al., 2002; Buboltz et al., 2001; Jean-Louis et al., 1998; Lund et al., 2010; Oginska & Pokorski, 2006). Considerations of college students' sleep should also explore the differentiation between quantity of sleep and quality of sleep. Researchers have found that quality of sleep may be a better predictor of success among college students than quantity of sleep (Buboltz et al., 2001; Curcio, Ferrara, & De Gennaro, 2006). A broad look at sleep has suggested that quality is a key consideration and may drive considerations of quantity (Eliasson, Eliasson, King, Gould, & Eliasson, 2002; Pilcher, Ginter, & Sadowsky, 1997).

So what is causing these sleep problems? As James Maas (the man who introduced us to the term "power nap") suggests, "Stress is the main culprit; that and caffeine after two in the afternoon, and any liquor within three hours of bedtime and certainly drugs—all can lead to stress" (cited in Bhattacharjee, 2014). Arnett, in his work on emerging adulthood, suggests that in the period when young people are slowly transitioning from adolescence and into adulthood, they are testing the waters, learning about what being an adult entails, embracing the most self-focused period of life, and using the time as a period of exploration and possibilities. Young people at this developmental stage are merely delaying the adoption of adult responsibilities that likely signal "the end of independence, the end of spontaneity, the end of a sense of wide-open possibilities" (Arnett, 2004, p. 6).

If you combine Maas's ideas with the developmental stage of students in which they are continually exposed to new ideas and stimuli, an internalized drive to maximize their college years, delays in adopting the behaviors associated with being an adult, and campuses increasingly catering to student demand as part of the customer service approach, then it is not difficult to understand the lack of sleep and associated concerns experienced by college students.

In fact, campuses are likely working against sleep supportive environments in a number of ways. A growing number of campuses are catering to the on-demand world of students by making more spaces available 24/7. Additionally, campuses have been partnering with stimulant beverage companies ("energy" drinks), increasing late-night activities, and scheduling more early morning classes (usually driven by classroom space needs and growing enrollment). Combine these administrative actions, often driven by student requests, and it is not difficult to see why students may be experiencing pressures to trade sleep as a discretionary time for other activities, resulting in less than adequate quantity and quality of sleep and the potential for negative academic experiences.

Sleep and Quality of Life

There are many factors of life that can be impacted by sleep. While seven of these are explored in this chapter, there is simply not enough room to address them all. Additionally, the seven described here are not independent of each other. These examples were selected for inclusion as they have a distinct relationship to academia and may intersect in any number of ways for a student. As you explore these areas, consider that these may combine in additive or synergistic manners whereby sleep disruptions (quality or quantity) may have greater impacts.

Academic Performance

Sleep difficulties are a common, but often ignored or overlooked, problem among college students that has notable implications for student academic success. Researchers have repeatedly found that sleep behaviors are associated with academic performance. The theme across the studies is consistent and clear; sleep is necessary for solid and sustained academic performance. Findings include impaired concentration when in the classroom (Ban & Lee, 2001), wake times as an element of sleep behaviors having a particularly notable relationship with grade point variability (Trockel, Barnes, & Egget, 2000), strong correlates between GPA and quantity and quality sleep measures (Murphey, Lamonda, Carney, & Duncan, 2004; Peters, Joireman, & Ridgway, 2005), and students with sleep disorders being more likely to be academically at risk and experience greater academic performance consequences (Gaultney, 2010). Given the academic pressures of students and the role of sleep in memory consolidation (Stickgold, Hobson, Fosse, & Fosse,

2001), achieving and maintaining good quantity and quality of sleep become a key need for supporting students as they cope with, absorb, and process the new information being gained through classroom experiences (O'Quinn, 2003; Yang, Wu, Hsieh, Liu, & Lu, 2003).

Addressing sleep quantity and quality issues does appear to moderate the negative impacts on academics (Taras & Potts-Datema, 2005). That being said, some students appear to self-regulate and prioritize sleep based on perceptions of future elements and success, suggesting that the relationship between sleep and academic performance is being driven by a desire for high grades, with students thus electing to prioritize sleep (Peters et al., 2005).

It is worth noting that the directionality of the relationship between sleep and academic performance is primarily assumed. While some controlled studies have measured performance and problem selection when sleep is limited, most of the studies are using correlational models. As such it may be worth considering the possibility that students who perform at higher levels have skills and strategies that may include prioritization of sleep. Simply put, it is possible that high achievers are able to sleep more and better because they do well, not assuming that they do well because they are sleeping in greater quality and quantity.

Working

Sleep is well documented to have impacts on work. It is not just work performance that can suffer; sleep also contributes to absenteeism and increased workplace injuries. Individuals doing shift work are at increased likelihood of sleep concerns, along with those working extended hours. On the other side, presenteeism (the practice of being present at work or school—despite health or other reason to be absent; often associated with lower productivity) is more common in people with the sleep disorder insomnia ("Presenteeism," 2015). Though these individuals have difficulty sleeping and may be at work more often, they, too, are more likely to see negative consequences of sleep disruptions in the workplace (Swanson et al., 2011).

For individuals who work and attend postsecondary education, there may be a combined effect that impacts both key areas. The working student may face unique challenges in scheduling the needed 7–9 hours of sleep and may benefit from situation-specific support. One area to consider is having academic advisors discuss with working students the need to manage the number of courses taken in a given term. While it may take longer to complete the academic degree, the student's broader well-being is being considered in trying to find a work/school balance without sacrificing sleep.

Relationships

The idea of relationships can be broadly defined. Relationships with self, romantic partner, classmates, faculty, administrators, family, coworkers, supervisors, friends, and many more can be impacted by sleep.

Sleep problems are associated with greater aggression and violence, suggesting that if not obtaining a sufficient amount of quality sleep a person may be more likely to react in a negative manner in a host of relationship situations (Kamphuis, Meerlo, Koolhaas, & Lancel, 2012). Lack of sleep is also tied to impaired emotional function and mood regulation. Researchers have established a link between insufficient sleep and the inability to reprocess and manage emotional experiences (van der Helm & Walker, 2009). Given that sleep helps people process relationship experiences and regulate mood, it becomes critical for college students to have a good quantity and quality of sleep. Students are balancing a wide-range of relationships, and sleep is one part of ensuring the needed tools are available for cross-relationship success.

There is a known connection between relationship quality and sleep (quality and duration) (Troxel, Buysse, & Matthews, 2009; Troxel, Robles, Hall, & Buysse, 2007), but more recent research also connects relationship history (stable relationships) with better sleep quality. This research suggests that maintaining healthy, lasting relationships is beneficial to sleep (Troxel et al., 2010). A logical follow-on to the studies indicates that individuals struggling with relationships may also experience lower sleep quantity and quality. In an effort to better understand how to support sleep among students, it is wise to consider the broad range of factors that may be contributing to poorer sleep hygiene.

Athletics

Whether intercollegiate or intramural, there is a connection between sleep and athletic performance. Mixed results from various studies leave the exact relationship yet to be fully understood. What is known is that student athletes report low quality and quantity of sleep (Birge, 2014) and that disrupted sleep has an impact on athlete mood, especially on the night prior to a competition (Lastella, Lovell, & Sargent, 2014).

Regular exercise is known to support quality and quantity of sleep, though mostly when completed three or more hours before bedtime. Because physical activity is associated with improved sleep it may be logical to believe that athletes do better with sleep. However, because athletes report lower sleep, schedule variability must be taken into consideration. There are some positives to consider. Increasing sleep time has been shown to improve athletic performance (Mah, Mah, Kezirian, & Dement, 2011) and decrease risk for athletic injury (Milewski et al., 2014). Overall, loss of sleep is broadly associated with reduced athletic performance, and athletes report less than the recommended 7–9 hours of sleep per night (Halson, 2013).

Technology and Sleep Disruptions

One of the recommendations for improving sleep quantity and quality is limiting or stopping the use of electronic devices at least an hour before bedtime. Associations with television use near and at bedtime are known disruptors to sleep, including the delaying of going to sleep, but the widespread use of other devices (phones, laptops, tablets) by younger people has been shown to cause even greater disruptions to sleep (Gradisar et al., 2013). The more engaging the device (cognitive and psychosocial arousal), the more likely people are to put off going to sleep, resulting in a loss of sleep quantity. Further, the sounds made by a phone (e.g., text message notification) have been shown to disrupt quality of sleep.

Broadly speaking, the increased use of media devices (e.g., TV, phone, computers, video games) is associated with reductions in sleep time (Van den Bulck, 2004). Given that college students are already established as having lower amounts of sleep (quantity), the potential for further disrupting sleep and the associated consequences is increased. More recent studies have found that the increasing disruptions to quality of sleep from devices like mobile phones are more prevalent in extroverted individuals, introducing further complexity to the relationship between technology and healthier sleep behaviors (White, Buboltz, & Igou, 2011).

Other Quality of Life Impacts

INJURY

Sleep deprivation increases the risk of injury, especially motor vehicle crashes, among college students and young adults (Carskadon & Acebo, 2002). Drowsy driving peaks during the college-age years and increases risk for motor vehicle crashes (Pack et al., 1995; Taylor & Bramoweth, 2010). In fact, research suggests that drowsy driving may produce higher levels of impairment than alcohol (Dawson & Reid, 1997; Roehrs et al., 1994). When combined, alcohol and sleep deprivation may result in a synergistic effect that exponentially increases the risk of motor vehicle crashes and other negative consequences among college students.

ALCOHOL

Alcohol has a bidirectional relationship with sleep. The consumption of alcohol is known to disrupt sleep quality and can result in broadly defined declines in performance in and out of the classroom (Lund et al., 2010; Roehrs & Roth, 2001). Sleep deprivation is also associated with increased alcohol consumption (Brown et al., 2002), and some students report using alcohol as a mechanism to address poor sleep (Taylor & Bramoweth, 2010; Yang et al., 2003). While alcohol is a depressant and may contribute to falling asleep, a person who has consumed alcohol will not sleep as deeply, will be less likely to experience REM sleep, and may experience other disruptions. The combined effect is sleep of lower quality. Further, students that fell asleep in school had higher reported consumption of alcohol, though they did not identify any causality in the relationship. Researchers have also suggested that daytime sleepiness may increase vulnerability to substance use (Jean-Louis et al., 1998).

Beyond the individual impact, a person consuming alcohol could disrupt the sleep of others as an indirect negative sleep issue associated with alcohol consumption. Health professionals tend to give consideration to the impact of alcohol on the sleep of the person who consumed alcohol (Wechsler et al., 2002) but rarely to the impact of alcohol-related behaviors on disturbing sleep for others. For example, consider an intoxicated person making noise in a residence hall and how that may impact sleep for other residents.

Tips for Good Sleep

There are a few key ideas that promote good quantity and quality of sleep.

- Go to bed and wake up around the same time every day, even on weekends.
- Exercise regularly, but finish up at least three hours before planning to sleep.
- Create a sleep environment that is quiet, dark, cool, and comfortable.
- Use the bed for one primary activity: sleep.
- Meditate, read, listen to music, take a bath, give/receive a massage, or do some other relaxing activity that will help take the mind off of the day's stresses and excitements and allow easing into slumber land.
- Try a white noise machine if there are potential noise distractions.
- Limit daytime naps to one of no more than 30 minutes.
- Avoid using the bed for studying, socializing, or other nonsleep activities.
- Avoid caffeine, alcohol, or nicotine close to bedtime.
- Avoid eating right before going to sleep.
- Avoid exposure to bright lights right before going to bed.

Adapted with permission from Alice! Health Promotion, Columbia University, *The Downside of Sleep Deprivation* (2015).

Living and Learning Environments

Living Environment

Students living on campus spend most of their time on and near campus. Add in the facts that many campuses have a finite amount of space and students are transient, and the on-campus living environment becomes somewhat of a fixed structure. The traditional model of on-campus living included students in shared living environments. However, there are some campus opportunities for greater consideration to be given to sleep, including when designing new or renovating existing residential spaces. For example, if the spaces are set up as two-room doubles, the typical setup is one student per room with bed, desk, and so forth. Instead, give consideration to separating the spaces into sleeping room (two beds) and living/study room (two desks). This creates a clear indicator that the bedroom is a space for sleeping and other activities are designed to occur in the living/study space.

Other considerations for sleep-supportive living environments include the following:

- Room darkening shades/blinds/curtains
- Considerations of external lighting
- Interior lighting, not a single overhead light
- Dimmer features for overhead lighting
- Placement of rooms within building to minimize exterior sound
- Soundproofing rooms
- Sound attenuating walls
- Limitations of Internet bandwidth at night
- Quiet hours, seven days a week.

In addition to structured living environments that are maximized to support sleep, it is also necessary to ensure that policies and staff training match the other sleep-promoting efforts occurring on campus. Quiet hour policies are the most common example available. Students and professional staff living and working in residential spaces are often trained to enforce policy but are rarely trained on how to encourage proper quantity and quality of sleep or the available campus resources for sleep.

With college students tending to experience more sleep deprivation, they also build up "sleep debt" that reduces alertness and functional ability (Carskadon & Acebo, 2002). This debt accumulation tends to lead to the idea of wanting to "catch up" on sleep. Unfortunately this myth of catching up is perpetuated by systemic factors. For example, those living off campus may believe that the weekend will provide "extra time" to sleep and initially forget the desire to use weekend time for socializing, other responsibilities (work, family, etc.), or homework that is intended to be completed using weekend hours. Simply put, it is not possible to catch up on sleep. A person can, however, return to a point of balance (or homeostasis) with regard to sleep.

Far too often, students talk of "catching up" on the weekend or during academic breaks. When students engage in sleep binges, especially during prolonged breaks, the inconsistent sleep cycle is reinforced. The sustained inconsistency actually works against the students' best interests, potentially leading to greater sleep challenges and disruptions when they return to the classroom. Additionally, inconsistent sleep that becomes routine during the college years may continue when students transition to the next life phase (work, raising a family, etc.) and may lead to challenges in achieving goals in those respective domains.

Learning Environment

The college years are a time of distinctive learning in and out of the classroom. Campuses often approach learning as a blend of formal academic experiences and broader co-curricular learning opportunities. The Framework for Assessing Learning and Development Outcomes (FALDOs) considers good sleep (quantity, quality, or both) a key element of learning (CAS, 2006). While some of the following may seem difficult to achieve, campus professionals should aim for learning environments that are attuned to the sleep needs of the student population. Learning environments' considerations include:

- Limiting or eliminating late-night hours of libraries
- Limiting early morning and late-night classes
- Discouraging all-nighters
- Closing classroom buildings at night
- Closing computer labs at night
- Eliminating the sales of stimulant beverages
- Restricting the sales of caffeinated beverages at night
- Offering required classes at different times of the day (when more than one section)
- Training academic advisors to encourage and support positive sleep behaviors
- Restricting online course access during late-night hours
- Require the submission of online assignments no later than 9:00 p.m.

Ultimately campuses should be working toward creating environments that maximize efficiency and support sleep. The broad and ever evolving landscape of the learning environment requires continuous re-evaluation of efforts and considerations of sleep when making substantive changes.

Social Environment

When students enroll in postsecondary education, they enter an environment that provides a less formal structure, especially from a time management perspective. If a student is enrolled in 15 credit hours, he or she will spend only a fraction of the week in the classroom, allowing significant freedom for how the balance of time will be allocated. This may not be exactly the same among students who work, or working adults returning to school, but for a notable portion of college students there exists a scheduling flexibility that will not be as open again until they reach retirement.

Because the typical student has classes during the day, the majority of social opportunities are shifted to nights and weekends. Researchers have identified a shift in weekend bedtimes and wake times compared to weekday sleep patterns among college students. This shifting of times contributes to inconsistencies in sleep schedules and may contribute to sleep deprivation (Taylor & Bramoweth, 2010). Less consideration has been given to the time between classes or creation of designated programming blocks. Some campuses have moved to a schedule that creates a designated daytime opportunity for co-curricular activities (such as student organization meetings) as a mechanism for encouraging involvement and social connections while not always shifting these activities to nights and weekends.

Other considerations regarding the co-curricular social environment include a generational tendency to be hyper-involved and a fear of missing out. Campuses should consider limiting the number of leadership roles each student may have and the number of organizations to which a student belongs, and ensure there are structural and advisor-supported efforts that help with co-curricular involvement/development without overscheduling students (potentially resulting in compromised sleep quantity or quality). The current generation of students grew up during a time in which much of their lives was highly scheduled and promoting the glorification of "busy." As a result, these young people have a tendency to want to do everything and cannot imagine missing something. As a result these young people may be quick to trade sleep for other activities so as to stay "connected."

Recognizing Sleep Problems Among Students

So how would a faculty/staff member or classmate recognize sleep concerns in a student? The logical answer is falling asleep in class, not paying attention, glazed eyes, or being disconnected. However, in-class sleeping could be the result of a number of potential contributors, not just a lack of quantity and quality of sleep. Some medications, for example, can produce sleepiness in many individuals.

To truly determine if a student is experiencing challenges with sleep, the best approach is to discuss concerns directly with the individual. This direct approach allows faculty, teaching assistants, and classmates to share any concerns, along with providing referrals to supports, as appropriate. Most likely a pattern will need to develop before the issue rises to the point of concern. Any individual may have an off-day that manifests in symptoms including drowsiness.

Other symptoms of potential sleep issues include difficulty staying on topic or concentrating, assignments suddenly going down in quality, and missing class more often. As might be expected, all of these symptoms may also be the result of nonsleep-related causes or may be the result of a combination of issues (e.g., learning disability and coursework leading to less sleep).

Benefits of Sleep

There are many benefits of sleep. Check out this list of how sleep helps us:

- Promotes memory consolidation of what is studied
- Affects processing speed so that a person can learn faster
- Makes people feel refreshed and ready for work or exams
- May help a student to pay attention in class
- Boosts immune health
- Helps maintain energy balance
- Improves athletic performance by enhancing motor skills
- Is closely related to stress. Experiencing stress often can be the cause of sleep troubles, and lack of sleep can, in turn, be very stressful.

Adapted with permission from Alice! Health Promotion, Columbia University, *Sleep Resources* (2015).

Sleep and Disability

The most frequent thinking on sleep is that in contemporary society people do not make it a priority and do not get enough. Rarely do we explore the idea that sleep may occur too often, in ways that are unanticipated, or that quantity and quality are not the main issue. These ideas are where sleep and disability frequently intersect. For example, with college students there are frequent efforts to increase sleep quantity and quality but little consideration is given to disorders, like sleep paralysis and narcolepsy. Researchers have found that sleep paralysis and narcolepsy are associated with a variety of factors, including student status, and that issues like sleep paralysis are likely over-represented in student populations (Sharpless & Barber, 2011). As a result it is important for campus professionals and faculty to not assume all sleep-related issues are related to lower quantity/quality problems and to know that there are distinct sleep-related support needs for students with sleep disorders. Consider reaching out to the campus disability services team to gain a better understanding of students with sleep-related disabilities. While talking with them, consider that the issue of sleep may take other directions for students with nonsleep-related disabilities as well.

Recommendations

Throughout this chapter there have been multiple recommendations on how campuses can improve environments and practices that are designed to respect the academic and co-curricular learning functions while also making the campus sleep-supportive. The following are additional recommendations, organized by audience, that can further these concepts.

Faculty

For faculty, including teaching assistants, it is important to remember that dozing off in class is not necessarily a reflection on teaching ability or engagement with material. As instructors, there are a number of potential strategies to help encourage supportive sleep behaviors among students.

SLEEP STATEMENT

Placing a simple wellness-oriented statement on a syllabus and course online platform serves to remind students that health and associated behaviors have a role in supporting academic performance. Making a statement regarding sleep at the beginning of the term, perhaps including some of the research on sleep and academics, and repeating it at key times (prior to exams, major assignments, etc.) can help to remind students of the importance of proper rest. Faculty can also remind students to not put off studying or reviewing until the last minute—and how time management can link to quality of sleep.

CURRICULUM INFUSION

Faculty teaching a wide variety of courses can use sleep-related information and examples to illustrate course principles and support other learning.

- *Advertising/Public Relations* faculty could assign students projects related to creating and testing sleep promoting messages.
- *Architecture* faculty could task students with designing sleep-supportive environments.
- *Health Professions* faculty could include sleep ideas in nearly any part of the curriculum.
- *Mathematics* faculty could model formulas to determine how long it will take students to return to a rested baseline (homeostasis) related to sleep, following different intervals of disruptive or missing sleep.
- *Psychology* faculty can use sleep as an example of individuals sacrificing health-supporting behaviors in the pursuit of other goals.
- *Research* faculty can use data on sleep and academics for teaching data analysis strategies.
- *Sociology* faculty can assign projects for students to determine the role of peers and other social forces related to sleep decisions.

ONLINE TEACHING

When teaching online or blended model courses, faculty are wise to use the reporting tools found in most online platforms to see when students are accessing materials. Time-of-day and day-of-week access data may help faculty to determine if students are potentially sacrificing sleep in an effort to do their work. Faculty can consider limiting access during typical sleep times, accounting for students who may be in different time zones. Additionally, online faculty (and other faculty as well) can restrict deadlines for submitting materials to no later than 9:00 p.m.

PARTNERSHIPS

Faculty and co-curricular partnerships have many benefits for the faculty, administrators, and students. When it comes to sleep, like students, faculty members have access to campus administrators and community resources to help promote sleep. Each campus can give thought to how working with others on and off campus can support students in the achievement of personal and academic goals. Further, the broad missions of the institution (research, teaching, service, etc.) are all furthered when sleep is supported.

Administrators and Staff Members

Administrators and staff members, such as those in student affairs, tend to suggest that students seek more late-night spaces for studying, socializing, and other activities. As a result, a growing number of campuses offer some spaces that are available to students 24 hours a day. A delicate balance exists between providing spaces as requested by the students and choosing the sleep-supportive policy of closing buildings overnight. Reviews of the literature suggest that because students intentionally defer sleep, the demand for space is driven by a need to fill that deferred sleep time with other activities (e.g., study, student group meetings, late-night programming). No research exists to suggest students would make enrollment, campus engagement, or other key decisions (e.g., transfer consideration) based on availability of late-night or overnight space.

Administrators and staff members can consider the development, implementation, and evaluation of a sleep education and skill-building program. One such program, Sleep Treatment and Education Program for Students (STEPS), resulted in significantly improved sleep quality and sleep hygiene behaviors (e.g., consistent bedtime, less caffeine) at post-treatment. The STEPS program also showed an impact by preventing worsening sleep behaviors as an academic semester progressed. As part of educational efforts, campuses can consider the inclusion of sleep education in first-year orientation courses as a step toward preventing negative sleep quality and sleep hygiene behaviors (Brown, Buboltz, & Soper, 2006).

Further, campuses may consider expanding training for student leaders to incorporate sleep information. Key student leader groups that may benefit from information and skill-building training regarding sleep are resident assistants, commuter student organizations, student government, student-parent organizations, and many others.

Students

Because students have been shown to trade sleep time for other activities (Brown, Buboltz, & Soper, 2001; Machado, Varella, & Andrade, 1998), sleep outcomes may be improved by considering increased student involvement with scheduling and time management. Students are encouraged to develop time management priorities for creating a balanced, health-promoting, and sustainable schedule. The recommended order for adding time to a blank schedule is (1) sleep (7–9 hours per night), (2) meals (2–3 hours a day), (3) classes and academic work (classroom hours + 5–8 hours per class per week), and (4) everything else. Sleep and meals come before classes as proper sleep and good nutrition both contribute to academic success. Like Maslow's hierarchy of needs, the scheduling of sleep and meals before all other activities is driven by the fact that sleep and nutrition support the effectiveness of all tasks that follow in a schedule.

These priorities for time management are not impacted by variables like full-time or part-time student status, age, hours spent working or volunteering, and so forth. Linking back to the concepts of being overinvolved, setting unrealistic schedules, glorifying being "busy," and the fear of missing out, students may overschedule when adding more than sleep, meals, and academics. Although students should not focus only on academics and directly connected items, postsecondary education is a time focused on learning, and the co-curricular opportunity to learn about balance that supports immediate and long-term goals is an important lesson for students.

Students can do it all; but it does not need to be in the same day, week, month, semester, year, or academic experience.

Finally, students have the opportunity to lead by example on the topic of sleep. The influence of peers in higher education is well documented. Rather than always rely on policy and administrators, students can lead on the topic of sleep by challenging the glorification of nonsleeping or reduced sleep, encouraging and engaging in positive sleep behaviors (consistent bedtimes, dark sleeping spaces, eliminating distractions from the sleep environment, 7–9 hours of sleep per night), and advocating for more sleep-supporting environments on campus.

Parents and Families

While students may deny it at times, they frequently look to parents and other trusted family members for guidance and advice. Because of this trusted relationship, parents and family members have an opportunity to encourage students to obtain sufficient sleep of high quality. Leveraging the wisdom gained with greater life experience, parents and family members can offer specific viewpoints to promote healthier sleep choices. Examples of actions and advice for parents and families to offer include:

- Discourage oversleeping
- Dispel the false myth of "catching up" during weekends, breaks, visits
- Actively encourage 7–9 hours of sleep per night
- Assist in setting schedules that include proper sleep time
- Provide guidance on creating quality sleep environments (reduce light, sound, etc.)
- Share on- and off-campus resources for sleep (sharing them with students during peak times—e.g., start of term, exams, major assignment due dates).

Summary

While the reasons for sacrificing sleep among college students may be as unique as the individual, the need for and benefits of sleep are quite clear. Sleep supports students in the achievement of academic and life goals, positively contributes to physical and psychological health, and has many other benefits (improved athletic performance, relationship well-being, etc.). Many of the issues connected to health may be bidirectional, yet there is a historical reluctance to take on sleep as an area for improvement with college students.

The time has come to stop glorifying nonsleeping as a badge of honor, a rite of passage, or an expectation of the college years. Time spent in postsecondary education is every bit the "real world" as that experienced by students when they complete their program of study. We must challenge people who talk of "all-nighters" and be sure to lead by example through our practice of healthier sleep behaviors.

Students may lack the wisdom of life experience, have trouble separating want from need, find difficulty achieving balance in schedules, and not yet realize the negative impacts that sleep may be having. The balance between students' perceived need for and benefits of sleep continues to present challenges for campuses. As such there are many opportunities for students, faculty, administrators, and even parents/families to work in partnership to address sleep needs. Working across the socioecological model, campuses can promote sleep and the associated benefits through intra- and interpersonal efforts, create sleep-promoting campuses (including policies), develop sleep-supportive environments, and build a community that values and practices good sleep behaviors (quantity and quality).

References

Alice! Health Promotion, Columbia University. (2015). *The Downside of Sleep Deprivation*. Retrieved from http://goaskalice.columbia.edu/downsides-sleep-deprivation

Alice! Health Promotion, Columbia University. (2015). *Sleep Resources*. Retrieved from https://sleep.health.columbia.edu/resources

American College Health Association. (2013a). *Spring 2013 reference group data report*. Retrieved from http://www.acha-ncha.org/docs/ACHA-NCHA-II_ReferenceGroup_DataReport_Spring2013.pdf

American College Health Association. (2013b). *Spring 2013 reference group executive summary*. Retrieved from http://www.acha-ncha.org/docs/ACHA-NCHA-II_ReferenceGroup_ExecutiveSummary_Spring2013.pdf

Arnett, J. (2004). *Emerging adulthood: The winding road from late teens through the twenties*. Oxford: Oxford University Press.

Ban, D. J., & Lee, T. J. (2001). Sleep duration, subjective sleep disturbances and associated factors among university students in Korea. *Journal of the Korean Medical Society, 16*, 475–480.

Bhattacharejee, A. (2014, February 26). Sleepless and slow. *Mercury*. Retrieved from http://utdmercury.com/sleepless-and-slow

Birge, M. E. (2014). *Sleep quality and quantity of Portland State University intercollegiate student-athletes: A case study* (Master's thesis). Retrieved from http://pdxscholar.library.pdx.edu/open_access_etds

Brown, F. C., Buboltz, W. C., Jr., & Soper, B. (2001). Prevalence of delayed sleep phase syndrome in university students. *College Student Journal, 35*, 472–476.

Brown, F.C., Buboltz, W.C., Jr., & Soper, B. (2002). Relationship of sleep hygiene awareness, sleep hygiene practices, and sleep quality in university students. *Behavioral Medicine, 28*, 33–38.

Brown, F. C., Buboltz, W. C., Jr., & Soper, B. (2006). Development and evaluation of the Sleep Treatment and Education Program for Students (STEPS). *Journal of American College Health, 54*, 231–237.

Buboltz, W. C., Jr., Brown, F., & Soper, B. (2001). Sleep habits and patterns of college students: A preliminary study. *Journal of American College Health, 50*, 131–135.

Carskadon, M. A., & Acebo, C. (2002). Regulation of sleepiness in adolescents: Update, insights, and speculation. *Sleep, 25*, 606–614.

Centers for Disease Control and Prevention (CDC). (2014). Youth risk behavior surveillance—United States, 2013. *Morbidity and mortality weekly report*. Retrieved from http://www.cdc.gov/mmwr/pdf/ss/ss6304.pdf

Clement, M., Jankowski, L. W., Bouchard, L., Perreault, M., & Lepage, Y. (2002). Health behaviors of nursing students: a longitudinal study. *Journal of Nursing Education, 41*, 257–265.

Council for the Advancement of Standards in Higher Education (CAS). (2006). *Framework for assessing learning and development outcomes*. Washington, DC: Author.

Curcio, G., Ferrara, M., & De Gennaro, L. (2006). Sleep loss, learning capacity and academic performance. *Sleep Medicine Reviews, 10*, 323–337.

Dawson, D., & Reid, K. (1997). Fatigue, alcohol and performance impairment. *Nature, 388*(6639), 235.

Eliasson, A., Eliasson, A., King, J., Gould, B., & Eliasson, A. (2002). Association of sleep and academic performance. *Sleep and Breathing, 6*, 45–48.

Engle-Friedman, M., Reila, A., Golan, R., Ventuneac, A. M., Davis, C. M., Jefferson, A. D., & Major, D. (2003). The effect of sleep loss on next day effort. *Journal of Sleep Research, 12,* 113–124.

Gaultney, J. F. (2010). The prevalence of sleep disorders in college students: Impact on academic performance. *Journal of American College Health, 59,* 91–97.

Gradisar, M., Wolfson, A. R., Harvey, A. G., Hale, L., Rosenberg, R., & Czeisler, C. A. (2013). The sleep and technology use of Americans: Findings from the National Sleep Foundation's 2011 Sleep in America Poll. *Journal of Clinical Sleep Medicine, 9,* 1291–1299.

Halson, S. L. (2013). Sleep and the elite athlete. *Sports Science Exchange, 26*(113), 1–4.

Jean-Louis, G., von Gizycki, H., Zizi, F., & Nunes, J. (1998). Mood states and sleepiness in college students: Influences of age, sex, habitual sleep, and substance use. *Perceptual and Motor Skills, 87,* 507–512.

Kamphuis, J., Meerlo, P., Koolhaas, J. M., & Lancel, M. (2012). Poor sleep as a potential causal factor in aggression and violence. *Sleep Medicine, 13,* 327–334.

Lastella, M., Lovell, G. P., & Sargent, C. (2014). Athletes precompetitive sleep behaviour and its relationship with subsequent precompetitive mood and performance. *European Journal of Sports Science, 14,* s123–s130.

Lund, H. G. Reider, B. D., Whiting, A. B., & Prichard, J. R. (2010). Sleep patterns and predictors of disturbed sleep in a large population ot college students. *Journal of Adolescent Health, 46,* 124–132.

Machado, E.R.S., Varella, V.B.R., & Andrade, M.M.M. (1998). The influence of study schedules and work on the sleep-wake cycle of college students. *Biological Rhythm Research, 29,* 578–584.

Mah, C. D., Mah, K. E., Kezirian, E. J., & Dement, W. C. (2011). The effects of sleep extension on athletic performance of collegiate basketball players. *Sleep, 34,* 943–950.

Milewski, M. D., Skaggs, D. L., Bishop, G. A., Pace, J. L., Ibrahim, D. A., Wren, T. A., & Barzdukas, A. (2014). Chronic lack of sleep is associated with increased sports injuries in adolescent athletes. *Journal of Pediatric Orthopaedics, 34,* 129–133.

Murphey, D.A., Lamonda, K.H., Carney, J.K., & Duncan, P. (2004). Relationships of a brief measure of youth assets to health-promoting and risk behaviors. *Journal of Adolescent Health, 34*(3): 184-191.

Oginska, H., & Pokorski, J. (2006). Fatigue and mood correlates of sleep length in three age-social groups: School children, students, and employees. *Chronobiology International, 23,* 1317–1328.

O'Quinn, S. (2003). Inadequate sleep hygiene practices: Level of community awareness. *Canadian Journal of Respiratory Therapy, 9,* 21–29.

Pack, A.L., Pack, A.M., Rodgman, E., Cucchiara, A., Dinges, D.F., & Schwab, C.W. (1995). Characteristics of crashes attributes to the driver having fallen asleep. *Accident Analysis & Prevention, 27*(6), 769–775.

Peters, B. R., Joireman, J., & Ridgway, R. L. (2005). Individual differences in the consideration of future consequences scale correlate with sleep habits, sleep quality, and GPA in university students. *Psychological Reports, 96,* 817–824.

Pilcher, J. J., Ginter, D. R., & Sadowsky, B. (1997). Sleep quality versus sleep quantity: Relationships between sleep and measures of health, well-being and sleepiness in college students. *Journal of Psychosomatic Research, 42,* 583–596.

Pilcher, J. J., & Walters, A. S. (1997). How sleep deprivation affects psychological variables related to college students' cognitive performance. *Journal of American College Health, 46,* 121–126.

Presenteeism. (2015). Dictionary.com. Retrieved from http://dictionary.reference.com/browse/presenteeism

Roehrs, T., Beare, D., Zorick, F., & Roth, T. (1994). Sleepiness and ethanol effects on simulated driving. *Alcoholism, Clinical & Experimental Research, 18*(1), 154–158.

Roehrs, T. & Roth, T. (2001). Sleep, sleepiness, sleep disorders, and alcohol use and abuse. *Sleep Medicine Reviews, 5*(4), 287–297.

Sharpless, B. A., & Barber, J. P. (2011). Lifetime prevalence rates of sleep paralysis: A systemic review. *Sleep Medicine Review, 15,* 311–315.

Smith, D. R. (1996). Healthy children are prepared to learn. *School health: Programs in action.* Austin: Texas Department of Health.

Stickgold, R., Hobson, J.A., Fosse, R., & Fosse, M. (2001). Sleep, learning, and dreams: off-line memory reprocessing. *Science, 294*(5544), 1052–1057.

Swanson, L. M., Arnedt, J. T., Rosekind, M. R., Belenky, G., Balkin, T. J., & Drake, C. (2011). Sleep disorders and work performance: Findings from the 2008 National Sleep Foundation Sleep in America poll. *Journal of Sleep Research, 20,* 487–494.

Taras, H., & Potts-Datema, W. (2005). Sleep and student performance at school. *Journal of School Health, 75,* 248–254.

Taylor, D. J., & Bramoweth, A. D. (2010). Patterns and consequences of inadequate sleep in college students: Substance use and motor vehicle accidents. *Journal of Adolescent Health, 46,* 610–612.

Trockel, M. T., Barnes, M. D., & Egget, D. L. (2000). Health-related variables and academic performance among first-year college students: Implications for sleep and other behaviors. *Journal of American College Health, 49,* 125–131.

Troxel, W. M., Buysse, D. J., Hall, M., & Matthews, K. A. (2009). Marital happiness and sleep disturbances in a multi-ethnic sample of middle-aged women. *Behavioral Sleep Medicine, 7,* 2–19.

Troxel, W. M., Buysse, D. J., Matthews, K. M., Kravitz, H. M., Bromberger, J. T., Sowers, M., & Hall, M. H. (2010). Marital/cohabitation status and history in relation to sleep in midlife women. *Sleep, 33,* 973–981.

Troxel, W. M., Robles, T. F., Hall, M., & Buysse, D. J. (2007). Marital quality and the marital bed: Examining the covariation between relationship quality and sleep. *Sleep Medicine Reviews, 11,* 389–404.

Tsai, L. L., & Li, S. P. (2004). Sleep education in college: A preliminary study. *Perceptual and Motor Skills, 99,* 837–848.

U.S. Department of Health and Human Services. (2010). Office of Disease Prevention and Health Promotion. *Healthy People 2020.* Retrieved from http://www.healthypeople.gov/2020/topics-objectives/topic/sleep-health

Van den Bulck, J. (2004). Television viewing, computer game playing, and Internet use and self-reported time to bed and time out of bed in secondary-school children. *Sleep, 27,* 101–104.

van der Helm, E., & Walker, M. P. (2009). Overnight therapy? The role of sleep in emotional brain processing. *Psychological Bulletin, 135,* 731–748.

Wechsler, H., Lee, J. E., Kuo, M., Seibring, M., Nelson, T., & Lee, H. (2002). Trends in college binge drinking during a period of increased prevention efforts. Findings from 4 Harvard School of Public Health College Alcohol Study surveys: 1993–2001. *Journal of American College Health, 50,* 203–217.

White, A. G, Buboltz, W., & Igou, F. (2011). Mobile phone use and sleep quality and length in college students. *International Journal of Humanities and Social Science, 1,* 51–58.

World Health Organization. (1996). *Promoting health through school.* Geneva: Author.

Yang, C. M., Wu, C. H., Hsieh, M. H., Liu, M. H., & Lu, F. H. (2003). Coping with sleep disturbances among young adults: A survey of first-year college students in Taiwan. *Behavioral Medicine, 29,* 133–138.

11
Nutrition
Eating to Survive or Thrive
ANNANN HONG

Introduction: Eat to Live or Live to Eat

When it comes to our health and day-to-day survival, we cannot choose to eat in the same manner that we can opt to exercise or opt to meditate. However, similar to the human dynamic between sex, pleasure, and procreation, we are one of the few species that eats for more than sustenance. Eating has become a deeply nuanced and rich part of the human experience, embedded with meaning and significance, not just to support bodily functions. We eat not only to provide the basic calories required to engage in our activities of daily living but also to nourish ourselves in social, spiritual, and emotional ways. We connect with our food emotionally, and it can have healing qualities. Many of us have fond memories that can be evoked by smelling a particular dish or even simply conjuring a dish from memory that we associate with positive feelings from our past. Eating can also be a painful and unpleasant experience for those who have a negative relationship with food (either generally or specific to a food) or who might have chronic conditions that prohibit them from consuming certain foods that disagree with their bodies. But the one constant that remains across humanity is that we all require sustenance of some kind in order to survive. The question then becomes: are we eating to thrive?

We need to collectively engage in more critical thinking and discourse around our food choices and the food we consume every day. There are considerations we might not entertain as many of us mindlessly push our shopping carts through aisles of processed food, autopilot our way through the fast food drive-through, or seek to define "food preparation" as the process of cutting open prepackaged food that might require some minimal handling and heating. We live in a food culture in which time is our enemy and convenience is our friend.

Our basic understanding of what constitutes "food" in the modern world and the ways in which we nurture our bodies seem to reflect a sense of loss. We eat largely out of synch with our hormones and metabolism, which may be a more compelling culprit in weight gain than our need to consume more low-fat products. Furthermore, we seem to be searching for ways to satisfy our hunger, and yet what we have seems unfulfilling, perhaps precisely because many of the foods we are consuming really no longer constitute what our bodies truly need. Our bodies can't recognize the long list of chemical ingredients found on many food labels. Many of the foods we have manufactured today have little to no redeeming nutritional value and may be contributing more harm than sustenance—there is sufficient controversy over items on the "generally recognized as safe," or GRAS list, to support legitimate questions about what we are truly putting into our bodies.

Unfortunately, we cannot always find consensus about what constitutes good nutrition, and "diet" frequently becomes another four-letter word instead of the pursuit of a balanced intake of nutrients. Constantly evolving research and conflicting science reports add to the confusion and misinformation. Because all of us have grown up with certain messages about food and eating, and the fact is we all eat, there is a tendency to believe we might all be our own experts in nutrition. However, the fact remains that there is controversy around some of the messages we have been taught about nutritional intake (Walsh, 2014).

This chapter will first provide a brief overview of the socio-political-historical framework for what food and health have become in the United States. Next, the chapter will tackle several of the most common myths and misconceptions about nutrition. Providing the latest science behind nutrition will hopefully spur the transformative educational movement necessary to create a nutrition revolution that challenges what many of us have come to accept today as a normative way to eat.

Next, we need to support students in translating those nutrition guidelines into effective strategies for caring for themselves while on our campuses and then develop the necessary life skills to support their nutritional wellness as they leave the relative sanctuary of our campuses. Lastly, suggestions for campus-level policy and programmatic review and implementation will be highlighted that focus on enlisting campuses in a nutrition revolution. The study of food and eating from a cross-disciplinary perspective, integrating literary, psychological, economic, political, historical, sociological, and anthropological perspectives, among others, can yield rich discussions, debates, and new insights about one of the most compelling and universal human behaviors.

We Are What We Eat, but What Are We Eating?

Jonathon Bailor, author and blogger, tries to illustrate for us the evolution of the human diet by looking at the history of eating as if it were scaled across a single 24-hour period. If 12:00 a.m. represented the dawn of our first ancestors and we are at one second before midnight nearly 24 hours later,

> [f]or 23 hours and 57 minutes (up until 11:57 pm) our ancestors stayed healthy and fit, eating vegetables, seafood, meat, eggs, fruit, nuts and seeds. At 11:57 pm, people started farming, became "civilized," and began eating starch and a small amount of sweets. Two seconds ago, people started eating processed starches and sweets. Only right now—one second before midnight—did people start getting most of their calories from manufactured starch- and sweetener-based food products. That means the diet recommended by the government's Dietary Guidelines was not possible for 99.8% of our history.
>
> (Bailor, 2012)

For the vast majority of our evolution, our diet has involved one way of eating that has provided the necessary sustenance for survival. In that same time period, humans have changed relatively little from a physiological standpoint, yet our dietary landscape has been drastically altered without correlating to improvements in nutritional wellness.

One of the first times that food and food production seemed to enter into a more public zone of controversy was when Upton Sinclair published his novel *The Jungle*. Although written as a fictional account documenting the survival story of a young Lithuanian immigrant and his family in Chicago, Sinclair did first-hand research, immersing himself in the meatpacking plants in order to accurately depict the working conditions, hazardous health violations, unsanitary practices, deep poverty, and hopelessness found in that environment. Upon investigation, it was revealed that the U.S. Department of Agriculture (USDA) had misrepresented working conditions and bribed inspectors to file erroneous reports that skewed the truth. What followed was the passage of the Pure Food and Drug Act, which was handled strictly as consumer protection legislation around the adulteration of consumable goods, not as an opportunity to address the deplorable, inhumane working conditions of low-wage laborers.

There are far-reaching social and economic implications of a country transitioning out of a largely agrarian model, where families were much more self-sufficient in their food supply in the early 1800s, to a post–Industrial Revolution reality by the late 1800s. The advent of industrial agriculture results in far-reaching consequences not only to the demise of farming families and communities (Henke, 2008) but also even for climate change (Bunyard, 1996).

By World War II, we had mastered the ability to manufacture highly processed food made cheaply and conveniently for mass distribution. Popkin (2006) has documented a "nutrition transition" toward the greater use of refined vegetable fats, for example, in the decade following WWII, greatly reducing the cost of producing a variety of baked goods, spreads, and oils that once required animal fats. The increased consumption of cheap vegetable oils, added sweeteners, and animal proteins also aligns with a shift away from the consumption of fruits, vegetables, and whole grains and coincides with a growing epidemic of obesity.

There is a concomitant change in three other arenas to cultivate the kind of health problems we see today: (1) a reduction in human energy expenditure due to technology often precluding the necessity of such activity; (2) a reduction in meal preparation time as we redefine work to mean only that which we do outside the home to earn a paycheck; and (3) an increase in the production and consumption of high-calorie sodas, juices, and other beverages to replace our water consumption. Post-WWII, as Hawkes (2007) documents, large, monopolistic transnational food corporations (TFCs) began to take over our food system, with real impacts on food production at all levels. Today, many agricultural commodities continue to be controlled by only a relatively small number of processors and retailers that also happen to wield significant lobbying power. Imagine the power leveraged not only by our food industry but also by our pharmaceutical and diet/fitness industries to shape the very nutritional guidance that has become the foundation of our current habits.

Since 1980, the United States has adopted a set of national dietary guidelines advocating a low-fat, high-carbohydrate diet (LF-HC) as key to addressing our growing obesity epidemic. These guidelines were based on a Senate committee report published three years earlier entitled "Dietary Goals for the United States." Ottoboni and Ottoboni (2004) have indicated that "there is considerable concern today that the diet the Pyramid illustrates is responsible for the current epidemic of cardiovascular disease. The concurrent epidemics of obesity and type-2 diabetes are unintended consequences that can also be attributed to this diet" (pp. 109–110), prompting Harvard's Health Eating Plate alternative, which focuses on shifting toward the quality of calories consumed (Harvard School of Public Health, 2011).

The Science of Misinformation: Weighing Fact and Fiction

The area of nutrition has been, for several reasons, a quagmire of conflicting science and even at times predatory techniques that prey on the vulnerable. What follows are some of the most common things one might hear, along with some of the most current research, to encourage more honest dialogue and debate about things that aren't quite as black and white as we once thought.

"I can eat whatever I want; I don't seem to gain any weight!"

Health is more than just what is reflected in the numbers that are collected by sphygmomanometers, scales, and blood tests. While these are interesting indicators that are suggestive of how one compares to others who have taken the same tests, they are not predictive of life span. Even the manner in which those tests are used to make a diagnosis of high blood pressure or diabetes is a moving target. While it's not to discredit the prevention principles behind making an early diagnosis, it is to point out that numbers can be made to mean different things. It begs the question of how one defines or measures health.

If health is purely the quantitative pursuit of weight loss and "normal" cholesterol levels, then it becomes more complicated to reconcile what to do about the "obesity paradox," the notion that skinnier people are not, in fact, any healthier nor do they live longer than overweight or even obese individuals. While compelling longitudinal studies like the Framingham Heart Study (Wong, Levy, & Narula, 2013) have correlated obesity-related risk factors and health status, these studies have typically overlooked the role of physical activity and fitness and have resulted in a culture that demonizes fat in a manner that has many destructive psychosocial consequences. As analysis of data from other studies shows (Hu et al., 2004; Wessel et al., 2004), it is the compelling lack of exercise and fluctuation in weight over time, not necessarily being overweight, that are the greatest risk factor for chronic illness. BMI is a singular numeric calculation that cannot distinguish variance in body composition (muscle versus fat).

Similarly, the notion of "the freshman 15," or the weight gain that is often associated with the first year of college, creates an interesting psychosocial dilemma.

On the one hand, some students are still developing physically and have not yet settled into their adult weight; therefore, weight gain is just a natural process of ongoing maturation. Couple this with some likely scenarios that if the students are no longer living at home, they may not be paying the same kind of attention to their nutritional and caloric intake as they were before. Add to this the often-found reality of less sleep during the college years, which then compromises the production of the hormones leptin and ghrelin that are responsible for controlling hunger and weight. Furthermore, students may have a precipitous drop in their activity level if they are not participating in sports as they were in high school, and their access to food may now be 24/7. Lastly, they may also be experiencing the possible intake of more empty calories through alcohol consumption, for example.

While weight gain and loss *are* simply a mathematical equation of calories in versus calories out (at a rate of 3,500 calories per pound), it is ultimately a questionable way to place value on health, wellness, and fitness. In reality, the quantity of our fuel, while not completely irrelevant, cannot overshadow the importance of considering the quality of our calories. There is truth to the saying, "You are what you eat." While some students in their infinite wisdom of youth will play roulette with their health in the short term, there isn't ultimately any way to exercise your way out of poor nutrition in the long term. Your body needs to receive necessary macro- and micronutrients in order to run efficiently. One can use the metaphor of a car; while it's possible to run your vehicle without regularly checking and changing your oil and filter, it is by no means the most effective way to run your vehicle, and you eventually face the greater cost of repair that comes with neglecting preventive maintenance.

"If I eat fat, I will get fat."

In a similar theme as earlier, there is the notion that fat is the ingredient to be feared above all else; but not all fats are created equally. In fact, when compared to a control group that consisted of a low-fat diet, subjects eating primarily plant-based foods with added fats from olive oil and nuts were found to have a lower risk of peripheral artery disease, demonstrating not only how powerful nutritional intake might be for health but also that fat can't possibly be the singular enemy we have made it to be (Ruiz-Canela, Estruch, Corella, Salas-Salvadó, & Martinez-Gonzalez, 2014). Similarly, fats have been shown to have a differential influence on brain activity. Taking our auto maintenance analogy even further, keeping our brains well-oiled by investing in high-quality oil will measurably improve brain performance!

For quite some time now, the prevailing wisdom was that both saturated fats and trans fat were equal culprits in cardiovascular disease because of their role in raising low-density lipoproteins (LDL), which are the type of cholesterol that lodges in the arteries. On the other hand, high-density lipoproteins (HDL) offer a protective role against cardiovascular disease through their anti-inflammatory and antioxidant properties (McGrowder, Riley, Morrison, & Gordon, 2011). The research actually shows that saturated fats might raise the benign form of LDL (known as pattern A) but not the smaller and more dangerous dense form of LDL (pattern B), and thus a recent large-scale meta-analysis found no connection between saturated fat consumption and cardiovascular risk (Chowdhury et al., 2014).

On the other hand, the case against trans fat is sound, justifying what many considered at the time to be drastic but now seemingly effective measures to legally ban the use of artificial trans fat in New York City restaurants beginning in 2007 (Angell et al., 2012; Lichtenstein, 2012). Artificial trans fats are found primarily in food items containing partially hydrogenated vegetable oils. Hydrogenation is a chemical process that converts liquid vegetable oils to a solid or semisolid state to increase their shelf life. Trans fats are used as a less expensive replacement for animal fats, particularly in the baking process, and have proven to be artery-clogging culprits of heart disease (Mozaffarian, Katan, Ascherio, Stampfer, & Willett, 2006).

The fear that remains unfounded, however, is that eating fat alone will make one fat. In fact, eating particular fats, such as those in certain oils, nuts, and avocados, is essential for good health and cognitive benefits. Eating "low-fat" foods often means consuming something that might still be high in calories, sodium, and even sugar (to offset the loss of flavor that comes with taking out the natural fats), or now has other artificial ingredients introduced that create new risks.

"Butter is the spawn of the devil."

In the summer of 2014, *Time* magazine boldly declared on its cover, "Eat Butter." The distant cousin to the myth that all fats must be avoided like the plague, butter has earned a reputation in that same vein, spawning many butter alternatives. While some margarines, especially more solid-state ones, are more harmful because they contain partially hydrogenated oils, some spreads that are fortified with plant stanols and sterols are known to have heart-healthy benefits by reducing the circulation of LDL cholesterol concentration (Ellegård, Andersson, Normén, & Andersson, 2007; Myrie, Mymin, Triggs-Raine, & Jones, 2012). However, butter itself is now redeemed by the latest science that reveals that saturated fat, which in the case of butter comes from animal fat, is not what we should fear most after all.

Instead, we need to be more discerning of the other options that have been pushed on us in lieu of butter over the years. For example, avoid cooking with seed oils that are manufactured through complex industrial procedures. These are processed vegetable oils, like soybean oil, sunflower oil, corn oil, canola oil, cottonseed oil, and safflower oil. They are high in one of our two essential fatty acids, omega-6 polyunsaturated fats, which most people today consume in excess and out of balance with omega-3 fatty acids, which is harmful at a cellular level. Over time, excess omega-6 fats (commonly stored as linoleic acid—LA) lead to structural changes in our fat stores and cell membranes.

"Is breakfast really the most important meal of the day?" or *"I'll just cut back on calories and skip some meals to get bikini ready."*

If you ever heard your mother say this first statement, she really was right! Many students never think about breakfast as a meal that is meant to "break a fast." Taking time to eat a nutritious meal in the morning that consists of more than a sugar-laden Danish or bowl of cereal is key to jump-starting metabolism for the day! Chronic meal-skipping as a way of cutting back on daily caloric intake is actually very counterproductive to weight loss, never mind dangerous to one's health in the long term. Skipping meals puts the body into a stressful "fight or flight" response mode. The body is programmed for self-preservation; if it's fearful about where or when it might next get its calories, it will store the next calories consumed as fat in a protective manner in order to draw upon the stores when needed.

Methods that involve caloric restriction also tend to result in binging behavior. In contrast, the "grazing" approach seems to yield better results. The idea is that one consumes much smaller portions of food every few hours in order to control hunger before it hits full force and results in a binge. It also helps to keep metabolism and energy levels at a more constant high. Finally, periods of caloric restriction also increase the production of the stress hormone cortisol, which in turn depresses the immune system and exacerbates weight gain because it triggers the release of insulin and over time can contribute to insulin resistance (Tomiyama et al., 2010).

"It says it's organic so it must be healthy."

Food labeling is a tricky business in today's marketplace. While the concept of eating organically, with its emphasis on pesticide- and hormone-free production and sustainability, is a compelling message, we also have to exercise reasonable judgment as the consumer. Not everything that is labeled organic is automatically better. Some items are just as processed as the nonorganic options (although with generally fewer problematic ingredients) and can be equally high in sodium, for example. While it's flawed to assume that all things organic are better, there is something to be said about most of the wholesome foods that have been grown organically, especially if they are grown locally and spend far less time losing their nutrient content during transport between farm and table. In general, organically farmed produce hasn't necessarily been shown to be more nutritious, but the benefit of foods containing fewer chemicals and hormones is surely inarguable.

"Eggs are good. No, eggs are bad. Actually it's okay to eat eggs. Don't eat too many eggs. Eggs are beneficial to your health."

Given our often single-minded focus on things that are "good" and "bad" when it comes to nutrition, we have demonized foods like eggs because they are high in cholesterol. However, some now consider eggs to be one of the most nutritious items we could consume because they contain such a diverse array of nutrition, especially when enriched with omega-3. For most people, even though eggs are high in cholesterol, eating them does not raise the cholesterol levels in their blood. In fact, studies of whole egg consumption have shown an increase in HDL levels

(Blesso, Andersen, Barona, Volek, & Fernandez, 2013; Mutungi et al., 2010); one study found that two eggs per day for six weeks increased HDL levels by 10% (Schnohr et al., 1994).

"I drink several cans of soda a day, but it's diet soda so it's okay!"

Carbonated water surprisingly dates back to 1772, a discovery that earned the English scientist Joseph Priestley an induction into the French Academy of Sciences! After several more key discoveries and inventions that would support its mass production, what we know as our modern-day soda pop finally emerged in the late 1800s, with Coca-Cola making its appearance in 1886 and Pepsi in 1893. Today, it is a ubiquitous beverage option and carries one of the lowest consumer per-unit costs in the food and beverage marketplace.

In addition to fueling our national caffeine addiction, soda is implicated in both obesity and diabetes, prompting many fast food chains to no longer offer soda as the default option for kids' meals. Because high-calorie beverages like soda do not trigger any sense of satiety, those calories do not detract from our normal consumption of calories from solid foods in a corresponding number, thus resulting in an overall daily increase in caloric consumption and decrease in water consumption, which most people can ill afford. Present in many of our sodas is high fructose corn syrup (HFCS), a cheaper but highly processed alternative sweetener to sugar, converting some of the glucose from corn syrup into fructose, and with powerful addictive qualities not unlike that of cocaine (Citizens for Health, 2013; Poupart, 2013).

Making the choice to consume diet sodas is not a clear winner either. The calorie-free artificial sweetener found in many diet sodas, aspartame, has undergone massive scrutiny since receiving FDA approval in 1981. It becomes an interesting academic exercise in critical thinking to engage students in discussion and debate about the veracity of the claims that vehemently declare that aspartame is or is not safe for human consumption (Butchko et al., 2002; Thomas, 2005).

"What's the deal with sugar?" or "High fructose corn syrup is just sugar, right?"

A major point of the 2014 documentary *Fed Up* is that sugar, not fat, is at the crux of the obesity epidemic. The American Heart Association (AHA) recommends that women consume no more than 6 teaspoons (25 grams) of added sugar per day and men consume no more than 9 teaspoons (38 grams) of added sugar per day. The limit for children ranges between only 3 and 6 teaspoons (12–25 grams) per day. In actuality, the average American consumes nearly 20 teaspoons of added sugar every day, or 66 pounds of sugar annually (Ervin & Ogden, 2013). Following our previous discussion of soda consumption, it should be noted that an average 12-ounce soda can have as many as 11 teaspoons (46 grams) of sugar alone, close to twice the recommended intake for an adult! Added sugar can be found in some very surprising food items, so a consumer must be vigilant in reading food labels for unexpected sources of sugar.

The overconsumption of added sugar can lead to several issues. It increases glucose in our bloodstream, which causes the pancreas to release insulin. Higher levels of insulin cause the body to store more food calories as fat. Insulin also affects a hormone called leptin, which functions as a natural appetite suppressant by triggering a message of satiety.

Add to these concerns the phenomenon of "sugar addiction." When Princeton researchers studied the effects of sugar on rats, they found it triggers production of the brain's natural opioids, giving the sense of euphoria or high that can be linked to the addiction process, not unlike becoming addicted to morphine or heroin (Avena, Rada, & Hoebel, 2008; MacPherson, 2008).

We also have to exercise caution with sweetener substitutes, such as honey, agave nectar, or stevia, although there are some potential benefits and cautions to each of these alternatives. For example, honey is packed with many disease-fighting antioxidants (Gross, 2004), and local honey in particular has been known to provide benefits to allergy sufferers. It is, however, important to find raw, unprocessed, and unfiltered honey. The same can be said about any alternative sweeteners; look for products that have gone through the least amount of processing.

"I don't eat that well, but I can just take a multivitamin."

It often seems like the prevailing American wisdom is that we can always find a way out of what ails us through some magic bullet, whether it's a diet, a pill, or some other cure. The notion of prevention does not always seem to have quite the same curbside appeal as what our technology might offer us in terms of treatment options. A person who wants to supplement or fortify his or her way out of poor nutrition is really not unlike the person who will search for the perfect hangover cure instead of just choosing to drink less. While in very specific instances, the idea of supplementation might make sense (e.g., an iron supplement for anemia or calcium supplement for osteoporosis prevention), most people supplementing with vitamins might risk toxicity when we also have so many foods on the market today that have been enriched and fortified in some way. As a result, it would be easy to exceed the recommended safe daily limits for certain vitamins and minerals. For example, routinely exceeding 4,000 international units (IUs) of vitamin D can pose heart problems for adults. Seek either specific supplements for confirmed deficiencies, or select a multivitamin that provides less than 100% of the recommended daily value (DV) to avoid vitamin toxicity.

The other issue is that our bodies simply cannot metabolize cheaper, synthetic versions of vitamins and minerals in quite the same way as they can those in their natural form in the foods we eat, nor can the synthetic versions ever fully simulate the complex cocktail of benefits of eating whole food vitamins and minerals. If the ultimate decision is to supplement, take the supplements along with or just after a meal so that the vitamins and minerals are better absorbed. Also, don't be misled by the notion that enriched grains are any healthier for you. In fact, during processing, enriched grains are stripped of their most nutritious component, the fiber. Instead, opt for whole grains for the most nutrition.

"What I eat can't possibly have anything do with my grades."

There is a growing body of evidence that there are, in fact, foods one can eat to boost brain power ("Brain Superfoods," 2012; Heller, 2010; Kamal & Kamal, n.d.; Sorgen, n.d.). These include foods that increase essential omega-3 fatty acids that help the brain function optimally, that provide folic acid or alpha linolenic acid (ALA) and promote blood flow to the brain to increase mental alertness and memory, or simply provide a long-lasting energy source that aids in concentration. Consider researching "power foods," such as mixed nuts (particularly almonds and walnuts) and unhydrogenated nut butters; blueberries in any form—frozen, fresh, or freeze-dried; kale and spinach; salmon and sardines; dark chocolate; avocados; beans; flax seeds; broccoli and other cruciferous vegetables; eggs; and whole grains. It is also important to drink enough water. At a loss of only 1% of hydration, mental performance and physical coordination can become impaired. What we eat could make the difference between a "B" and an "A" or between failing and passing a course!

The list of myths, misconceptions, and sources of confusion will surely continue to grow as what constitutes food continues to evolve over time. Likewise, we hope that scientists will continue to seek and use more refined techniques to find valid answers to our basic questions about what is beneficial and what is harmful to humans. One must exercise the skills of an intelligent health consumer through health literacy to weed through what is credible and promising information from that which has little to no research-based grounding (National Network of Libraries of Medicine, n.d.; UCSF Medical Center, n.d.).

Strategies for Change

Ideas for Students: Eating on a Budget, Mastering Grocery Shopping, and Preparing Food

- Making smoothies is a fantastic way of packing an amazing amount of nutrition into something that is prepared simply with largely raw ingredients and consumed easily, even on the go. While there are many small appliances that one could invest in to aid in this endeavor, one suggestion is for a community of residents or roommates to work collaboratively to invest in a high-quality blender. Through such an appliance, bananas, strawberries, and ice, for example, can be easily blended into a simple, healthy freeze that even the pickiest of eaters can enjoy within minutes. The product's owners can rotate the task of researching or creating on their own new fruit and vegetable combinations to share each day (e.g., how many versions of a green smoothie can be produced to satisfy the palates of all who participate?).
- In the same vein, the idea of "firehouse" food preparation and consumption is really just the lost art of a family sitting down at the end of the day to eat a

meal—the same meal—together. Eating as a social phenomenon should not be underestimated. This approach to communal cooking can also appeal to the resource-poor, as it allows one to use limited resources in a more targeted fashion by investing in fewer ingredients that can be purchased in bulk and/or on sale.

- Try "Meatless Mondays." Traditional animal proteins can be very costly, not only directly to the wallet but also in terms of their total carbon footprint on environmental wellness. A "Meatless Monday" campaign boasts that "if the world ate just 15% less meat, it would be like taking 240 million cars off the road each year" ("Meatless Mondays," n.d.). When you simultaneously increase your fruit and vegetable intake, you can add to that the benefits to your health, such as improved weight management and prevention of chronic disease (CDC, 2011).

- When possible, try to focus less on eating according to a set schedule, but learn to read your body's cues for impending hunger or eat smaller meals on a more frequent basis, rather than waiting for the "set mealtime." When you wait until you experience that overwhelming sense of intense hunger, you are much more likely to binge and consume more calories. You can also try drinking water, since we sometimes confuse thirst for hunger. Eating more often helps to maintain a more consistent blood sugar level over the course of the day, and the smaller portions also help to keep blood sugar from spiking and then crashing. Additionally, more frequent eating can actually boost metabolism.

- Never shop on an empty stomach. Grocery shopping on an empty stomach triggers our modern-day fight or flight response and psychologically drives us to hoard food and purchase different types of food than we would if we were feeling sated at the time. Tal and Wansink (2013) discovered in their research that not only did short-term food deprivation increase our overall grocery shopping by nearly 19%, but also, in particular, it led shoppers to buy almost 45% more in specifically high-calorie foods than those who shopped under more sated conditions. Lastly, when faced with more options, the research shows that we tend to eat more. Kahn and Wansink (2004) and Wansink (2004) cite several studies where subjects consumed more volume of food when presented with more choices. Keep options of calorie-dense foods to a minimum as a strategy for reducing intake, but increase the variety of nutrient-dense foods for increasing intake!

- Plan your menu based on items in season, shop with a basket versus a cart, and shop with a list. We might think the store is just a repository of goods from which we are making independent choices and purchases. However, Lindstrom (2011) describes his visit to a grocery store as a sales laboratory for one of the world's largest consumer goods manufacturers, where staged supermarkets are designed specifically to test buying patterns in response to varied marketing techniques. Add to this the consumer-specific research that is driven by your own purchasing habits being tracked through unique frequent shopper identification codes; sale items and coupons are then pushed directly to you to also influence what you buy and where and when you do your grocery shopping (Duhigg, 2012).

- From a marketing standpoint, grocery stores put their most appealing and/or expensive items at consumer eye level, where target shoppers are most likely to focus their attention. As a result, be sure to scan the top and bottom shelves for your best deals and avoid end caps of aisles. Consumers need to research and be familiar with typical pricing for products that are purchased most often. Both the engineering of the food marketplace and the eating environment are salient factors in implicating food producers, stores, and restaurants in contributing the lion's share of the current obesity problem.
- Given the layout of most grocery stores, your best bet is to avoid the center of the store and shop only on the perimeter. The perimeter is generally where you will find your fresh produce and nonprocessed food items.
- Whether shopping or preparing food for one or many, learning how to spot the real deals on bulk purchases is a handy skill you acquire with experience. Not every bulk purchase is necessarily the more cost-effective option. When it does make cost-effective sense to purchase in bulk, however, also prepare in bulk, then portion and freeze the rest. Instead of having to pull into a drive-through for a quick meal, enjoy the benefits of creating your own freezer store of "convenience" meals that can be reheated when time is short.
- Invest in a basic slow cooker, which can be acquired for a reasonable investment. It is incredible how many simple but delicious meals can be prepared in a single pot with so little commitment of time! Ingredients can be prepped the night before and stored in the stoneware insert. Set the slow cooker to cook during the day, and it will produce a hot meal on one's return home.

Strategies for Higher Education Professionals

- Encourage dialogue, exploration, and critical thinking among students in both curricular and co-curricular ways. To what degree are there curriculum infusion opportunities to embed discussions around food and nutrition into the curriculum (i.e., anthropology, art, business, economics, English, health, history, psychology, sociology) through class presentations, research projects, or even field trips? Are there extracurricular student health/health promotion programs available to students who wish to explore and learn about nutrition in more in-depth ways?
- Assess and evaluate the campus environment and norms regarding food and nutrition (e.g., dining halls, vending machines). What are the hours of operation? Do students have access to food on a 24-hour basis? What parameters are in place to assess the nutritional value of the food served? How are meals portioned for students? How much variety is provided? What are the sizes of the plates on which food is served? Are there intentional placements of nutritional messages alongside the dining/eating options?
- Explore the marketing tactics and partnerships that exist on campus. Does the school engage fast food vendors? Are such establishments allowed to furnish coupons or sponsor school events? Are fliers posted around campus or advertisements placed in the school newspaper?

- Don't underestimate the potential to leverage campus policies to enact change. In just two years' time, research found that New York City's bold public health approach in 2007 to legally ban the use of artificial trans fat resulted in measurable reductions in consumption of trans fat by making the default option the healthier one (Angell, Cobb, Kurtis, Konty, & Silver, 2012; Lichtenstein, 2012). What kinds of policies can be implemented that can galvanize change around how students view food and what is made available to them?
- Support a student initiative to run a campus garden if there isn't one already; find natural partnerships with local farmers. Focus on programs like "Sustainable Table" that encourage knowledge and social action both personally and collectively at the point of food production, purchase, and preparation. Even in urban environments we are seeing programs documented by Kremer and DeLiberty (2011) regarding urban sustainability. Urban rooftop and outdoor gardens in a variety of unique environments not only offer a unique approach to sustainability but also address environmental justice issues around urban "heat islands" (Chow, Brennan, & Brazel, 2012; Gonzalez, 2013; "New Roots," 2012; "San Francisco Giants," 2014; U.S. Environmental Protection Agency, n.d.; Vigilante, 2012). Are there any available partnerships to be cultivated for outdoor classrooms? Is there a local community-supported agriculture (CSA) or farmers market that is accessible for students?
- Consider integrating service learning projects that actively engage students in learning about food and nutrition that then, in turn, inspire them to work for social change. Can we ensure that all of our students leave our institutions with the knowledge and skills to prepare at least 10 meals on their own? How can we inspire students to become leaders and champions for the future of our food? How do we teach our students about environmental sustainability and the reduction of their carbon footprint?
- Evaluate and re-engineer the ways in which professional and paraprofessional staff model particular behavioral norms around food and nutrition. Do faculty/staff/administrators eat with students? Are there communal food preparation opportunities that provide cross over between various campus entities and expose younger students to role models of realistic but healthier food consumption on campus? Are there individuals whose personal stories and/or challenges can be highlighted as a way of making nutrition and the profile of sound nutrition practice a salient topic of discussion?

Conclusions

We have become complacent about food in America. Many of us may put very little thought each day into what is available for us to eat and unquestioningly accept what is offered to us in lieu of real food. We are in dire need of a nutrition revolution that challenges us all to recognize the need to develop an awareness of the myriad of food controversies that we face that have profound historical, economic, and sociopolitical roots. It is difficult for the average consumer to identify, nevermind also accurately analyze, some of the major myths and misconceptions around basic nutrition, especially when it turns out that much of our conventional wisdom about eating is based on flawed science and corporate interests.

The best that we can do is to seek and then interpret the best available research we have on the neuroscience behind various foods. To that end, we should be focused on promoting and consuming some very basic power foods that have had a long history of supporting human survival, not on ways of manufacturing new foods. This latter process has yet to yield compelling results. We have already created a challenging marketplace for most people to make reasonable choices about their nutritional intake; the last thing we need is to make that process even more complex. The goal is not to let the pendulum swing the other way, to what Dr. Steven Bratman (1997) has coined "orthorexia," which is characterized by an unhealthy and excessive obsession with the quality, composition, and preparation of the particular food one consumes to the detriment of functional living. Instead, a reasonable expectation is simply that we live in a society that makes a commitment to an environment of nutritional excellence rather than manufacturing an apparently more profitable culture of nutrient deficiency. By utilizing an ecological framework for change that examines the built environment around food and eating, as well as exploring the psychological variables that contribute to individual decision-making about food and eating, we can create an opportunity that both encourages and enables us to make choices that allow us not just to survive but also to thrive.

References

Angell, S.Y., Cobb, L.K., Curtis, C.J., Konty, K.J., & Silver, L.D. (2012). Change in trans fatty acid content of fast-food purchases associated with New York City's restaurant regulation. *Annals of Internal Medicine, 157*, 81–86.

Avena, N.M., Rada P., & Hoebel, B.G. (2008). Evidence for sugar addiction: Behavioral and neurochemical effects of intermittent, excessive sugar intake. *Neuroscience and Biobehavioral Reviews, 32*, 20–39. doi:10.1016/j.neubiorev.2007.04.019

Bailor, J. (2012, May 17). The simple scientific cause of the obesity epidemic. Retrieved from http://thesmarterscienceofslim.com/thecause

Blesso, C.N., Andersen, C.J., Barona, J., Volek, J.S., & Fernandez, M.L. (2013). Whole egg consumption improves lipoprotein profiles and insulin sensitivity to a greater extent than yolk-free egg substitute in individuals with metabolic syndrome. *Metabolism, 62*(3), 400–410. doi:10.1016/j.metabol.2012.08.014

Brain superfoods. (2012, September 19). *Huffington Post*. Retrieved from http://www.huffingtonpost.com/2012/09/18/brain-food-superfoods_n_1895328.html

Bratman, S. (1997). The health food eating disorder. Retrieved from www.orthorexia.com/original-orthorexia-essay/

Bunyard, P. (1996). Industrial agriculture—Driving climate change? *Ecologist, 26*(6), 290–298. Retrieved from http://go.galegroup.com/ps/i.do?id=GALE%7CA19313822&v=2.1&u=mcc_estm&it=r&p=AONE&sw=w&asid=f59c4947131893972232c03490436de1

Butchko, H.H., Stargel, W.W., Comer, C.P., Mayhew, D.A., Benninger, C., Blackburn, G.L., ... Mendenhall, C.L. (2002). Aspartame: Review of safety. *Regulatory Toxicology and Pharmacology, 35*(3), S1–S93. doi:10.1006/rtph.2002.1542

Centers for Disease Control and Prevention. (2011). Strategies to prevent obesity and other chronic diseases: The CDC guide to increase the consumption of fruits and vegetables. Retrieved from http://www.cdc.gov/obesity/downloads/FandV_2011_WEB_TAG508.pdf

Centers for Disease Control and Prevention. (2012, September 27). Nutrition basics. Retrieved from http://www.cdc.gov/nutrition/everyone/basics/index.html

Chow, W.T.L., Brennan, D., & Brazel, A.J. (2012). Urban heat island research in Phoenix, Arizona: Theoretical contributions and policy applications. *Bulletin of the American Meteorological Society, 93*(4), 517–530.

Chowdhury, R., Warnakula, S., Kunutsor, S., Crowe, F., Ward, H.A., Johnson, L., . . . Di Angelantonio, E. (2014). Association of dietary, circulating, and supplement fatty acids with coronary risk: A systematic review and meta-analysis. *Annals of Internal Medicine, 160,* 398–406.

Citizens for Health. (2013, June 6). New research suggests high fructose corn syrup triggers addictive consumption similar to drugs: Industrial sweetener implicated as cause of global obesity epidemic. Retrieved from http://search.proquest.com.ezproxy1.lib.asu.edu/docview/1365001067/fulltext?accountid=4485

Duhigg, C. (2012, February 16). How companies learn your secrets. *New York Times.* http://www.nytimes.com/2012/02/19/magazine/shopping-habits.html?pagewanted=all&_r=0

Ellegård, L.H., Andersson, S.W., Normén, A.L., & Andersson, H.A. (2007). Dietary plant sterols and cholesterol metabolism. *Nutrition Reviews, 65*(1), 39–45. doi:10.1301/nr.2007.jan.39–45

Ervin, R.B., & Ogden, C.L. (2013). *NCHS Data Brief, No. 122: Consumption of added sugars among U.S. adults, 2005–2010.* Centers for Disease Control and Prevention. Retrieved from http://www.cdc.gov/nchs/data/databriefs/db122.pdf

Gonzalez, L. (2013, April 4). Whole Foods to grow produce on rooftop garden. PSFK. Retrieved from http://www.psfk.com/2013/04/whole-foods-rooftop-garden.html

Gross, H. (2004, March 28–April 1). *Effect of honey consumption on plasma antioxidant status in human subjects.* Paper presented at the 227th American Chemical Society National Meeting, Anaheim, CA.

Harvard School of Public Health. (2011, September 14). Harvard researchers launch Healthy Eating Plate. Retrieved from http://www.hsph.harvard.edu/news/press-releases/healthy-eating-plate

Hawkes, C. (2007). *Globalization, food and nutrition transitions.* World Health Organization. Retrieved from http://www.who.int/social_determinants/resources/gkn_hawkes.pdf

Heller, S. (2010). *Get smart: Samantha Heller's nutrition prescription for boosting brain power and optimizing total body health.* Baltimore, MD: Johns Hopkins University Press.

Henke, C. (2008). *Cultivating science, harvesting power: Science and industrial agriculture in California.* Cambridge, MA: MIT Press.

Hu, F.B., Willett, W.C., Li, T., Stampfer, M.J., Colditz, G.A., & Manson, J.E. (2004). Adiposity as compared with physical activity in predicting mortality among women. *New England Journal of Medicine, 351,* 2694–2703. Retrieved from http://www.nejm.org/doi/full/10.1056/NEJMoa042135

Kamal, R., & Kamal, T. (n.d.). Top 10 brain foods that help you study and get better grades [Web log post]. Retrieved from http://www.campustalkblog.com/top-10-brain-foods-that-help-you-study-and-get-better-grades/

Lichtenstein, A.H. (2012). New York City trans fat ban: Improving the default option when purchasing foods prepared outside the home. *Annals of Internal Medicine, 154,* 144–145.

Lindstrom, M. (2011, October 21). What your supermarket knows about you. *Time.* Retrieved from http://ideas.time.com/2011/10/21/what-your-supermarket-knows-about-you/?xid=rss-topstories&utm_source=feedburner&utm_medium=feed&utm_campaign=Feed%3A+time%2Ftopstories+%28TIME%3A+Top+Stories%29

Kahn, B.E., & Wansink, B. (2004). The influence of assortment structure on perceived variety and consumption quantities. *Journal of Consumer Research, 30,* 519–533.

Kremer, P., & DeLiberty, T.L. (2011). Local food practices and growing potential: Mapping the case of Philadelphia. *Applied Geography, 31,* 1252–1261. doi:10.1016/j.apgeog.2011.01.007

MacPherson, K. (2008, December 10). Sugar can be addictive, Princeton scientist says. *News at Princeton.* Retrieved from http://www.princeton.edu/main/news/archive/S22/88/56G31/index.xml?section=topstories

McGrowder, D., Riley, C., Morrison, E.Y.St.A., & Gordon, L. (2011). The role of high-density lipoproteins in reducing the risk of vascular diseases, neurogenerative disorders, and cancer. *Cholesterol,* 1–9. doi:10.1155/2011/496925

Meatless Mondays. (n.d.). NGOs lack incentive to address meat consumption role in climate change. Retrieved from http://www.meatlessmonday.com/articles/ngos-lack-incentive-to-address-meat-consumption-role-in-climate-change/

Mozaffarian, D., Katan, M.B., Ascherio, A., Stampfer, M.J., & Willett, W.C. (2006). Trans fatty acids and cardiovascular disease. *New England Journal of Medicine, 354*(15), 1601–1613. doi:10.1056/NEJMra054035

Mutungi, G., Waters, D., Ratliff, J., Puglisi, M., Clark, R.M. Volek, J.S., & Fernandez, M.L. (2010). Eggs distinctly modulate plasma carotenoid and lipoprotein subclasses in adult men following a carbohydrate-restricted diet. *Journal of Nutritional Biochemistry, 21*(4), 261–267. doi:10.1016/j.jnutbio.2008.12.011

Myrie, S.B., Mymin, D., Triggs-Raine, B., & Jones, P.J.H. (2012). Serum lipids, plant sterols, and cholesterol kinetic responses to plant sterol supplementation in phytosterolemia heterozygotes and control individuals. *American Journal of Clinical Nutrition, 95*, 837–844. doi:10.3945/ajcn.111.028985

National Network of Libraries of Medicine. (n.d.). Health literacy. Retrieved from http://nnlm.gov/outreach/consumer/hlthlit.html

New Roots on the Rooftop urban farm is first in the country. (2012, May 17). *PR Newswire.* Retrieved from http://go.galegroup.com/ps/i.do?id=GALE%7CA290144050&v=2.1&u=mcc_estm&it=r&p=ITOF&sw=w&asid=e7b1df489c9eeab379123fae8926e8eb

Ottoboni, A., & Ottoboni, F. (2004). The food guide pyramid: Will the defects be corrected? *Journal of American Physicians and Surgeons, 9*(4), 109–113. Retrieved from http://www.jpands.org/vol9no4/ottoboni.pdf

Popkin, B.M. (2006). Technology, transport, globalization, and the nutrition transition food policy. *Food Policy, 31*(6), 554–569. doi:10.1016/j.foodpol.2006.02.008

Poupart, J. (2013, May 22). Addiction to unhealthy foods could help explain the global obesity epidemic. Canadian Association for Neuroscience. Retrieved from www.eurekalert.org/pub_releases/2013-05/cafn-atu051613.php

Ruiz-Canela, M., Estruch, R., Corella, D., Salas-Salvadó, J., & Martinez-Gonzalez, M. (2014). Association of Mediterranean diet with peripheral artery disease: The PREDIMED randomized trial. *Journal of American Medical Association, 311*(4), 415–417.

San Francisco Giants and Bon Appétit Management Company open the Garden at AT&T Park. (2014, June 24). *Business Wire.* Retrieved from http://www.businesswire.com/news/home/20140624005730/en/San-Francisco-Giants-Bon-App%C3%A9tit-Management-Company#.VGmcKIdM7YM

Schnohr, P., Thomsen, O.O., Riis, H.P., Boberg-Ans, G., Lawaetz, H., & Weeke, T. (1994). Egg consumption and high-density-lipoprotein cholesterol. *Journal of Internal Medicine, 235*(3), 249–251.

Sorgen, C. (n.d.). Eat smart for a healthier brain. WebMD. Retrieved from http://www.webmd.com/diet/features/eat-smart-healthier-brain

Tal, A., & Wansink, B. (2013). Fattening fasting: Hungry grocery shoppers buy more calories, not more food. *Journal of American Medical Association Internal Medicine, 173*(12), 1146–1148. doi:10.1001/jamainternmed.2013.650

Thomas, P. (2005). Aspartame. *Ecologist, 35*(7), 36–36.

Tomiyama, A.J., Mann, T., Vinas, D., Hunger, J.M., DeJager, J., & Taylor, S.E. (2010). Low calorie dieting increases cortisol. *Psychosomatic Medicine, 72*, 357–364.

UCSF Medical Center. (n.d.) Evaluating health information. Retrieved from http://www.ucsfhealth.org/education/evaluating_health_information

U.S. Environmental Protection Agency. (n.d.). Green roofs. Retrieved from http://www.epa.gov/heatisland/mitigation/greenroofs.htm

Vigilante, R. (2012). Aeroponics at O'Hare. *Organic Gardening, 59*(2), 83.

Walsh, B. (2014, June 23). Don't blame fat. *Time*, 29–35.

Wansink, B. (2004). Environmental factors that increase the food intake and consumption volume of unknowing consumers. *Annual Reviews of Nutrition, 24*, 455–479. doi:10.1146/annurev.nutr.24.012003.132140

Wessel, T. R., Arant, C. B., Olson, M. B., Johnson, B. D., Reis, S. E., Sharaf, B. L., . . . Merz, C.N.B. (2004). Relationship of physical fitness vs. body mass index with coronary artery disease and cardiovascular events in women. *Journal of American Medical Association, 292*(10), 1179–1187. doi:10.1001/jama.292.10.1179

Wong, N. D., Levy, D., & Narula, J. (2013). Legacy of the Framingham Heart Study: Rationale, design, initial findings, and implications. *Global Heart, 8*(1), 3–9. doi:10.1016/j.gheart.2012.12.001

12

Exercise

Hey, Millennial, It's Time to Get Physical!

LINDA A. KNIGHT, JENNIFER R. FISHER, AND PARTH K. PATEL

Thomas Jefferson once said, "Leave all the afternoon for exercise and recreation, which are as necessary as reading. I will rather say more necessary because health is worth more than learning" ("Jefferson," n.d.). Exercise has been valued for personal health and well-being for many years, long before the days of treadmills and fitness apps. Exercise has changed and evolved with each generation, adding bells and whistles in some places, while returning to basics in others. Today, all people, especially college students, need to get a healthy amount of exercise. Integrating exercise into a college student's busy schedule, along with academics and other extracurricular activities, can be challenging; however, it is not impossible.

It is worth noting the definitions of exercise, physical activity, and physical fitness because the average person often easily confuses them when reading and trying to interpret exercise recommendations. Exercise is defined as "a type of physical activity consisting of planned, structured and repetitive bodily movement done to improve and/or maintain one or more components of physical fitness" (American College of Sports Medicine [ACSM], 2014a, p. 2). Physical activity is defined as "any bodily movement produced by the contraction of skeletal muscles that results in a substantial increase in caloric requirements over resting energy expenditure" (ACSM, 2014a, p. 2). Therefore, it is possible for people to accumulate physical activity throughout the day without officially exercising. Further, physical activity differs from physical fitness, which is "a set of attributes or characteristics individuals have or achieve that relates to their ability to perform physical activity" (ACSM, 2014a, p. 2). Examples of such attributes, also referred to as components, are muscular strength and cardiovascular endurance. As such, someone performing physical activity to improve one of the components of fitness might have different goals than someone performing physical activity to attain health benefits.

In this chapter we will talk about the benefits of exercise. We will describe the millennial and what type of student that is, and also what motivates him or her. While we understand that not all students fall into the millennial age group, we feel it is important to understand them. Our chapter information will also be applicable for nontraditional students. We cite trends in exercise as well as recommendations for different aspects of exercise. We will provide recommendations and resources for the higher education professional (student affairs, administration, and faculty) and hope this will provide understanding and support the value and importance of exercise for the college student.

Benefits of Exercise for College Students

Exercise has a myriad of benefits for college students, ranging from increased academic performance to decreased stress and improved mental health. For starters, just moving is beneficial for health. "There are health benefits in concurrently reducing total time engaged in sedentary pursuits and also by interspersing frequent, short bouts of standing and physical activity between periods of sedentary activity, even in physically active adults" (Gerber et al., 2011, p. 1334). Such benefits include a decreased risk for developing heart disease and type 2 diabetes and increased weight management and quality of life. Individuals should be encouraged to get physical activity throughout the day, even if it is not a structured workout in the gym. For college students, some examples include walking around campus between classes, taking the stairs instead of the elevator, and parking further from their destination. Activity trackers are a great way to encourage individuals to get more physical activity throughout the day, and many campuses have incentive programs that involve pedometers. Online tracking is also available through resources such as America on the Move.

The higher education professional needs to understand the importance of fitness and exercise for many other areas of a student's life, including leadership and grade point average. Matt Howard (2010) explains the importance of fitness for successful leaders:

> Fitness does so much more than just keep the extra weight off and prevent us from blaming the cleaners for shrinking our clothes. It increases mental stamina and endurance as well. It helps one weather stressful events with aplomb, and to keep one's head when all around them are losing theirs. The leader of the group, the one expected to make a good decision under stress and chart an effective course, should take advantage of the extra mental acuity and sharpness that comes with being physically fit.

Additionally, Neubert (2014) conducted a study at Purdue University and found that:

> Students who visited Purdue's recreational sports center 15 or more times during the 16-week fall 2013 semester, held a 3.08 GPA, which is 8.77 percent higher, compared to 2.81 for those who did not use the facility at all. The difference on the letter scale is a B and B–. More than 60 percent of the students who visited the Co-Rec at least once a week earned a B or better during the fall semester.

There are many studies that show that exercise can have a positive benefit on a person's mental health, especially when referring to depression and self-esteem. Weir (2011) refers to a study that shows the direct benefit of exercise on depression:

> Blumenthal has explored the mood-exercise connection through a series of randomized controlled trials. In one such study, he and his colleagues

assigned sedentary adults with major depressive disorder to one of four groups: supervised exercise, home-based exercise, antidepressant therapy or a placebo pill. After four months of treatment, Blumenthal found, patients in the exercise and antidepressant groups had higher rates of remission than did the patients on the placebo. Exercise, he concluded, was generally comparable to antidepressants for patients with major depressive disorder.

Regular exercise can help ease depression in a number of ways. These ways include releasing "feel-good" brain chemicals, such as endorphins, reducing certain immune system chemicals that can worsen depression, and increasing body temperature, which may have calming effects (Mayo Clinic Staff, 2014).

The Context of the College Student—The Millennial Generation and Beyond

Many of today's college students are part of the millennial generation, and it is important to understand who they are and what motivates them in order to best serve them. A millennial is someone born in the 1980s or later—someone brought up using digital technology and mass media ("Millennial Generation," 2015). Richard Sweeny (2006, p. 1) summed up the millennial generation's thirst for new technology:

Millennials are "natives" of this new, digital, consumer driven, flat, networked, instant satisfaction world. While some in the older generations may adapt quickly, they will always be immigrants and will never be as competent, resourceful or "natural" as the Millennial "natives" born into this new culture.

Millennials are a perfect example of the experiential learning theory, which places an emphasis on learning through direct experience (Center for Learning and Teaching, n.d.). Some examples of experiential learning activities are multiplayer games, computer simulations, social networking, and social media. These activities allow individuals to learn by doing the experience rather than reading about the activity. An exercise-related example is outdoor recreation, where students learn through practical experience. Experiential learning allows for immediate feedback, which is ideal for millennials, who crave instant gratification. Millennials feel a need to constantly know how they and their peers are progressing. They are practical and results-oriented, and prefer merit-based systems to other systems because of the ability to measure productivity and goals.

Technology integration into the fitness world has made measuring productivity and goals much easier. Some of the more noticeable advancements are the interactive displays on equipment. These displays allow students to connect their mobile devices to the machine, which enables them to listen to music and track progress; smartphone applications even give students direct, immediate feedback using numbers and charts about their workout and their progress. Activity trackers have been around in various forms for decades. Heart rate monitors, pedometers, and accelerometers have all taken a new form in the recent decade and can now be housed in a device that is no bigger than a wristwatch, such as Fitbit, Motorola Up, and Nike FuelBand. They give visual feedback at any point in time and can be worn all day, not just during a workout; users see daily, weekly, monthly, and yearly progress. It is easy for students to set goals using these devices since they can see how far along they are and how much further they have to go. The visual feedback also allows students to seek approval and support from friends via social media. Negative feedback can be controlled by students as they can limit their friend circle on their choice of social media.

Today's millennials are also motivated by autonomy-supported learning. The autonomy-supportive learning context allows students to progress at their own pace without outside pressure (Perlman, 2013). Free from additional pressure, they feel supported to pursue their internal desires and reach outside of their comfort zone. A sense of caring and guidance for students during challenging tasks can come through social media, where they post their progress and hear from their peers via comments or likes. The accumulation of support and encouragement is called social capital. Social capital can be simply described as resources collected through relationships (Ellison, Steinfield, & Lampe, 2007). Connecting through social media can be best described as bridging social capital, or what network researchers like to call "weak ties." Weak ties are loose connections between peers who provide useful information and perspectives but normally not emotional support (Ellison et al., 2007). At this point in the students' lives, when students are away from their parents, social media such as Facebook, Twitter, and Instagram are now the place to which students turn to seek approval, gain appreciation, and feel unique. Social media connects students with like interests, such as health and exercise, providing them with support and motivation to engage in activities they might not otherwise attempt.

Fitness Trends

According to the American College of Sports Medicine's "Worldwide Survey of Fitness Trends for 2015: What's Driving the Market," the number one fitness trend projected for 2015 is body weight training (Thompson, 2014). Body weight training programs use minimal equipment, which make it a very versatile and inexpensive way to exercise. One type of body weight leverage equipment that has grown in popularity in recent years is the TRX Suspension Trainer. Created by a Navy SEAL, this type of training can be used by anyone, from the beginner exerciser to the professional athlete.

The second predicted fitness trend for 2015 is high-intensity interval training (HIIT) (Thompson, 2014). HIIT classes are typically less than 30 minutes and combine short bursts of high-intensity exercise, at 80%–100% of maximum heart rate, followed by rest or recovery periods. HIIT can be easily modified for people with different fitness levels and can be done using a variety of exercise modes, including walking, running, and cycling. Current research shows similar results to continuous endurance training (such as 30–60 minutes of continuous running or cycling) with fewer workouts (Kravitz, 2014). Due to the increased recovery period (referred to as "excess post-exercise oxygen consumption" or EPOC) after an intense workout like HIIT, caloric expenditure can be 6%–15% higher than after a low-intensity, longer-duration aerobic workout on cardio equipment, such as the elliptical machine. One concern among some health and fitness professionals is the potential for a higher injury rate with HIIT workouts. As such, both HIIT and continuous aerobic workouts yield physiological and metabolic benefits. The recommendation is to incorporate a balance of both programs into cardiovascular training programs (Kravitz, 2014). Individuals should make modifications to high-intensity workouts as needed, according to their own fitness level.

The third projected fitness trend for 2015 is "educated, certified and experienced fitness professionals" (Thompson, 2014, p. 11). As the market for fitness professionals becomes more competitive, there is an increasing interest in regulation, such as offering degree programs at colleges or universities. Currently, several colleges and universities provide personal trainer and group fitness instructor training courses, of which some are accredited. Even if students are not looking to go into personal training or group fitness as a career, participating in educational training programs such as these can prepare them for a national certification in fitness, helpful for part-time work or interim employment following graduation. Some universities offer courses for academic credit, and others consider them noncredit courses. College students who go through the training can find a part-time job as a personal trainer or group fitness instructor at their student recreation center while in college. Most colleges and universities offer personal training services and group fitness classes at affordable rates.

Themed races such as "color runs" and zombie runs and obstacle course races, such as Tough Mudder, are becoming more popular among college students. Tough Mudder races feature a 10–12-mile course with intense challenges, such as diving into ice-cold water, running through live, low-voltage electrical wires, and crawling through mud. In 2013, approximately one in seven Tough Mudder participants was between the ages of 18 and 23, with college student participation in obstacle course challenges reported to be dramatically increasing (Vendituoli, 2013). A new type of obstacle course race called "Campus Carnage" has also entered the obstacle course scene, though these campus-based events often omit more dangerous obstacles, such as freezing water, electrical wires, and fires (Vendituoli, 2013).

CrossFit is another fitness-based community present in most towns and even some colleges and universities. This fitness regimen involves "constantly varied functional movements performed at relatively high intensity" ("What is CrossFit?," 2015). To dedicated CrossFit enthusiasts, CrossFit is more than just a workout; it is a way of life. They apply a nutrition regime consisting of meat and vegetables, nuts and seeds, some fruit, little starch, and no sugar. Due to the space and equipment required and an expensive initial training, adding CrossFit on a college campus can pose challenges. Some college campuses have managed to address the challenges and offer CrossFit as part of their small group training program. There are typically 4–10 participants in small group training, allowing the instructor or trainer to provide more individualized attention as well as maintain the group dynamic that provides support and motivation. The same support and motivation can also be found in group fitness classes.

The traditional types of group fitness classes, such as Zumba and indoor cycling, are currently not as popular as they once were. Classes such as bodyweight training, boot camp, strength training, and core conditioning are growing in popularity (Schroeder & Donlin, 2013). Sometimes offered at no charge and other times for a fee, group fitness classes provide a variety of different exercise formats for students of various skill and fitness levels. With fun music, motivating instructors, and group camaraderie, fitness classes can provide both motivation and structure to help individuals stick with an exercise program. Group fitness classes are most commonly 60 minutes in length; however, a current trend is shorter classes (e.g., 30 minutes), which are easier to fit into a busy schedule. Combination or "fusion" classes that combine different types of exercise formats (e.g., cardio and strength training) are also popular. Although it lost a little popularity for a period of time, yoga is now back in the top 10 fitness trends (Thompson, 2014). One of the appeals of yoga is that it is a "mind-body" exercise; classes incorporate a focus on breathing along with movement and also normally include an opportunity for meditation and relaxation at the end of class. With college students being pulled in many different directions, taking time to focus on the present moment through practices such as meditation can benefit their mental health.

Workouts such as restorative yoga and self-myofascial release are projected to increase in 2015 (Brown, 2014). Perhaps this is due to the popularity of high-intensity workouts like HIIT and the fact that people are getting very sore and even injured. Foam rollers and other self-myofascial release tools have been used by athletes and physical therapists for years and are now gaining in popularity in the general population, often used as part of warm-ups and cool downs (Brown, 2014). Self-myofascial release can be a compliment to stretching because it relaxes muscles and improves range of motion (Penney, 2013).

Recommendations for Cardiovascular Exercise

The first exercise recommendations in 1975 were produced by the American Heart Association. At the same time, the American College of Sports Medicine (ACSM) produced "Graded Exercise Testing and Exercise Prescription" documents. These documents were the beginning of a growing movement toward clinically focused recommendations about exercise that were based on specific health outcomes. Prior to that, the "science" around exercise recommendations was focused on athletic or performance-related outcomes. These highly structured exercise recommendations caused most people to believe that exercise not meeting these specific criteria would be of limited or no value (U.S. Department of Health and Human Services [USDHHS], 2007).

Starting in 1990, ACSM distinguished its recommendations for physical activity for health from those for fitness. ACSM acknowledged that while lower levels of physical activity might not accomplish the same fitness goals, such as increased cardiorespiratory endurance, certain levels of moderate-intensity physical activity could still help to reduce the risk of certain chronic diseases (ACSM, 2014a).

In 1995, the CDC and ACSM recommended that "every US adult should accumulate 30 minutes or more of moderate-intensity physical activity on most, preferably all, days of the week" (ACSM, 2014a, p. 7). The recommendations were meant to increase public awareness of the important health-related benefits of moderate-intensity physical activity. However, even a decade later, in 2005, nearly 25% of adults reported they were sedentary (Haskell et al., 2007). Changes to the previous exercise recommendations had to be made.

In 2007, ACSM and AHA issued updated recommendations for physical activity and health, further specifying intensity, duration, and frequency. These recommendations stated that "healthy adults aged 18–65 years should participate in moderate intensity, aerobic physical activity for a minimum of 30 minutes on five days per week or vigorous intensity, aerobic activity for a minimum of 20 minutes on three days per week" (ACSM, 2014a, pp. 7–8). The recommendations also stated that individuals who wanted to further improve their health and/or fitness may benefit from additional amounts of physical activity (ACSM, 2014a).

In 2008, the Office of Disease Prevention and Health Promotion within the U.S. Department of Health and Human Services compiled the first Physical Activity Guidelines for Americans (USDHHS, 2008a). The Physical Activity Guidelines originated from a review of current exercise recommendations and scientific literature by the Physical Activity Guidelines Advisory Committee, which clearly demonstrated that sedentary behavior increases health risks (USDHHS, 2008b). In their scientific research, the committee found that the total volume of physical activity (or the combination of frequency, intensity, and duration of physical activity) *per week* was the most important predictor of health benefits, rather than frequency, intensity, and duration of individual exercise sessions (ACSM, 2014a, p. 8). Therefore the guidelines encouraged at least 150 minutes of moderate-intensity physical aerobic activity or 75 minutes of vigorous-intensity aerobic physical activity per week, or an equivalent combination of moderate- and vigorous-intensity aerobic activity per week to incur health benefits. For additional, more extensive benefits, adults should increase their physical activity to 300 minutes of moderate-intensity physical activity or 150 minutes of vigorous activity per week. According to the guidelines, aerobic activity should be performed in bouts of at least 10 minutes, and regular physical activity is better than sporadic physical activity. However, if individuals are not able to meet the weekly physical activity recommendations, doing some activity is better than doing none. The guidelines also give more specific recommendations for different populations, such as children and adolescents, older adults, and adults with disabilities. The weekly goal of 150 minutes of moderate-intensity aerobic physical activity is more realistic for the average person to accomplish than previous recommendations of 30 minutes or more per day.

There is substantial evidence to support the inverse relationship between physical activity and premature mortality, chronic diseases and other health conditions, and 150 minutes per week is what is recommended for "substantial health benefits" (USDHHS, 2008a). However, even if individuals are not able to meet the 150 minutes per week minimum, benefits can still be obtained from doing some physical activity. It is not exactly clear yet whether less exercise than the recommended 150 minutes per week can extend life expectancy, but one study found that doing only half the recommended weekly amount of exercise still has health benefits. The prospective cohort study demonstrated that 90 minutes per week of moderate-intensity exercise, or 15 minutes per day, can still be beneficial for health, even for those at risk of cardiovascular disease (Wen et al., 2011). It is important to remember that anything in excess is typically not healthy, and exercise is no exception. Overexercise can lead to health concerns, such as injuries, decrease in immune function, bone problems, and menstrual irregularities (Lein, 2015).

Recommendations for Strength Training

Although most of the research conducted on the health benefits of exercise focuses on aerobic activity, benefits can also be obtained from strength training. The ACSM-AHA Primary Physical Activity Recommendations state that "every adult should perform activities that maintain or increase muscular strength and endurance for a minimum of 2 days per week" (ACSM, 2014a, p. 8). ACSM gives more detailed information about the intensity, type, number of sets and repetitions, length of rest intervals, and progression to follow specific to different strength-training goals. The health benefits of strength training include a lower risk of all-cause mortality, fewer cardiovascular disease events, lower risk of developing physical function limitations, and lower risk of nonfatal disease (Gerber et al., 2011). Additional benefits include improvements in body composition, blood glucose levels, insulin sensitivity, and blood pressure. According to ACSM, one of the primary goals of strength training should be to maintain bone mass (Kohrt, Bloomfield, Little, Nelson, & Yingling, 2004). Although it is still ambiguous whether strength training actually increases bone mineral density, studies suggest that age-related decline in bone mineral density can be slowed and the relative risk for fracture reduced in people who are physically active (Kohrt et al., 2004). The most effective exercise "prescription" for preserving bone health, according to ACSM, is resistance training exercises for all major muscle groups, along with a combination of weight-bearing endurance activities (e.g., stair climbing and walking with at least some periods of jogging) and activities that involve jumping, commonly referred to as "plyometrics." High-intensity activities, such as plyometrics, have shown to increase bone mineral density in children and adolescents, and there is some evidence that these gains are maintained into adulthood (Kohrt et al., 2004). Participating in bone density building and maintenance activities when individuals are younger is advantageous. During childhood and adolescence, bone density is accrued at a rate greater than it is broken down, so the skeleton grows in both size and density. According to the National Institutes of Health (NIH), "Up to 90 percent of peak bone mass is acquired by age 18 in girls and by age 20 in boys" (2012). Bone mass can keep increasing until around age 30, at which point bones reach their maximum strength and density, known as peak bone mass. Given that a greater peak bone mass decreases the risk of osteoporosis later in life, it is especially important that individuals younger than 30 years old make efforts to build and maintain bone mass/density (NIH, 2012).

This is why encouraging adolescents and college-aged students to participate in strength training and other activities to build or maintain bone mineral density is so important. There is a stigma associated with strength training, particularly for females, that lifting weights will cause individuals to "bulk up." This common misconception is untrue for several reasons. Females do not have the same testosterone levels as men, and these levels vary even for males. So it is significantly more difficult for women to put on muscle mass than men. Second, a certain type of strength training program or "prescription" is designed to increase muscle mass, such as the type used by bodybuilders. The general, ACSM recommendations for muscle conditioning are exercises for all major muscle groups, 2–3 days per week, and 2–4 sets of 8–12 repetitions. This type of program is not designed to cause major increase in muscle mass. Third, in order to put on muscle weight or mass, individuals must increase their caloric consumption, something that the average female is not intentionally doing. Females should be encouraged to participate in strength training activities because biologically they are predisposed to lose bone mineral density at a greater rate than men once menopause starts. Young women whose periods stop because of extremely low body weight (a condition that often accompanies eating disorders, such as anorexia) may lose significant amounts of bone density, which may not return even after they start getting their periods again (NIH, 2012).

Many college and university recreation centers offer strength training classes, such as weight training, body sculpting, or BODYPUMP. These classes can be fun, motivating ways for women and men to participate in strength training activities on campus. For students who want to learn more about weight lifting, colleges might also offer weight training clubs or even weight training academic classes. ACSM suggests that a goal of a health-related resistance training program for adults should be to "make activities of daily living (ADLs) (e.g., stair climbing, carrying bags of groceries) less stressful physiologically" (ACSM, 2014a, p. 181). This type of strength training, also referred to as functional training, has recently become very popular. In functional training, body weight exercises or workouts using small equipment, such as medicine balls or kettlebells, are commonly used to attempt to increase functionality of ADLs. Functional training is popular for use with personal trainers and is also often incorporated into group fitness classes such as boot camp.

Recommendations for Stretching and Flexibility

While stretching is an important part of any comprehensive exercise program, it is an area less researched than aerobic fitness or strength training. There is still controversy around stretching, with often more questions than answers regarding the benefits versus the risks of stretching (ACSM, 2014b). The main goal of stretching is to increase flexibility, which is "the degree to which a joint moves throughout a normal, pain-free range of motion" (ACSM, 2014b, p. 432). Increasing range of motion can help improve athletic or exercise performance in the joints that are stretched and also improve activities of daily living. Stretching can also help to improve postural stability and balance (ACSM, 2014a). It is often thought that stretching can decrease the risk of injury, but the research is not consistent in this area. One study found that stretching was more likely to reduce injury for individuals participating in sports or exercises involving more explosive skills and movements. Two risks of flexibility training include joint hypermobility, or extreme range of motion, and a short-term decrease in performance (ACSM, 2014b). There is also some evidence to suggest that static stretching, holding the stretch "to the point of feeling tightness or slight discomfort" for 10–30 seconds, may acutely result in a short-term decrease in muscle strength, power, and sports performance.

The most common types of stretching to increase flexibility after workouts are static stretching and proprioceptive neuromuscular facilitation (PNF) stretching. PNF stretching is the "contract, relax" method of stretching. It involves a contraction of the muscle group, followed by a static stretch of the same muscle group. A 3–6-second contraction followed by a 10–30-second assisted stretch (often provided by another person) is recommended. PNF stretching should be performed only by trained practitioners, as there is a risk for overstretching if the technique is not completely understood. All stretches, both static and PNF stretches, should be repeated 2–4 times for each muscle group. Flexibility exercises should be performed at least 2–3 days per week, with daily being the most effective. In order to maximize benefit and decrease risk for injury, PNF and static stretches should be performed when muscles are warm. A third type of stretching, called dynamic stretching, incorporates movements along with the development of muscle tension. The goal of this type of stretching is to move the joint in a controlled manner through a normal range of motion, progressing to a larger range of motion (ACSM, 2014b). Dynamic stretching is often used in sport-specific warm-ups because it mimics activities that will be performed in the workout or competition. For example, soccer players often incorporate a footwork drill called "carioca" into their warm-up routines, which prepares them for the fast footwork that will be required in the game. So, while some controversy remains regarding how effective stretching really is for the general population, flexibility exercises performed to increase range of motion in specific joints might still be useful for individuals, depending on their needs and abilities.

Hydration and Nutrition for Exercise

A less controversial, but still often confusing, part of exercise is hydration: what to drink, how much, and how often. Staying optimally hydrated during exercise has several benefits, including a decreased strain on the heart, improved endurance, better sweat rates, and improved cooling (ACSM, 2014b). Yet, most people do not stay optimally hydrated. Many people rely on thirst as the signal to consume fluids, but when the thirst sensation occurs the person has already lost 1 to 2 liters of fluid. In order to stay hydrated, individuals should consume fluids at fixed time intervals throughout the day. Individuals should prehydrate several hours before physical activity, and drink slowly to enable absorption of fluids. Because sweating rates and electrolyte losses vary between individuals and between different types of exercise, ACSM recommends that individuals develop customized fluid replacement programs (Sawka et al., 2007). Four hours before exercise, an individual should consume about 5–7 milliliters of fluid per kilogram of body weight (for a 150-pound individual, this would be about 11–16 ounces). If the individual is not producing urine, or the urine is dark, approximately two hours before exercise, he/she should consume approximately 3–5 milliliters of fluid per kilogram of body weight (for a 150-pound individual, this would be about 7–11 ounces) (Sawka et al., 2007).

During exercise, individuals should drink enough fluids to "prevent excessive dehydration (>2% body weight loss from water deficit)" (Sawka et al., 2007, p. 384). Because sweat rates vary with individuals, and the intensity of activities vary, there do not seem to be clear recommendations for hydration during exercise for short-term duration activities (less than one hour). ACSM recommends consuming fluids at regular intervals, at a rate equal to the sweat rate. Athletes should monitor body weight changes during training sessions and in competition to estimate sweat losses.

After exercise, individuals should drink at least 16–24 fluid ounces per pound of body weight that was lost during exercise (ACSM, ADA, & the Dietetics of Canada, 2009). This should be consumed within two hours after exercise (ACSM, 2014b).

The type of fluid consumed can also be important, and sports drinks including carbohydrates and electrolytes are recommended for exercise lasting more than one hour. Carbohydrates help to refuel muscles and provide energy, and electrolytes (such as sodium) help to maintain blood volume, critical to sweat rates and performance (Sawka et al., 2007). Studies have shown that sports drinks containing a 6%–8% carbohydrate solution and 100–200 mg of sodium per cup are most effective for reducing mental and physical fatigue, improving performance, and for gastric emptying and intestinal absorption (ACSM, 2014b).

Consuming sodium will also help recovery by stimulating fluid retention and thirst (ACSM, 2014a). A hydration-related issue that has arisen in recent years is hyponatremia, a state of low sodium concentration in the blood. Exercise-associated hyponatremia was first reported in endurance runners but has also been reported in soldiers and a number of participants from a variety of recreational activities. Participants have been hospitalized and have even died from this condition. The major contributing factors to exercise-associated hyponatremia are the overdrinking of low-sodium fluids and an excessive loss of total body sodium. Therefore, while it is important that individuals hydrate before, during and after exercise, they should be careful not to drink too much water.

Another concern around exercise is proper nutrition for weight control and also for optimal exercise performance. Food energy is measured in kilocalories (kcal). If a person consumes more energy than is expended, the excess energy is stored and body weight will increase. If a person consumes less energy than is expended, body weight will decrease. Consistently consuming too little energy to meet energy needs will burn enough lean muscle mass that the body's metabolic rate will actually decrease. The result of a lower metabolic rate is usually higher body fat and thus an increased body weight because the body cannot burn the energy that is consumed. Therefore, it is important to maintain an energy-balanced state or deviate only slightly from it. Individuals wishing to lose weight by decreasing body fat should decrease no more than 300–400 kcal per day, depending on body size, while maintaining a regular strength training schedule to maintain lean muscle mass. Those wishing to gain weight by increasing muscle mass should increase daily caloric intake by 300–400 kcal, while performing appropriate strength training exercises needed for building muscle (ACSM, 2014b).

What to eat before, during, and after exercise depends on the person and the activity. The greater the person's body weight and the more activity that an individual does, the more energy and calories he or she needs in order to have energy for activity. In general, maintaining an energy balance throughout the day by consuming small but frequent meals (approximately every three hours) is a good strategy for active individuals. This style of eating keeps the metabolic rate steady and improves fat burning and also glucose tolerance and insulin response (which make it less likely that fat will be produced from foods consumed). Other benefits are better maintenance of muscle mass and improved physical performance (ACSM, 2014b). The quantities of carbohydrate, fat, and protein included in meals eaten around exercise depend on the intensity and duration of the physical activity. For example, more intense activity (such as jogging or running) requires more fuel from carbohydrates than lower-intensity activity (such as walking). The protein requirement for physically active people is about double that of nonathletes. However, most individuals naturally consume more protein than they need just in the foods they eat. This is one reason that most individuals wanting to gain muscle mass do not need to consume protein powder. Protein from natural sources, such as meat and eggs, is better-quality protein than protein powders and is more readily absorbed and processed by the body. If more protein is consumed than an individual needs or can physically use for tissue-building purposes (about 1.5 grams per kilogram of body weight) that protein will be burned as a source of energy (which can lead to dehydration if the body is trying to get rid of excess nitrogenous waste on a regular basis) or stored as fat (ACSM, 2014b). Fat is a source of energy and necessary for essential body functions. How much fat a person consumes depends on the activity they are performing and their energy needs. Some athletes must have a lower body fat for performance-related reasons. It is important that athletes not allow their body fat to drop to lower than essential fat levels, in order to keep their bodies functioning appropriately and not cause any long-term physiological problems.

Before exercise, individuals should consume a well-balanced meal (higher in carbohydrates and lower in fat) three to four hours before exercising. An example of a pre-exercise breakfast meal is oatmeal with almonds, plus a banana and skim milk. An example of a pre-exercise lunch meal is a turkey and cheese sandwich, plus fruit. Thirty to sixty minutes before activity, a light-carbohydrate snack (such as a piece of fruit) can be consumed (Sports, Cardiovascular, and Wellness Nutrition [SCAN], 2010a).

During exercise lasting one hour or less, there is usually no need to consume food during the workout. With long-duration endurance activities, such as cycling or running events lasting several hours, consumption of solid, easy-to-digest, carbohydrate foods is encouraged, along with carbohydrate-containing beverages. Some endurance athletes prefer to consume foods such as bananas and pretzels, and others prefer to consume carbohydrates in the form of gels and gummies. Carbohydrates should be consumed 15–60 minutes following exercise, depending on the intensity of the activity (SCAN, 2010b). The more intense the activity, the more quickly carbohydrates should be consumed in order to replace glycogen stores. Following exercise, muscles are more receptive to replacing stored glycogen because the level of the enzyme that enhances the conversion of carbohydrates to stored glycogen is higher. Immediately following activities, 200 to 400 kcal of carbohydrates should be consumed and then an additional 200 to 300 kcal within the next several hours (ACSM, 2014b). Protein should be consumed to aid in repair of damaged muscle tissue and also to stimulate the development of new tissue (SCAN, 2010b). An example of a postexercise snack is a smoothie made with yogurt and frozen berries and an example of a postexercise meal is stir-fry with chicken, vegetables, and brown rice. Since many college students have a campus meal plan, finding healthy options to aid in the recovery process is relatively simple.

Weight Control and Exercise

Many students entering college are concerned about the "freshmen 15." According to a study published in the *Social Science Quarterly* in December 2011, the freshmen 15 is just a myth. The study found that the average student gains between 2.5 and 3.5 pounds during the freshman year (Zagorsky & Smith, 2011). The reason college freshmen gain weight can be explained by a variety of factors, including a change from home-cooked meals to free rein over an all-you-can-eat-style buffet at the cafeteria, increased stress, less sleep, and less physical activity. Students who were previously involved in structured exercise, such as participating on sports teams in high school, do not have that same schedule if they do not become college athletes. Also more schoolwork and studying, along with participating in extracurricular activities, socializing with friends, and maybe even holding a part-time job decrease time for exercise. During the 1990s the U.S. Surgeon General actually found that the largest declines in physical activity took place during adolescence (Zagorsky & Smith, 2011). The National College Health Assessment shows that only 51.3% of college students are meeting the recommended amount of aerobic physical activity (American College Health Association, 2014).

Regular physical activity can help prevent weight gain and improve weight loss and is also a good habit for students develop in college. According to ACSM, a minimum of between 150 and 250 minutes per week of moderate-intensity physical activity can be effective in preventing weight gain. This level of activity will provide only modest weight loss, unless moderate diet restriction is included. However, more than 250 minutes of moderate-intensity physical activity per week can improve weight loss (Donnelly et al., 2009). While resistance training does not increase weight loss, it does increase lean body mass, which can increase loss of fat mass and therefore can decrease risk for chronic diseases. It is also likely that individuals vary in their response to physical activity for weight maintenance, weight loss, and prevention of weight gain. The concern about 66.3% of U.S. adults being overweight and obese is that these conditions increase the risk for a variety of chronic diseases and other health conditions (Donnelly et al., 2009). These include heart disease, hypertension, diabetes, and some cancers. The prevalence of obesity among 18- to 24-year-olds has steadily increased, with overweight status exceeding 25% of the population and almost 20% of this age group meeting the criteria for obesity (Bjerke, 2013).

Exercise Adherence and Motivation

It seems that most college students and young adults are well aware of the risks associated with overweight and obesity and yet, due to a variety of reasons, still gain weight in college and adopt unhealthy behaviors. In fact, for a myriad of behaviors (including smoking and drinking alcohol), individuals can be well educated and informed of the risks and still choose to participate in those behaviors. Therefore, listing the benefits of exercise is not enough to encourage most college students to exercise. A more effective method is to look at strategies for motivating individuals to adopt a behavior change. Two important strategies associated with prevention of weight gain are lifestyle approaches and planned physical activity (Donnelly et al., 2009). Individuals who make lifestyle changes (e.g., eating more fruits and vegetables) are more successful at maintaining a healthy weight than those who make changes to their diet and exercise routines in order to achieve a short-term goal (e.g., cutting calories drastically in order to lose weight for a wedding). Having a plan for physical activity involves scheduling days and times for exercise and making it a priority so other activities will not get in the way.

There are a variety of theory-based approaches for helping individuals to both adopt and adhere to exercise. One of these theories is called the theory of planned behavior. According to this theory, strategies for encouraging individuals to adopt exercise are exploring attitudes related to change, introducing enjoyable activities, utilizing group activities or buddy systems, and identifying and engaging social support (ACSM, 2014b). Another theory that supports healthy behaviors is the self-determination theory. It is concerned with supporting our natural or intrinsic tendencies to behave in effective and healthy ways. Individual motivation and benefits are influenced in a linear progression: (a) social or learning context, (b) support for psychological needs, (c) motivational level, and (d) associated benefits/experiences (Perlman, 2013). The linear progression displays characteristics of the driving forces and factors of motivation. Within the first progression, social or learning context, individuals interact with others. This is the start of the motivation chain, and if there is no success at this stage, then the progression comes to a halt. The decision to start the chain comes from an individual's personal choice and the environment.

College professionals can help point students in the direction of groups and programs that will provide an environment of social support and structure, such as intramural sports, sport clubs, group fitness classes, and physical activity academic classes (e.g., yoga and weight lifting). There are also other fitness-based "communities" of people that exist on and off campuses all over the country. There are training groups available for a variety of fitness and sport-related events, such as running and biking. Some local bike and running stores will also offer weekly rides or runs for the community.

Since approximately 50% of individuals who start a physical activity program drop out within the first six months, strategies to encourage exercise adherence are also important (ACSM, 2014b). Three of the strongest theory-based concepts related to exercise adherence are self-efficacy, motivation for exercise, and self-worth. Self-efficacy is defined as an individual's confidence to do something successfully. The higher a person's self-efficacy, the more willing he or she is to put forth effort toward the activity. Strategies for increasing self-efficacy include overcoming barriers, regulating behaviors, and accessing social support. Barriers can be a variety of factors, such as lack of time, weight status, fitness level, or even family and friends. Barriers can also be a fear of injury or failure (ACSM, 2014b). Having the experience of successfully completing a challenging but attainable task can increase a person's self-efficacy. Setting and achieving small goals (such as exercising three times in one week or going to one fitness class) are a good place to start. Individuals often become overwhelmed by big goals (e.g., running a half-marathon) and big commitments (e.g., purchasing a 30-pack of personal training sessions). The important thing is to get started doing something. The motivation will not come to those who wait for inspiration.

Motivation for exercise can be intrinsic or extrinsic. When individuals are intrinsically motivated, they choose to exercise for internal reasons, such as the enjoyment of the activity or the feeling of accomplishment after the workout. Individuals who are extrinsically motivated exercise to achieve external outcomes, such as weight loss and appearance. External motivation is not associated with long-term exercise adherence because of concerns about what will motivate the person once the external goal is achieved. In most cases, individuals just starting to exercise will be extrinsically motivated. Strategies for shifting individuals' motivations toward intrinsic motivation and autonomy are important to introduce early on. Some of these strategies are planning exercise, goal-setting, and self-monitoring. Several studies have shown the effectiveness of utilizing self-monitoring techniques in physical activity interventions, and research shows that including at least one other technique (such as goal setting) is even more effective. Many tools exist for self-monitoring, including mobile phone apps, workout logs, the Internet, heart-rate monitors, and pedometers (ACSM, 2014b). Many web-based tools are interactive and can provide peer support through discussion boards, blogs or chat rooms, video demonstrations of exercises, online journaling, and online coaching.

Self-worth is the satisfaction individuals have with themselves. Research shows that an increased self-worth leads to more participation in exercise and vice versa (ACSM, 2014b). Self-worth and self-esteem also have a reciprocal relationship. As individuals gain confidence in their ability to do something, such as exercise, they will start to feel better about themselves. Feeling good about oneself will further aid in successfully overcoming barriers and achieving goals and will also spill over to other areas, such as diet and other healthy lifestyle behaviors.

Conclusion

Given the many benefits of exercise, it is important that higher education professionals—student affairs staff, faculty, and others—encourage students not only to exercise but also to live physically active lifestyles. In general, it is important to avoid placing an emphasis on exercising for aesthetic reasons. For individuals who may have an obsession with exercising to be thin or to "get big," focusing on exercise to change one's appearance may foster obsessions with weight loss, promote an addiction to exercise, lower self-worth, and place individuals at risk for developing eating disorders (Druxman, 2003). The key is to focus on behaviors and feelings. Encourage students to exercise in reasonable amounts, according to the guidelines provided by ACSM, and to exercise for reasons such as enjoyment and stress relief.

The world in which we live enables students to take shortcuts instead of doing hard work to get better and healthier results. In a culture of quick fixes and instant gratification, it is important to remind students that there is no magic bullet when it comes to exercise and health. Diet pills, smoking, and liposuction may help people to lose body weight and fat, but at what cost? Making lifestyle modifications, such as diet and exercise, are harder and take more work, but in the long run they will also have the greatest benefits. Exercise and physical activity actually used to be viewed by the medical world as essential to humans as medicine. Prior to the beginning of the twentieth century, when Western medicine became more focused on "sick care," it was common for physicians to focus on the promotion of health and the prevention of disease. The strong emphasis on health, rather than disease, dates back to Hippocrates, who wrote two books on "regimen," stating that "eating alone will not keep a man well; he must also take exercise. For food and exercise work together to produce health" (Berryman, 2010, p. 1). The classical Western medical notion was that one could improve one's health through one's own actions, which included breathing fresh air, healthy eating, sleep, and exercise.

Studies show that behavioral causes currently account for 40% of all deaths in the United States, with the top causes of premature death being obesity and physical inactivity combined, along with smoking (Schroeder, 2007). Recent data suggests that nearly two-thirds of patients would be more interested in exercising to stay healthy if they were advised to do so by their doctor (Berryman, 2010). Today there is a global health initiative managed by the American College of Sports Medicine, called "Exercise Is Medicine," which is focused on encouraging physicians and other healthcare providers to include physical activity when designing treatment plans for patients. Exercise Is Medicine is committed to the belief that physical activity is integral in the prevention and treatments of many common chronic health conditions and should be regularly assessed as part of medical care (ACSM, 2015).

In order to ensure that our students have the best quality of life possible, we must encourage them to view exercise in the way that Hippocrates did, as a regimen that is just as essential to health as eating.

There are many benefits of exercise for a person's overall well-being. Exercise is a key component in helping our students to flourish during their time at college. Many institutions look at recreation as a luxury for the students, faculty, and staff. This chapter shows you it is much more than a luxury. We talked mostly about the benefits for students, but those benefits also apply to faculty and staff. There are some universities that give faculty and staff extra time off during the day to exercise because that makes the employee healthier and more productive. This is a benefit more universities should provide. In a college setting fitness professionals need the support of faculty, student affairs, and administration to be able to help the students flourish through exercise. Resources are often not available for equipment, staff, and training. Without these resources fitness professionals cannot provide the quality programs that the students, faculty, and staff deserve. Many fitness programs offer classes and personal training with instructors who are not certified, which can be a risk management concern. There needs to be a general commitment from the university in terms of the importance of exercise in students' lives. This commitment includes sufficient professional staffing, training, facilities, and budget. Exercise is not a luxury—it is essential to the overall success of students during their time at college. By encouraging students to live physically active lifestyles, higher education professionals can help students achieve success in all aspects of college life, both in and outside the classroom.

References

American College Health Association. (2014). *National College Health Assessment II: Undergraduate students reference group executive summary, spring 2014*. Hanover, MD: American College Health Association.

American College of Sports Medicine (ACSM), American Dietetic Association (ADA), & the Dietetics of Canada. (2009). Joint position statement: Nutrition and athletic performance. *Medicine and Science in Sports and Exercise, 41*(3), 709–731. doi:10.1249/MSS.0b013e318190eb86

American College of Sports Medicine. (2014a). *ACSM's guidelines for exercise testing and prescription* (9th ed.). Baltimore, MD: Lippincott Williams & Wilkins.

American College of Sports Medicine. (2014b). *ACSM's resources for the personal trainer* (4th ed.). Baltimore, MD: Lippincott Williams & Wilkins.

American College of Sports Medicine. (2015). Exercise is medicine. Retrieved from http://www.exerciseismedicine.org

Berryman, J. (2010). Exercise is medicine: A historical perspective. *Current Sports Medicine Report, 9*(4), 195–201.

Bjerke, W. (2013). Health and fitness courses in higher education: A historical perspective and contemporary approach (anthropomorphism). *Physical Educator, 70*(4), 337–358.

Brown, J. (2014, September 5). Fitness trend forecast for 2015: 6 trends on the rise. *Huffington Post*. Retrieved from http://www.huffingtonpost.com/jill-s-brown/fitness-trend-forecast-fo_b_5753458.html

Center for Teaching and Learning. (n.d.). Experiential learning defined. Retrieved from http://ctl.utexas.edu/teaching/engagement/experiential-learning/defined

Donnelly, J., Blair, S., Jakicic, J., Maore, M., Rankin, J., & Smith, B. (2009). American College of Sports Medicine position stand: Appropriate physical activity intervention strategies for weight loss and prevention of weight regain for adults. *Medicine and Science in Sports and Exercise, 41*(2), 459–471. doi:10.1249/MSS.0b013e3181949333

Druxman, L. (2003). The body image we see and feel. *IDEA Health & Fitness Source.* Retrieved from http://www.ideafit.com/fitness-library/body-imagethe-body-image-we-see-and-feelthe-body-image-we-see-and-feelw

Ellison, N., Steinfield, C., & Lampe, C. (2007). The benefits of Facebook "friends": Social capital and college students' use of online social network sites. *Journal of Computer-Mediated Communication, 12*(4), 1143–1168.

Gerber, C. E., Blissmer, B., Deschenes, M., Barry, F., Lamonte, M., Lee, I., & Swain, D. (2011). American College of Sports Medicine position stand: The recommended quantity and quality of exercise for developing and maintaining cardiorespiratory and muscular fitness in healthy adults. *Medicine and Science in Sports and Exercise, 43*(7), 1334–1359. doi:10.1249/MSS.0b013e318213fefb

Haskell, W., Lee, I., Pate, R., Powell, K., Blair, S., Franklin, B., . . . Bauman, A. (2007). *Physical activity and public health updated recommendation for adults from the American College of Sports Medicine and the American Heart Association.* Retrieved from http://circ.ahajournals.org/content/116/9/1081.full.pdf

Home. (2015). Self-determination theory. Retrieved from http://www.selfdeterminationtheory.org

Howard, M. (2010). Leadership and physical fitness. *Weekly Leader.* Retrieved from http://weeklyleader.net/2010/leadership-and-physical-fitness

Jefferson, T. (n.d.). BrainyQuote.com. Retrieved from http://www.brainyquote.com/quotes/quotes/t/thomasjeff164329.html

Kohrt, W. M., Bloomfield, S. A., Little, K. D., Nelson, M. E., & Yingling, V. R. (2004). American College of Sports Medicine position stand: Physical activity and bone health. *Medicine & Science in Sports & Exercise, 36*(11), 1985–1996.

Kravitz, L. (2014). *ACSM information on high intensity interval training.* Retrieved from www.acsm.org/docs/brochures/high-intensity-interval-training.pdf

Lein, S. (2015). Overexercise. Retrieved from http://www.eatingdisordersonline.com/explain/exercise.php

Mayo Clinic Staff. (2014). Depression and anxiety: Exercise eases symptoms. Retrieved from http://www.mayoclinic.org/diseases-conditions/depression/in-depth/depression-and-exercise/art-20046495?pg=1

Millennial generation. (2015). Dictionary.com. Retrieved from http://dictionary.reference.com/browse/millennial+generation

National Institutes of Health (NIH). (2012). Osteoporosis: Peak bone mass in women. Retrieved from http://www.niams.nih.gov/Health_Info/Bone/Osteoporosis/bone_mass.asp

Neubert, A. (2014). New college students who visit campus gym regularly see boost in GPA their first semesters. *Purdue University News.* Retrieved from http://www.purdue.edu/newsroom/releases/2014/Q3/new-college-students-who-visit-campus-gym-regularly-see-boost-in-gpa-their-first-semesters.html

Penney, S. (2013). Foam rolling: Applying the technique of self-myofascial release. National Academy of Sports Medicine. Retrieved from http://blog.nasm.org/training-benefits/foam-rolling-applying-the-technique-of-self-myofascial-release/#sthash.CBYAjhjC.dpuf

Perlman, D. (2013). Manipulation of the self-determined learning environment on student motivation and affect within secondary physical education. *Physical Educator, 70,* 413–428.

Sawka, M., Burke, L., Eichner, R., Maughan, R., Montain, S., & Stachenfeld, N. (2007). American College of Sports Medicine position stand: Exercise and fluid replacement. *Medicine & Science in Sports & Exercise, 39*(2), 377–390. doi:10.1249/mss.0b013e31802ca597

Schroeder, S. A. (2007). We can do better: Improving the health of the American people. *New England Journal of Medicine, 357,* 1221–1228. doi:10.1056/NEJMsa073350

Schroeder, J., & Donlin, A. (2013). 2013 IDEA Fitness Programs & Equipment Trends Report. *IDEA Fitness Journal, 10*(7), 34–45.

Sports, Cardiovascular, and Wellness Nutrition (SCAN). (2010a). Eating before performing. *Nutrition Fact Sheet,* 3.

Sports, Cardiovascular, and Wellness Nutrition (SCAN). (2010b). Eating for recovery. *Nutrition Fact Sheet,* 1.

Sweeny, R. (2006). Millennial behaviors and demographics. New Jersey Institute of Technology. http://unbtls.ca/teachingtips/pdfs/sew/Millennial-Behaviors.pdf

Thompson, W. (2014). Worldwide survey of fitness trends for 2015: What's driving the market. *ACSM's Health & Fitness Journal, 19*(6), 8–17. doi:10.1249/FIT.0000000000000073

U.S. Department of Health and Human Services (USDHHS). (2007). Historical overview of physical activity recommendations. Retrieved from http://www.health.gov/paguidelines/meetings/200706/historical.aspx

U.S. Department of Health and Human Services (USDHHS). (2008a). 2008 physical activity guidelines for Americans summary. Retrieved from http://www.health.gov/paguidelines/guidelines/summary.aspx

U.S. Department of Health and Human Services (USDHHS). (2008b). *Physical Activity Guidelines Advisory Committee report.* Retrieved from http://www.health.gov/paguidelines/report/pdf/committeereport.pdf

Vendituoli, M. (2013, October 8). College students going obstacle course crazy. *USA Today.* Retrieved from http://www.usatoday.com/story/news/nation/2013/10/08/colleges-obstacle-courses/2945429

Weir, K. (2011). The exercise effect. *American Psychological Association, 42*(11), 48.

Wen, C. P., Wai, J. P., Tsai, M. K., Yang, Y. C., Cheng, T. Y., Lee, M. C., . . . Wu, X. (2011). Minimum amount of physical activity for reduced mortality and extended life expectancy: A prospective cohort study. *Lancet, 378*(9798), 1244–1253. doi:10.1016/S0140–6736(11)60749–6. PMID: 21846575 [PubMed—indexed for MEDLINE]

What is CrossFit? (2015). Retrieved from http://www.crossfit.com/cf-info/what-is-crossfit.html

Zagorsky, J., & Smith, P. (2011). The freshmen 15: A critical time for obesity intervention or media myth? *Social Science Quarterly, 92*(5), 1389–1407.

Section 5
Spiritual Wellness

Spiritual Devel _ _

Setting a Place at the Table for Spirituality

MARIA F. DiLORENZO

As children many of us were required to be home for dinner. This time served as an opportunity for families to reconnect, to review their days, and to find common understanding about the various topics and issues of the world. The challenge is that some of us learned from a young age that certain topics should remain, as they say, "off the table." Politics and religion were at the top of the list. We learned these topics could create discomfort or dissension, which clearly were not welcomed with Mom's spaghetti and meatballs.

It is no wonder that, decades later, we may still feel uneasy when religion comes up in casual conversation. And it is not simply religion that we squirm about but also matters of faith, spirituality, and moral thinking that often are lumped together. Admittedly, this is not the case for all, but I do believe it is an inherent challenge for educators who attempt to bring spirituality to the table. We have our own episodes of PTSD when a colleague or student brings up one of these forbidden topics, and there we are back at the family dinner table. Closing off. Shutting down. Ironically praying for the topic to change to who won last night's sporting events.

There is no question that in some homes, this does not happen. I happened to grow up in a family where academic dialogue and questioning were welcomed, especially about the inner life, where spirituality and religion reside. It clearly made a difference to me, as I never shied away from talking about those topics. I have witnessed my fair share of shock and unease from colleagues and students alike when I casually bring up a trending idea about spirituality, such as attendance at worship or use of prayer as a centering technique. I admit I am used to that kind of reaction, given the professional roles I have held, but it has stuck with me over the years. People struggle with spirituality, both on a personal and intellectual level, so it is no wonder that we struggle with teaching our students about its value.

I am referring to the fact that spirituality, along with religion, is a highly personal, subjective topic. I am even cautious to define the term spirituality because I recognize that the moment I do that, a host of connotations may surface. And while it is necessary to understand my terminology and approach, first ask yourself these three questions:

1. What is your reaction to the word "spirituality"?
2. Do you find yourself opening up or closing off when spirituality is addressed?
3. How do you create or continue the experience of openness to this topic?

Our mindset is essential to evaluate even before I delve into definitions and associations. Imagine the dinner table yet again where we are gathered at the end of the day. A nice meal is placed on the table lovingly by hands that prepared it. The family is all there—even our wacky Aunt Lou, who makes us blush when she blurts out her opinions—and we feel connected simply by being present. And then the topic of *spirituality* comes up. I challenge you to resist squirming or mindlessly picking at your plate. Take this opportunity to engage, listen, and learn how spirituality can be a welcomed topic at the table.

What Does Spirituality Mean?

I started this chapter using the terms spirituality, religion, and faith interchangeably. The fact is they are rarely understood in the same way, which complicates the terms even further. (No wonder this is so hard!) Language is limiting. The words we use to describe thoughts or ideas are never all-encompassing. It is rare when words fully express an idea, an emotion, or an experience. There is always more to say or a more perfect phrase to use, or, even worse, we simply cannot find the words to communicate what we really mean or feel. Spirituality falls victim to these circumstances.

Years ago, I came across two definitions of spirituality that simplified this complexity for me:

> Whatever the expression, everyone is ultimately talking about the same thing—an unquenchable fire, a restlessness, a longing, a disquiet, a hunger, a loneliness, a gnawing nostalgia, a wildness that cannot be tamed, a congenital all-embracing ache that lies at the center of the human experience and is the ultimate force that drives everything else. . . . Spirituality is, ultimately, about what we do with that desire . . . Spirituality is about what we do with our unrest.
>
> (Rolheiser, 1999, p. 4)

> Spirituality points to our inner, subjective life . . . it has to do with the values we hold most dear, our sense of who we are and where we come from, our beliefs about why we are here, and our sense of connectedness to one another and to the world around us.
>
> (Astin et al., 2011a, p. 4)

Rolheiser argues that we all contain a spirit—a fire—at our core. There are people who use this fire in an unhealthy way, who may fall apart or, at worst, self-destruct. There are also people who use this fire in a healthy way: to connect with anything that keeps them energized and integrated. As spiritual beings, we are constantly vacillating between that which builds us up and that which breaks us down. It is the constant struggle of humanity.

Astin et al. (2011a) reinforce the questions that are at the core of the spiritual quest: *Who am I? What do I value? How do I live out my values?* In the process of unpacking these questions, we perhaps come face-to-face with an awareness of our spiritual self, who understands his or her place in the world. These questions were directly addressed in the seven-year national study conducted by Astin et al. regarding how students change during the college years and the role that college plays in facilitating the development of their spiritual qualities. This study looked closely at many dimensions of the term spirituality and provided a few key findings to support spirituality as a developmental tool in college:

> Although religious engagement declines somewhat during college, students' spiritual qualities grow substantially.
>
> Exposing students to diverse people, cultures, and ideas through study abroad, interdisciplinary coursework, service learning and other forms of civic engagement helps students value multiple perspectives as they confront the complex social, economic, and political problems of our time.
>
> Meditation and self-reflection are among the most powerful tools for enhancing students' spiritual development.
>
> Providing students with more opportunities to connect with their "inner selves" facilitates growth in their academic and leadership skills, contributes to their intellectual self-confidence and psychological well-being, and enhances their satisfaction with college.
>
> (Astin et al., 2011b, "Key College Experiences," paras. 1–4)

As educators, we witness many circumstances where students become aware of their own unrest and questioning. Maturity does that for many—age, experience, and wisdom all contribute to the development of self-awareness. Student development theory tells us that during the traditional college ages of 18–22 there is exponential growth in self-awareness and identity (Chickering & Reisser, 1993). College-aged students are sorting out their complex selves to understand how they "fit" in the world and to what degree they have ownership over their natural developmental changes. Often we will see them explore their family of origin, which sometimes includes a religious or cultural tradition. Perhaps it should be no surprise that while growing increasingly more aware of their own selves, students also struggle to know what to *do* with this unrest. Therefore, spirituality is at the center of this struggle.

I would argue that there seems to be an undercurrent in Chickering's theory and more directly through the work of Sharon Daloz Parks (1991) and James W. Fowler (1981) that spiritual questioning and exploration are a component of human development. There is often reticence to tackle the spiritual realm in human development because we lack the precise language to use or we fear offending someone in the discussion process—not to mention the inherent mystery and uncertainty at the core of spirituality, as Rolheiser addressed. The struggle is real for us as humans. We have questions about our religious and spiritual selves, and these obstacles get in the way for healthy exploration. I contend that the more we name these obstacles and move past them, the stronger our spiritual identity becomes.

Spirituality and Wellness as Partners

This book is about wellness practices in higher education, and perhaps spirituality does not feel like an obvious partner. Sports autograph aficionados know the term "sweet spot," which identifies the perfect location on a ball for an autograph. While not as obvious, the sweet spot for wellness truly does lie at the intersection of the body, mind, and spirit. Finding this sweet spot can be a lifelong process, but we have an opportunity with students to begin or enhance the exploration of how to bring spirituality into the wellness conversation.

Dr. Bill Hettler, of the National Wellness Institute, identified six dimensions of wellness: emotional, occupational, physical, social, intellectual, and spiritual. He states,

> A person engaged in the process of spiritual wellness is willing and able to transcend oneself in order to question the meaning and purpose in his/her life and the lives of others. He/she is involved in the process of questioning all that is around him/her and has an appreciation for that which cannot be completely understood. This person seeks to find harmony between that which lies within and the social and physical forces that come from outside. Feelings of doubt, despair, fear, disappointment and dislocation as well as feelings of pleasure, joy, eagerness and discovery are part of this search for a universal value system.
>
> (Hettler, 1999, n.p.)

The harmony that Hettler refers to could also be demonstrated by Figure 13.1, which shows that wellness is achieved by the integration of the body, mind, and spirit.

We have to be more practiced at what brings about this intersection, or simply stated: we have to look for the sweet spot. How do we help students find their way to this often mysterious place where wellness is achieved? How do we as student affairs practitioners, faculty members, and other professionals in the campus community find this intersection for ourselves?

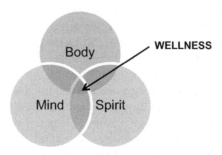

Figure 13.1 Integration of the Body, Mind and Spirit

It begins with understanding that human development is not linear nor fully complete; similarly, nor is spiritual development. It may be helpful to remember Jean Piaget's theory about the four key stages of cognitive development. Much of his research focused on children and how they made sense of the world as they grew into adults. A key piece of his findings was that the creation of knowledge, intelligence, and understanding is an active, ongoing process (Piaget, 1977).

It is a rare moment when our bodies are fit, well nourished, well rested, free of toxins, and perform freely without restraint or pain. Likewise is that rare moment when our minds are clear, focused, and free of worry or concern. The spirit, as discussed, is inherently at unrest. Ironically, that is the one constant of the spirit: the state of being unsettled! Achieving wellness, in fact, becomes a lifelong process. Perhaps it is better to say that wellness is not a state to be achieved but rather a process of balancing the needs of the body, the mind, and the spirit.

Case Study: Amy, First-Year Student

Amy came to my office one fall afternoon after her philosophy class. She had no appointment and was urgently wanted to talk to someone in Spiritual Life. Not knowing what sort of conversation was ahead, I welcomed her to share whatever was on her mind.

Amy told me the story of growing up in a two-religion home: Jewish and Christian. She primarily had Jewish friends in middle school and high school and likewise identified with being more culturally Jewish. Her family and friends observed the High Holy Days, but Amy felt distanced from the religious practice of either Judaism or Christianity. She shared a pivotal experience from high school that eventually led her to identify as an atheist: she was raped.

Amy was clearly practiced at telling this story, perhaps an indicator of counseling or therapy.

But my interest piqued when Amy shared that when she came to college, she felt uncomfortable about the religious identity that she had given herself. We explored some of the reasoning behind coming to be an atheist: feelings of abandonment by God when she needed help and disbelief in a benevolent force in the world. This rationale was not surprising, given what Amy had experienced, but I was surprised at her apparent discomfort as an atheist. The crux of her issue became clear as she circled back to her philosophy class. Amy shared that she participated regularly, and that day's topic touched on religious identity. Various comments from her classmates indicated a lack of acceptance of atheism as an identity. Amy felt defensive, but also unsure as to why she was defending atheism. She realized she had many, many questions about how to find a religious identity that truly resonated with her.

Thus, Amy came to my office seeking answers: *How do I know if I am truly an atheist? Do I have to identify with a specific religious tradition? Why do I feel pressured to be something or someone I may not be?*

The truth of this circumstance is that Amy's questions are not uncommon, especially among the traditionally aged college student. Exploring life's meaning and self-identity, specifically religious identity, is one of the most prominent developmental topics of their lives thus far (Parks, 1991). *Who am I? What do I value? How do I live out my values? What if those values are unpopular or different from my peer group?* I assured Amy that she was not alone in this process, and three things became important to communicate to her:

1. Amy was becoming aware that her own preferences could differ from her peers. This perhaps was the first time she either realized it or was confronted with a pivotal circumstance. Amy needed confirmation that her voice, both inner and outer, was uniquely her own. Learning to be comfortable with our own opinions and values in the presence of differing opinions and values is a mark of maturity.
2. Amy discovered the "blind followers" in her class of various religious traditions. Some of her peers admitted they had not given much thought to their own religious identity, but they were clear that her preference (as an atheist) was different and thus, somehow, unapproved. Amy wished she could be one of these "blind followers," mostly so she would fit in, but she was actually looking for permission to explore religious identity without judgment.
3. Amy was keenly aware that the trauma of rape had changed her in many ways. She deserved credit for that kind of self-awareness. For a first-year student, she was turning the mirror on herself at a much younger age than most. She needed to hear that the questions she was asking—*Who am I? What do I value? How do I live out my values?*—contribute to a lifelong process that she had only just begun.

Amy, while unique in many ways, was not unique in her line of thinking. College students are constantly bumping up against their peers on a host of matters, and their decision to shut down or open up is usually on the line. That decision is linked to popularity and belonging. Abraham Maslow (1943) would tell us the need to belong is intrinsic to their thinking; young adults thrive on peer approval. In fact, the need to belong can be so strong that sometimes physiological and basic safety needs can be overlooked. Religious identity is no different. Amy wanted to belong as an atheist, and yet, she also was aware there was dissent among her peers regarding that identity. She was at a crossroads. She could either venture forward on a path of self-discovery or cower at the realization that she held a differing preference. It was her choice, and I stood at the doorway inviting her in to explore further.

This is the point I want to make about students who seek help and support at these critical junctures. Religious identity is a deeply personal matter, and one that often changes as we grow, mature, and become more aware of the impact of life choices. I am always keenly aware of how fortunate we are in the United States to freely explore religious identity. I knew I had an opportunity to teach Amy to question, to wonder, to seek, to explore, to dig in, to feel unsettled, and to learn. These are fundamental concepts to unpacking the grey area of religious identity, as Astin et al. (2011a) argued. Amy was not on a linear path, which made her feel uneasy. Yet, she found comfort in the permission to seek the path that was right for her. I could not tell her Judaism, Christianity, or atheism was "the way," but I could tell her that it was okay to explore whatever religious identity suited her, even if that differed from her peers.

I offered Amy a few initial questions to guide her process of religious discovery. The end goal was not to provide a sequence diagram to direct her to a religious identity, but rather to give her questions, as well as some confidence, to facilitate introspection and foster possibilities to use her spirituality in the world:

- What kind of person do you want to be described as? Known for?
- How important is community to you?
- What characteristics do you value in others?
- How do you unwind or decompress from a long, stressful day?
- How do you know when you are "in your element" or "in the zone"?

I wanted Amy to consider the answer to these questions to aid in her process of self-discovery. As higher education professionals, I believe we have a responsibility to ask questions about that inner, subjective life and reassure students there is no perfect answer. Unlike mathematics, spiritual and religious exploration may not lead you to a defined answer. Rather, you may uncover more questions, more steps, and more things to consider. Students should see us as conduits to understanding themselves. The questions we pose begin that process.

Turning the Mirror on Ourselves

I had a colleague who lived by the mantra, "I never ask a student to do something I would not do myself." At the time, I thought it was admirable, but also a bit crazy because sometimes there were plenty of tasks I would rather have a student manage! Yet, this philosophy has stuck with me, and I often refer to it when confronted with the hard task of spiritual development.

I was asked several years ago to present to the student affairs division about spiritual life. Basic information was requested: trends of spirituality among our college's students (i.e., self-reported religious preferences and methods of spiritual practice), usage of the university's sacred space, and an overview of the campus climate when it came to spirituality and religious identity. This request was challenging for a few reasons. While I knew my colleagues were receptive to my position and the responsibility I had to manage spiritual life, I realized I lacked some basic information about my professional audience. Where did they stand when it came to spiritual development? Did they value the role of spirituality in a student's experience? Did they see the importance of spirituality in the landscape of student affairs? Love (2001) stressed the importance of student affairs professionals being comfortable with their own spirituality, and I knew this would have to be addressed.

These questions plagued me for weeks as I prepared my presentation. I felt it would be a missed opportunity to not address my inner struggle, but that upped the ante. I would have to be vulnerable with my colleagues about the questions I had, and I was uncertain how receptive they would be with that kind of approach. I was again reminded of Astin et al.'s (2011a) study, which showed that students whose professors encouraged them to explore questions of meaning and purpose are inclined to show larger-than-average increases in their inclinations toward spiritual questing. That is, "the seeking in us that can lead to a better understanding of who we are, why we are here, and how we can live a meaningful life" (Astin et al., 2011a).

I opted to throw a little caution to the wind. I began with this question: *How much do you care about spirituality?* I asked my colleagues to take a moment and jot down on a piece of paper a rating (from 1 to 5, 5 being high) and give a few comments as to why they rated it as such. I assured them their answers would remain anonymous. After a few initially awkward moments of people looking around the room looking for facial confirmation of *did she really just ask us that*, and they started writing feverishly. Here we were, inviting spirituality to the table without fear or concern that whatever was thought or written would be wrong. Instead, true and honest ratings were encouraged and welcomed.

I was onto something.

I spoke to them about the function of turning the mirror on ourselves. I referenced my colleague's mantra and simply stated, "No wonder talking about spirituality is so hard. We somehow expect students to sort through the questions *Who am I? What do I value? How do I live out my values?* without us even considering these questions for ourselves first." At that moment, I literally pulled out a mirror, held it up to my face, and simply asked myself out loud, "*Who am I? What do I value? How do I live out my values?*" My colleagues must have thought I had gone mad! *Is she going to answer that right now?*

I did not answer those questions in the moment, but I admitted that I had at least asked them before. I challenged them to recognize that we as practitioners must consider these questions first if we expect students to do so also. If we spend time practicing this method of introspection, I believe we can speak from a place of authenticity with students. They may see a reflection of their own doubt, struggle, hope, or encouragement in each of us. Those who are mental health professionals know reflective listening can be very effective. "What I hear you say is . . ." communicates that we have heard. This exercise promotes the same kind of understanding. If we ask ourselves these hard questions, we have an opportunity to speak from a place of personal understanding. Students may then see us as human beings confronted with similar challenges and questions as they.

While not all circumstances call for this level of vulnerability, perhaps we can explore the opportunities for these higher education professionals, whether serving as administrators, faculty members, or other campus leaders:

- The judicial coordinator or conduct officer who admits to an indiscretion or poor choice. Given the circumstance, this could be a pivotal moment of change for a student to see an authority figure who dealt with the ramifications of his or her actions.
- The mental health counselor who sought support from an external support system (i.e., another mental health counselor or social worker) when coping with a problem. Demonstrating that we all need various levels of help or support could bring you to an equal playing field with a student who feels awkward about seeking support.
- The spiritual life director who admits to questioning his or her faith. Normal- izing the seeking process may help a student embrace the unknown.
- The faculty member who was granted an extension to complete a deadline. Reciprocating this kind of consideration exhibits compassion for and understanding of a student's circumstance.

Creating a space for "I have been in your shoes" can be remarkably powerful and transformative for students. We should have a strong barometer for when these kinds of revelations may be appropriate without compromising any role we hold. To promote a healthy approach to self-discovery is to turn the mirror on ourselves.

The Function of Spirituality on a College Campus

As we began this chapter, I invited us to consider setting a place for spirituality at the table. Invite it into conversation and let it function as a welcomed friend, family member, or neighbor. Those of us on college campuses know how challenging that action may be, especially if our institutions affiliate with a religious tradition or simply remain secular in mission. Recognizing where spirituality should "sit" may be one of the most impactful efforts we can make as professionals in the higher education setting.

I have long advocated that those charged with the spiritual development of a campus community should not be acting independently of other campus partners. Some of the most effective partners for spirituality are wellness colleagues. Clinical psychologists, social workers, nurse practitioners, and registered nurses are among many who focus on the mental and physical needs of our students. What if they too could create space for students who seek spiritual development? What if they were able to pose *Who am I? What do I value? How do I live out my values?* without compromising their medical expertise? This may be a hard line to straddle. However, when wellness colleagues are able to simply ask, spirituality has a chance to enter.

What about those on campus who are *not* the traditional wellness colleagues? I contend there is room for them to be effective partners and promote this kind of engagement with students. Take faculty members, for example, who arguably have the most regular contact with students. There is an opportunity here for them to incorporate elements of connection into each class, regardless of the subject matter. I am thinking of the professor who begins each class with two minutes of deep breathing for relaxation and focus or the professor who shares a thought-provoking quote or video to spark conversation or reflection. There are innumerable ways for these nontraditional partners to create space for a student's deeper connection with self.

I have worked at a secular university where colleagues in our health and wellness center and counseling center truly embraced this line of thought. These practitioners were not afraid to set a place for spirituality at the table with students, and also recognized the effectiveness of referrals to spiritual life. We functioned as partners, not as experts in areas not our own but as professionals who understood the value of the body, mind, and spirit connection. I am not suggesting any single person impose personal belief systems or values that could sway students inappropriately. I am challenging us to guide students through thoughtful processes to decide what to do with that "fire within." I want all professionals in the higher education setting, whether in student affairs, teaching, or administrative roles, to be the ones to ask . . . to guide . . . to create space for a student to think through questions of self-discovery, which is an act of spiritual development.

Case Study: Bobby, Graduating Senior

Bobby came to see me via a referral from a colleague in the health and wellness center late in the spring semester. One of the nurses had suggested that he might like to speak with someone in Spiritual Life. He had recently lost his childhood best friend to suicide. Bobby emailed me to make an appointment to discuss his story, although he never once referred to seeking any spiritual guidance or support.

Bobby was a really friendly young man who appeared to be overwhelmed with the aftereffects of Matt's death. He shared Matt's story: troubled home, someone who often resided on the periphery of social circles, acted a bit odd at times, but ultimately forged ahead. Bobby and Matt were childhood friends who attended the same schools through high school. He recalled that Matt never really connected with the more popular students, but he appeared to get along fine nonetheless. His friendship with Matt was deep, though; they had bonded over many of the average things boys like, such as video games.

Bobby and Matt attended different colleges, and like most childhood friends, stayed in touch sporadically as they became accustomed to their new campuses. Bobby admitted to his lack of communication with Matt in the fall semester, which in many ways would plague him going forward. They connected in minor ways over the winter holiday break, and Matt committed suicide just before returning to classes in January.

Bobby came back to campus that spring semester having experienced a life-altering event. He struggled with how to normalize his life as a college student; meanwhile Matt's family was still reeling from the loss. Bobby shared that he became a point-person upon Matt's death, serving as the main source of communication and information about funeral services, as well as ways to support Matt's family. He told me about his cell phone ringing incessantly, and his feelings of responsibility to support Matt's family when they simply could not balance their needs.

Months later, Bobby realized he had not cried about Matt's death. He simply was too busy and too focused to notice otherwise. Now at a distance from home and Matt's family, Bobby was confronted with his own grief and ways to make sense of what had happened. Weeks away from his summer vacation, Bobby would return home to be around the many familiar things that would remind him of Matt and ultimately the loss.

Bobby and I spoke of plans. The fact was that, unlike Matt, Bobby *could* make plans. The summer months called for trips, vacations, internships, and opportunities to enjoy time away from campus. Yet, Bobby felt guilty that he had a life ahead of him, whereas Matt no longer did. He would have to go home and face the sadness he managed to escape while in school.

So we talked about the plans he could make. He spoke of hiking trips to be in nature and car trips with his dad. He craved time for himself after being present for everyone else after Matt's death. I was witnessing self-care in action, and I was curious if Bobby would be receptive to hearing about rituals to cope with loss. I asked a few probing questions like, "What could you do to mark Matt's death when you return home?" or "What could you do for yourself when you visit his gravesite?"

We brainstormed ideas, such as journaling, taking a long drive, looking at old photographs, or listening to music. The goal of these kinds of activities, while seemingly mundane, was to allow him some private time to decompress and be alone with his thoughts about Matt. It was clear that Bobby had not allowed much time for his own processing, and any activity that he enjoyed alone would give him space to accomplish that. The fact was that Bobby needed space and permission to find techniques that would comfort him, while also appropriately preparing him to be home, where memories of Matt would likely flood his mind.

The practices that were shared with Bobby probably seem simplified or perhaps not even identifiable as spiritual. The key to this interaction was that Bobby wanted to make sense of Matt's death while creating space for his own grief. He was a mature young man, most certainly, who wanted to be intentional about his summer experience. The ideas we brainstormed were ordinary, but in many ways that is what Bobby needed: simple activities that would allow his mind and heart to downshift and absorb the reality of the circumstance.

The role of any higher education professional, particularly those in student affairs, is to remind Bobby to carve out time to be introspective and consider the ways Matt's death would impact him. There are innumerable ways or techniques to do this, many more formalized or ritualized than the ideas he and I discussed. But did that make it any less of a spiritual encounter? Less of a spiritual practice? Ultimately Bobby was trying "to do something with that unrest." He was in the thick of practicing spirituality and probably never would name it that way. In my mind, it did not matter. Bobby was trying to reconnect with the center of this experience (i.e., his friend's unexpected death) and decide how he would respond. The fact that he invited me into that process with him was my privilege, courtesy of my colleague's referral.

The integration of spirituality could be the lifeblood of a campus, infusing itself into conversations between faculty, staff, administrators, and students. And, yet, there are perhaps more obvious places for spirituality to "sit" at the collegiate table. These opportunities often reside among events such as campus celebrations (e.g., convocation, baccalaureate, commencement), memorials (e.g., Virginia Tech massacre, Boston Marathon bombing, Sandy Hook Elementary School shooting), or community loss/bereavement gatherings (e.g., campus community members or friends/family of the university). Each event plays a very specific function for spirituality on college campuses and may create more opportunities for collaboration and partnerships. In addition, these events may allow campus community members to participate more fully in "spiritual events" while not taking a specific lead.

Celebration Events

Spiritual leaders are not the only ones on campus who can (or should) pray, invoke the spirit, or welcome members into a community at large-scale events. Yet, this is a very prominent role for spiritual life colleagues to play. As a community gathers to begin or end an academic year, campus leaders, particularly those with a spiritual focus in their professional positions, have an opportunity to set a celebratory tone and express gratitude. We often share messages at commencement to thank the faculty, staff, parents, and families who supported students along the way. Depending on whether the institution has a religious affiliation, prayers or general invocations may be offered. These opportunities publicly demonstrate an institution's appreciation for and support of spirituality on campus.

Memorials

Marking significant events that happen in the world is another responsibility of campus leaders as they promote the spiritual dimension of wellness. Tragic events like Sandy Hook or Virginia Tech are happening more frequently, and they invite our campuses to respond in a unique way. We have a responsibility not to ignore or shield our campus community from these acts but instead to invite togetherness where that has been broken elsewhere. These gatherings are often very useful for community members to express emotions and share mutual feelings about what happened. Answers are not the goal, but rather we want to create a safe space for reactions and questions. Moments like these often engender interest in spirituality overall, leading people to attend services, gather in churches/mosques/temples, or offer words of comfort in small groups. A question, then, is how to sustain this interest, and what role our institutions can play in the weeks, months, and years following these events.

Community Loss/Bereavement

The death of a community member, regardless of whether anticipated, is a profound event that bonds people. The web of connection grows as alumni and former employees learn of what has happened. Campus spiritual leaders have an opportunity to remind all of the value of each life, the mortality we all face, and the support we need to move through the grieving process. These are distinctive moments for a community, as there is no template for how to best to respond. The role a spiritual leader plays often shepherds a community through the natural steps of recovery and restoration.

It may be important to note that not every campus may have a designated professional to serve as spiritual leader. Sometimes these responsibilities fall to campus health professionals, usually in counseling centers. However, most private institutions will have at minimum a part-time professional with academic credentials in divinity or ministry with experience in the field. Public colleges and universities will vary the most in staffing, depending on budgets and the representation of students' affiliations. This further reinforces how all professionals, whether in student affairs, teaching, or administrative roles, should collaborate to support a campus through such events.

These three categories help secure a place for spirituality on college campuses. There will always be moments to celebrate and memorialize. And arguably then, spirituality will always have a seat at the table.

Bringing Spirituality Home

I previously discussed that spirituality is inherently individualistic. Yet, here is the great juxtaposition we face: it is also deeply communal because at the core of figuring out what to do with our "unrest," we are all confronted with making meaning out of our lives. We are all sorting through, deciding about, and considering the options for ourselves. I am reminded of Viktor Frankl's work as he chronicled his inmate experiences in an Auschwitz concentration camp. He created meaning of his experience by imagining a positive outcome (Frankl, 1959). The unrest is what connects us, but what we do with it is entirely our own.

There is no standardized road map for how spirituality impacts a campus community. This is complex because the makeup of the community is so varied: students of traditional age and nontraditional age, veterans, and transfers, to name a few. The argument here is that spirituality actually is at the heart of the members who make up the community, wherever they happen to be on the spectrum of their own development. And we have to be receptive and aware of the opportunities where spirituality may enter the conversation to support the student. Perhaps we are missing key moments in our everyday life where spirituality and wellness could be better partners, building bridges for students to live happier and healthier lives. Two examples come to mind here:

1. Graduating seniors are a unique population who often engage in self-discovery conversations with their faculty/staff mentors. They are on the cusp of change and ripe with unrest about their future. These are prime opportunities to reinforce wellness behaviors (i.e., proper nutrition, sleep, exercise) while deepening their exploration of *Who am I? What do I value? How do I live out my values?*
2. Many students engage in community service opportunities on our campuses. Connecting with community members in need often brings students to confront their own place of privilege and understand their value systems. Debriefing these kinds of experiences are perfect opportunities to unpack any unrest they may be feeling and consider choices they could make to improve a challenging life situation for someone else. In addition, these experiences may enrich and heighten a student's value of other human beings overall, often citing that they were the ones receiving the benefit, rather than the one in "need."

Even further, maybe we as practitioners are ignoring moments in our own lives to enhance the interactions we have with students. The poet Rumi challenges us to "be relentless in your looking" (Barks, 2004, p. 312). We have the benefit of longer lives filled with relationships, lessons, and wisdom obtained from each experience. We should not fear integrating these lessons in our approach with students. Use your personal experiences to fuel your understanding, compassion, and relatability with students. Give yourself permission to use your human experiences to be more present in your interactions with students. This kind of balance makes for higher education practitioners who not only understand the importance of spirituality and wellness but also have a lived practice of it.

Our spiritual dinner table has been set, and we begin our meal together finally. We know how vital the exploration of ideas and the vulnerability of each person are to our conversation. We prepare for the discomfort that may set in, but we resist changing the subject. We hear thoughts and questions with open minds and eager hearts. We consider how those thoughts and questions apply to us as individuals as well as educators. We may err in using certain terminology, but invite clarification and understanding. We chuckle when Aunt Lou shares her wacky opinions again, but we are reminded of this moment of connection. There is an intersection of body, mind, and spirit happening. Spirituality then has a home in each of us who prioritizes it. When we recognize and use the natural intersections of spirituality among the dimensions of wellness, we are inching toward the sweet spot of happy, healthy, balanced lives.

References

Astin, A., Astin, H., & Lindholm, J. (2011a). *Cultivating the spirit: How college can enhance students' inner lives.* San Francisco, CA: Jossey-Bass.

Astin A., Astin, H., & Lindholm, J. (2011b). A National Study of Spirituality in Higher Education: Students' Search for Meaning and Purpose. Retrieved from UCLA website: http://spirituality. ucla.edu/findings

Barks, C. (2004). *The essential Rumi.* New York, NY: HarperCollins.

Chickering, A., & Reisser, L. (1993). *Education and identity* (2nd ed.). San Francisco, CA: Jossey-Bass.

Fowler, J. (1981). *Stages of faith: The psychology of human development and the quest for meaning.* San Francisco, CA: Harper San Francisco.

Frankl, V. (1959). *Man's search for meaning: An introduction to logotherapy.* Boston, MA: Beacon Press.

Hettler, B. (1999). The History, Present, and Future of Wellness at UWSP. Retrieved from http://www. hettler.com/History/spirit.htm

Love, P. G. (2001). *Spirituality and student development: Theoretical connections.* In N. J. Evans, D. S. Forney, F. M. Guido, L. D. Patton, & K. A. Renn (Eds.), *Student development in college: Theory, research and practice* (pp. 194–211). San Francisco, CA: Jossey-Bass.

Maslow, A. (1943). A theory of human motivation. *Psychological Review, 50,* 370–396.

Parks, S. D. (1991). *The critical years: Young adults and the search for meaning, faith, and commitment.* New York, NY: HarperCollins.

Piaget, J. (1977). *The essential Piaget* (H. E. Gruber & J. J. Voneche, Eds.). New York, NY: Basic Books.

Rolheiser, R. (1999). *The holy longing: The search for a Christian spirituality.* New York, NY: Doubleday.

Contributor Biographies

David S. Anderson, PhD, George Mason University. David Anderson is Professor of Education and Development and Director of the Center for the Advancement of Public Health. Early in his career, he served as a student affairs administrator at the Ohio State University, Radford University, and Ohio University. He serves as project director and researcher on numerous national, state, and local projects, and has taught graduate and undergraduate courses on drug and alcohol issues, community health, and health communications. His strategic planning and program evaluation work emphasizes college students, youth, school and community leaders, program planners, and policy makers. Specialty areas include drug/alcohol abuse prevention, strategic planning and mobilization, communication and education, health promotion, and needs assessment and evaluation. His research includes the College Alcohol Survey (1979–2015), Understanding Teen Drinking Cultures in America, COMPASS: A Roadmap to Healthy Living, Best of CHOICES, IMPACT Evaluation Resource, and the Wellness Assessment for Higher Education Professionals. In 2000, he was the first recipient of the Visionary Award sponsored by the Network of Colleges and Universities Committed to the Elimination of Drug and Alcohol Abuse.

Shannon K. Bailie, MSW, University of Washington. Shannon Bailie is Director of Health & Wellness at the University of Washington. She created Health & Wellness as a unique blend of strategic outreach, intervention, and education employed by all programs: Suicide Intervention, Alcohol and Other Drug Education, Sexual Assault and Relationship Program, Student Care, and Peer-Health Educators.

Constance S. Boehm, MA, The Ohio State University. Connie Boehm is Director of the Student Life Student Wellness Center and Associate Director of the Higher Education Center for Alcohol and Drug Misuse Prevention and Recovery. She leads wellness efforts on campus and beyond by engaging campus leaders, students, faculty, and community members in comprehensive, innovative wellness initiatives for students. She has enjoyed working in student life for over 30 years in residence life, alcohol and drug prevention, and wellness.

M. Dolores Cimini, PhD, University at Albany, SUNY. M. Dolores Cimini has led campus-wide alcohol and other drug prevention and treatment efforts at the University at Albany for over two decades. She has served as Project Director for numerous grant-funded projects focused on the application of laboratory research to evidence-based prevention and intervention practice.

Maria F. DiLorenzo, MA, Bentley University. Maria F. DiLorenzo, a native of Dallas, Texas and resident of Boston, MA, is the former Director of Spiritual Life at Bentley University. She also served as a campus minister at Regis College in Weston, MA for several years prior to Bentley. She received her BA in psychology and religious studies from Loyola University, New Orleans, and MA in pastoral ministry from the Institute of Religious Education and Pastoral Ministry at Boston College (now the School of Theology and Ministry). She also serves on the Board of Directors for Sacred Threads Center, a Boston-based women's spirituality center, and currently works in the Center for Alumni, Parents and Friends at Bentley.

Heather Eastman-Mueller, PhD, CHES, CSE, FACHA, University of Missouri. Heather Eastman-Mueller is Coordinator of Sexual Health at the Student Health Center, Health Promotion and Wellness Department and is a certified health education specialist. She is Curriculum Coordinator and Supervisor of the Sexual Health Advocate Peer Education program. Her areas of expertise include survey and sexuality education curriculum development, gender identity and expression, and policy change. Her current research interests include gender and its impact on accessing testing for sexually transmitted infections. Her dissertation, which examined college student sexual health knowledge, attitudes, and behaviors, is published in the *Handbook of Sexuality-Related Measures*. She is an adjunct professor in the Department of Women's and Gender Studies. She was inducted as a fellow for the American College Health Association in 2014.

Jennifer R. Fisher, MS Ed, College of William and Mary. Jennifer R. Fisher is Assistant Director of Campus Recreation for Fitness and Wellness. She has been in the fitness and wellness industry for over 10 years and is certified as a health fitness specialist and personal trainer through the American College of Sports Medicine and as a group fitness instructor through the American Council on Exercise. She oversees the areas of group fitness, personal training, incentive programs and massage at the Student Recreation Center and teaches semester-long training courses for group fitness instructors and personal trainers. She also has an interest in mental health and has served on the Student Affairs Mental Health & Wellness Committee for several years at William and Mary.

Tom Hall, MSW, LCSW, University of Central Florida. Tom Hall is Director of the Alcohol and Other Drug Intervention and Treatment Program in Student Health Services at the University of Central Florida. He has over 20 years of experience providing substance abuse and mental health treatment. His research interests include developing brief intervention and treatment strategies as well as recovery services for college students. He has taught graduate-level social work and counselor education courses related to the treatment of substance use disorders, as well as group psychotherapy and family therapy. He is on the board of the Orange County Coalition for a Drug-Free Community and is active in local prevention and treatment efforts.

Annann Hong, PhD, MPH, Arizona State University, Estrella Mountain Community College. Annann Hong has worked in college health promotion for the last 25 years. Beginning her career as a prevention educator and student affairs professional, she transitioned to academia 10 years ago. In addition to working as a development officer for a charter school in the West Valley of Phoenix, she currently teaches as an adjunct with the Health Sciences and Psychology departments at Estrella Mountain Community College and as a faculty associate for the Exercise and Wellness program at Arizona State University. She has taught courses on general wellness, community health, health promotion program planning, nutrition, introductory psychology, and human sexuality. She also has an interest in cultural competency and social justice as it relates to health promotion.

Dori S. Hutchinson, ScD, CPRP, Boston University. Dori Hutchinson has worked at the Center for Psychiatric Rehabilitation at Boston University since 1984. She currently serves as Director of the Services Division, which assists people who live with mental health challenges assume their rightful roles as students, employees, residents, and members of their communities. She is Associate Clinical Professor at Sargent College of Health and Rehabilitation Services at Boston University. Currently, she serves as Chairwoman of the Board of the Psychiatric Rehabilitation Association (PRA), which trains and educates the global recovery workforce. She provides training nationally to universities, organizations, and providers who wish to deliver recovery-oriented services and conduct relevant program evaluations.

Lance C. Kennedy-Phillips, PhD, University of Illinois at Chicago. Lance Kennedy-Phillips is Associate Vice Provost for Institutional Research. His research interests include higher-education policy analysis, outcomes assessment, program evaluation, and applied institutional research. He is Co-editor of *Qualitative and Quantitative Research: A Mixed-Methods Approach in Higher Education* and *Measuring Co-Curricular Learning: The Role of the IR Office* as part of the New Directions for Institutional Research Series.

Jason R. Kilmer, PhD, University of Washington. Dr. Jason Kilmer received his PhD in clinical psychology from the University of Washington in 1997, and currently works at the University of Washington in both a student affairs and a research capacity. He is Associate Professor in Psychiatry and Behavioral Sciences, and serves as an investigator on several studies evaluating prevention and intervention efforts for alcohol and other drug use by college students. He is also Assistant Director of Health and Wellness for Alcohol and Other Drug Education in the Division of Student Life, working with different areas across campus (including health, counseling, Greek life, residence life, and athletics) to increase student access to evidence-based approaches. He also serves as Chairperson of Washington's College Coalition for Substance Abuse Prevention.

He was project faculty for both Dartmouth's National College Health Improvement Program (NCHIP) and NYU's National College Depression Partnership (NCDP). He was the 2014 recipient of the National Prevention Network's Award of Excellence for outstanding contributions to the field of prevention.

Linda A. Knight, MS Ed, College of William and Mary. Linda Knight is Director of Campus Recreation at the College of William and Mary. She has been involved with campus recreation for the last 29 years. The first 13 years of her career she was in charge of fitness and wellness at Emory University. During her time at Emory she was a certified personal trainer through American Council on Exercise (ACE). As director she has oversight of the fitness and wellness program and has remained involved with current trends in exercise and fitness. She does research on cardiovascular and weight equipment and purchases the equipment for the Student Recreation Center. Another area in which she is highly involved is hazing prevention, and she serves on the Board of Directors for HazingPrevention.org.

Kevin Kruger, PhD, NASPA is Student Affairs Administrators in Higher Education. He is President of NASPA. Before assuming the position as NASPA's first executive-level president in 2012, he served as Associate Executive Director of NASPA from 1994. His higher education career spans 35 years in a variety of student affairs positions, and he is widely published in leadership development, technology in student affairs, and trends in higher education. He received his PhD in counseling and personnel services from the University of Maryland College Park.

Michael McNeil, EdD, Columbia University. Michael McNeil is the Executive Director of Alice! Health Promotion, Student Health Insurance, and Immunization Compliance and a member of the faculty in Sociomedical Sciences at the Mailman School of Public Health, both at Columbia University. He holds a doctorate in higher education leadership, a master's in health education, and advanced training in public health, and he is a certified health education specialist (CHES) and a fellow of the American College Health Association (FACHA). Having spent 20+ years in college health and student affairs, he focuses on evidence- and theory-informed administration and practice. His other interests include health communication; linking health with academic success; technology in health and student affairs; and professional preparation. A widely respected colleague in student affairs and college health, he often presents at local, regional, and national meetings on a host of topics and works to publish practice-oriented pieces that are dedicated to supporting curricular and co-curricular student success.

Joleen M. Nevers, MAEd, CHES, CSE, University of Connecticut. Joleen Nevers is Health Education Coordinator in the Department of Wellness and Prevention Services. She is a certified health education specialist and a certified sexuality educator. Having more than 20 years of experience in sexual health, her areas of expertise include sexuality education in college health and peer education implementation and development. She presents both regionally and nationally at conferences, including BACCHUS Initiatives of NASPA, True Colors, American College Health Association, and American Association of Sexuality Educators, Counselors and Therapists. She developed a two-time nationally award-winning sexual health program (Rubberwear), and a nationally and regionally awarded peer education program (The UConn Sexperts). She has volunteered to teach several sexual attitude reassessments (SARs) and other sexuality courses to professionals, for AASECT certification. She is also an adjunct faculty at the UConn School of Public Health Graduate Program and at Manchester Community College.

Daniella Olibrice, EdD, Workforce Opportunity Services. Daniella Olibrice is Manager of University and Community External Affairs at a nonprofit organization in New York City, Workforce Opportunity Services. She has administered academic programs at the City University of New York's School of Professional Studies and Lehman College, and Teachers College at Columbia University. Her areas of experience and expertise are adult learning, employer-university partnerships for workforce development, prior learning assessment, and the development and implementation of academic programs and services for working adults and nontraditional students. She has served as an adjunct at the State University of New York, Empire State College's Harry Van Arsdale Jr. Center for Labor Studies.

Parth K. Patel, BA, College of William and Mary. Parth K. Patel is Graduate Assistant for Fitness and Wellness at the College of William and Mary. He is in the Higher Education Administration master's program. Prior to his time at William and Mary he received a BA in multidisciplinary studies (mathematics, psychology, and education) from Millersville University. His primary interest in fitness is in the area of personal training. He also has expertise in technology integration.

Bridget Guernsey Riordan, PhD, Emory University. Bridget Guernsey Riordan is Assistant Vice President for Alumni Relations, Parent and Family Programs in the Division of Campus Life at Emory University. Prior to this position she served Emory as Dean of Students, Assistant to the Vice President, and Director of Student Activities. She received her bachelor's degree from Ball State University. Upon graduation she worked for Alpha Chi Omega fraternity as a traveling consultant and then worked in student affairs positions at the University of Cincinnati and the University of Pittsburgh. She served as an adjunct faculty member at Georgia State University and received a certificate in higher-education law from the Stetson School of Law. She has served as President of the Association of Fraternity Advisors and has done research on fraternal organizations, alcohol policy development, and risk management issues.

Index

Note: Page numbers with *f* indicate figures; those with *t* indicate tables.

marijuana 124, 130*t*, 132–3; academic
achievement and 132–3; legal
issues with 133; as medicine 133;
tetrahydrocannabinol in 132
Marlatt, G. A. 110
Martens, M. P. 115
Marthur, A. 78
Maslow, A. 228
McNeil, M. 167–82
MDMA 130*t*
memorials, spirituality and 234–5
mental health 39–52; achieving, on
campuses 45; administrative support
and 45–6; caring communities and
48–9; collaboration and 46–7; faculty/
staff and 51; overview of 39; resiliency
framework for 49–50; signs of 41; social
media and 42–3; strategic planning
process for 47–8; students and 39–44;
students as peers/voices of 50–1;
technology and 57–9, 62–4; types of 41;
universities/colleges and, role of 44–5
MET *see* motivational enhancement theory
metacognition, as habit of mind 150
methamphetamine 129*t*
methylphenidate 129*t*
metrics, utilizing appropriate 13
Microsoft suite software 153
Miech, R. A. 123–4
millennials: described 39–40, 204; exercise
and 204–5; mental health and 39–40;
postsecondary education for 148–50;
strategies checklist for 25; stress
management and 23–5
Mills, C. W. 11–12
Mirsu-Paun, A. 8
Monitoring the Future study (MTF) 5, 123
Montalto, C. 37
Moreno, M. A. 133
morphine 128*t*
motivation: argument exploration tasks for
159; exercise and 215–17
motivational enhancement theory
(MET) 137
Motorola Up 205
MTF *see* Monitoring the Future study
multivitamins, nutrition and 193–4

narcotics 128*t*
Narcotics Anonymous 31, 139
NASPA *see* Student Affairs Administrators
in Higher Education
Nathan, R. 82

National Association of Manufacturers 147
National Center for Education Statistics
(NCES) 2, 23
National Center for Transgender Equality
(NCTE) 95
National College Health Assessment
(NCHA) 5, 19, 23–4, 124
National College Health Assessment II
(NCHA) 94, 97
National Depression Screening Day 47
National Institute of Justice 65
National Institute on Drug Abuse 127,
128–30*t*
National Institutes of Health (NIH) 209–10
National Survey of Student Engagement
(NSSE) 60
National Survey on Drug Use and Health
(NSDUH) 134
National Wellness Institute 226
Naylor, T. H. 90
NCES *see* National Center for Education
Statistics
NCHA *see* National College Health
Assessment, National College Health
Assessment II
NCTE *see* National Center for Transgender
Equality
Neff, K. 76
Neubert, A. 203
Nevers, J. M. 93–106
NIH *see* National Institutes of Health
Nike FuelBand 205
nontraditional students: defined 2;
postsecondary education for 148–50;
strategies checklist for 26–7; stress
management and 25–7
Northern Arizona, University of 82
NSDUH *see* National Survey on Drug Use
and Health
NSSE *see* National Survey of Student
Engagement
nutrition 185–98; change in, strategies for
194–6; for exercise 212–14; fact and
fiction statements about 188–94; future
directions of study for 197–8; higher
education professionals and 196–7;
human diet and 186–8; overview of
185–6
nutrition myths: "*Butter is the spawn of
the devil.*" 190; "*Eggs are good. No,
eggs are bad. Actually it's okay to eat
eggs. Don't eat too many eggs. Eggs
are beneficial to your health.*" 191–2;

Made in the USA
Monee, IL
15 May 2020